The Politics of Global Resources

The Politics of Global Resources

Population, Food, Energy, and Environment

James E. Harf and B. Thomas Trout

Duke University Press   Durham, 1986

© 1986 Duke University Press, all rights reserved
Printed in the United States of America
on acid free paper ∞
Library of Congress Cataloguing in Publication Data
appear on the last printed page of this book

In memory of my parents, Anna Marie and Ernest G. Harf, Jr.   JEH

To Jimi and Peg Trout, with special thanks.   BTT

Contents

Figures and Tables

Series Preface

This text is the final volume in a series of books on contemporary issues in the global environment. The Global Issues Series, of which it is a part, is the result of a multiyear project funded by the Exxon Education Foundation to develop educational resources on a number of problems arising from the shifting nature and growing interdependence of that environment. The issue areas addressed in this project have included such problems as global food, energy, population, and environment.

Four books have been published previously in this series. Each text examines one of the four issues within a systematic and integrated framework common to all. After establishing the substantive dimensions needed to provide the requisite foundation for analysis—such as the historical evolution, the structure of its global system, its basic contemporary characteristics—this framework is applied in separate chapters pursuing four distinct analytical inquiries: (1) Who are the global actors involved in the issue and what are the linkages among them? (2) What prevailing values are operating and how have the relevant actors responded to these values? (3) What policies are applied by these actors at the global level and how are these policies determined? and (4) What futures are represented in the values and policies of these global actors? The relationship among these perspectives and their connection to an analysis of the various issues are illustrated in figure 1. Each element—actors, values, policies, and futures—represents a distinct analytical approach.

In addition, differentiating this project and its product from other texts, each of the single-issue volumes incorporates exercises, or has them available from the Global Issues Project, that afford the student the opportunity to engage in a variety of active learning sequences—should the instructor so desire

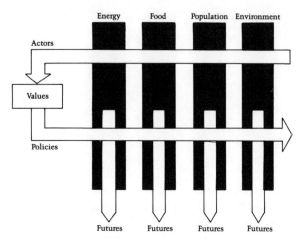

Energy   Food   Population Environment

Actors

Values

Policies

Futures   Futures   Futures   Futures

Figure 1   Global issues characteristics

—in order to understand better the complexities of the issue.

In realizing its goals, the project enlisted the participation of thirty-one prominent scholars who worked together with the project directors. These individuals contributed their substantial expertise both to specific areas and to the analytical development of the project as a whole. Although more than the four issues mentioned were included in the original materials development workshops, only those materials represented by the five volumes were completed in a form suitable for formal publication.

Each of the four single-issue volumes of the series represents the specific contributions of three principal authors and the editors. One author, the issues specialist, was responsible for the substantive introduction and, in some cases, the summary conclusion and for supervising and coordinating the efforts of the other two authors. Those authors applied the components of the perspective framework —actors, values, policies, futures—to the issue in separate chapters. The series editors designed the conceptual framework, assisted in the writing of some chapters (including primary responsibility for three chapters), and edited each individual volume together with the relevant issue specialist. These volume editors incorporated the feedback from pedagogical and substantive specialists as well as from field testers. The final volume represents a general introduction to global issues, emphasizing the substantive features of the four issues under investigation, and applying the conceptual framework to a series of case studies.

The project evolved through a series of stages centered on two materials development workshops—the first for the "issues" and "perspectives" specialists, and the second for all participants—and the elaborate field-test network of the Consortium for International Studies Education. The materials developed in the workshop were produced in field-test editions that were then used across the country in a variety of instructional settings. All the volumes have therefore been revised and refined based on actual classroom experience.

We wish to acknowledge formally the financial support of the Exxon Education Foundation, which provided the means to develop this project, and we wish to express our gratitude to several individuals: Roy E. Licklider of Rutgers University, who while serving with the Exxon Education Foundation encouraged us initially to pursue this venture; Richard Johnson, who as our contact at the Exxon Education Foundation shepherded this project to completion; and Suzanna Easton of the Department of Education, for her enthusiastic support and encouragement not only of this project but the entire education enterprise that it represents.

Duke University Press has published three texts from the Global Issues Project: *Energy in the Global Arena, Environment and the Global Arena,* and *The Politics of Global Resources: Population, Food, Energy, and Environment.* A fourth volume, *Population in the Global Arena,* first published by Holt, Rinehart and Winston, is now available from Duke University Press also, and a fifth, *Food in the Global Arena,* is being revised for publication by Duke as this volume goes to press. We are grateful to a number of individuals who encouraged us at various stages of the publishing process. First we worked with Patrick Powers, then a senior editor at Holt who believed in this project. Marie A. Schappert of Holt brought a sound, businesslike style to her task of overseeing the first two manuscripts. We are especially indebted to Richard C. Rowson, director of Duke University Press, who has continuously demonstrated a strong commitment to this project. Reynolds Smith, as editor responsible for the three Duke University Press manuscripts, translated them from final draft into print with a very high level of expertise and sound professional judgment. Both Mary Mendell and Bob Mirandon at Duke Press also contributed materially to the quality of the manuscript. We are also grateful for the help of our administrative assistant and typist, Edith Bivona, who delivered work of the highest quality under less than ideal circumstances. She brings a pleasant manner and much enthusiasm to her work, making our professional lives much easier. Finally, we would like to acknowledge the support of the Ohio State University's Mershon Center and its director, Charles F. Hermann, who was forthcoming with assistance when needed.

James E. Harf
B. Thomas Trout

Preface

This text serves as a general introduction and overview to international issues in the contemporary global arena. Its approach is characterized by five principal features. First, the text describes historical patterns and the contemporary character of the international system that serve to underscore why it is especially difficult for the world community to address today's issues. Second, it provides a conceptual foundation for examining specific issues. As outlined in the series preface and shown in figure 1 therein, for each issue area the analytical framework addresses the participants and those affected, the values they hold, the nature of policy-making and specific policy responses, and keys to the future. Third, the text examines in some detail the essential features of four specific issues: food, energy, population, and environment. Fourth, case studies of the application of the framework's four principal perspectives to the four issues are presented. Fifth, for those who wish to examine the conceptual foundation we provide a lengthy appendix, written by four specialists, that expands the analysis.

The text is divided into five parts and the appendixes. Part I describes both the evolution of global issues and their contemporary character. Each of the four chapters in Part II provides the essential elements of one of the four global issues featured in this volume. In Part III we apply the conceptual framework to the four issues in a series of case studies: food actors, energy values, population policy, and environment futures. In Part IV we summarize how far the global comunity has come in finding solutions for these issues and the tasks remaining in a complex, interdependent world. Finally, the appendix contains sections on the four major elements of the conceptual foundation: the role of actors in global issues, written by Robert S. Jordan; value orientations toward global issues, by Chadwick F. Alger; the policy context of global issues, by Richard W. Mansbach; and global futures, by Dennis Pirages.

A number of people contributed to the successful completion and publication of this manuscript. Joseph Rogers, Taeho Kim, Robert Donaldson, and Mark Denham provided research assistance. Mark Denham also helped with the editing, and Taeho Kim constructed the index. We would still be several steps away from a completed manuscript without the unique work habits of our administrative assistant and typist, Edith Bivona, assisted by Linda Anderson and Norma Turner, all of whom produced high-quality work in a timely fashion. Similarly, Mary Mendell, Bob Mirandon, and Reynolds Smith once again proved their worth at Duke University Press. Finally, and most important, we are especially grateful for the encouragement in the completion of this volume as well as the continuing commitment to the series given by Richard C. Rowson, director of Duke University Press. Dick demonstrated a level of professionalism and a sense of graciousness throughout this entire process not typically found in the publishing business. Our job was made easier as a consequence.

James E. Harf
B. Thomas Trout
November 1985

Part I
The New Global Agenda

We introduce in Part I the study of global issues. This set of problems is characterized by elements quite different from those of previous eras. We describe historical patterns that have influenced the contemporary nature of these global issues. Finally, we elaborate a framework for understanding the nature of these global issues. They constitute a new global agenda and we attempt to demonstrate the reasons why. The conceptual foundation describes the global actors involved in the issue and linkages among them, prevailing values and the implications of these values for policy, attempts at policy-making at the global level, and finally the nature of the future.

1 The Nature of Global Issues

The world as we know it today reflects both the slow, evolutionary changes of the centuries and the fast-paced impacts of the modern era. These forces exist, sometimes in harmony but frequently clashing, as they compete for domination in the creation of a new order. Science and technology have contributed to this competition by accelerating the process, increasing the magnitude of change, and making their impact greater. But these rapid intrusions on the current state of affairs must still occur simultaneously with forces that have been at work for centuries.

Historical Trends

Let us begin by examining both historical and contemporary trends that affect the global issues we will study. We will observe how these forces have resulted in the creation of a new global agenda for world leaders and would-be leaders. We will examine some long-term trends which now exist side by side with a number of post–World War II phenomena. Together these sets of factors have moved most of those in global leadership roles away from the traditional route to power through the acquisition of territory through either the threat or the use of traditional military force. In their place new definitions of power, new goals, new strategies, and new problems have appeared. Let us begin by moving back into history and observing some movements of the last few centuries.

Globalized Social Structure

Over the last five hundred years one principal trend has been the consistent but ever-accelerating movement toward a global social structure. The resultant multidimensional globalization, in turn, has affected the magnitude of the issues discussed in this book; in effect, it has allowed them to encompass the globe. This globalization has been strongly influenced by three historical events: (1) Western expansion, (2) the emergence and extension of capitalism, and (3) the rise and diffusion of modern science and technology. In the words of one observer, these three principal phenomena have "served to globalize the history, geography, economics, politics, culture, sociology, demography, ecology, and psychology of the human condition."[1]

World history is no longer a set of isolated and separate regional stories; rather, we have entered a period where every event has potential impact upon all corners of the globe—in effect, a period of global history. The development of rapid global transportation and communication systems has encouraged this impact, dramatically reducing the effect of geographic distance. The world's economics, even of the communist sector, are no longer independent but are quickly becoming part of a complex, interdependent global economy. Politically, a single worldwide interstate system has emerged, manifesting itself in the United Nations, in over three hundred other international governmental organizations, and in increased bilateral activities. In addition, most nations feel that it is important to attend even to political events far removed from their borders because they recognize the potential impact of such activity.

Individual cultures, long isolated against changes initiated from the outside, now find themselves part of an array of discrete "micro-" cultures confronting the encroachment of a more comprehensive, westernized, technologically oriented "macro-" culture encompassing the entire globe. Part of this change is the result of the increasing movement of private individuals, goods, services, and information across national boundaries to become global in scope. From a sociological perspective, the resultant impact has contributed to a globalized social structure. Demographically, urbanization has become a worldwide phenomenon. Ecologically the earth's environment is increasingly often affected by human activity. Humans can now move mountains, literally as well as figuratively, and no part of the earth is immune to the consequences.

Finally, this process of globalization has been accompanied by its own language. Phrases like "spaceship earth," the "global village," the "shrinking world," the "global shopping center," and the "global factory" are all part of a new rhetoric. It makes its presence increasingly felt in the language and visual imagery of communication and advertising. Psychologically, humans are being conditioned to see themselves as members of an increasingly larger community.

Recent Global Trends

In addition to the historical patterns suggested above, a number of trends characterize the contemporary global system. These changes touch upon political, economic, military, and social realms throughout the world. These trends include the military growth imperative, the shrinking globe, global interdependence (including resource dependencies), and unmet basic human needs for a substantial portion of the nations of the globe.

Military growth imperative

The ever-increasing expansion of the quality and quantity of military spending and activity has been estimated to exceed $818 billion in 1982, compared to "only" $291 billion ten years earlier and under $200 billion in 1960.[2] An estimated 28 million people are considered members of the military forces, seven million more than two decades ago. When one adds the number of civilians employed directly or indirectly by the military, the number of personnel exceeds 100 million, a significant portion of the total world population.[3]

The increase in military expenditures tells only part of the story. There have also been dramatic changes in the cost and quality of the military equipment purchased. It is generally acknowledged that prices for the same military item average about six times higher today than during World War II. A modern version of the same item used in World War II now costs two hundred times more, because of the technological sophistication of the new equipment. Today's basic stripped-down tank sells for two hundred times the price of the tank seen in old World War II movies. And those GIs of forty years ago never dreamed of doing with their tanks what today's soldier views as normal operating capability.[4]

This improvement has occurred not only in conventional weaponry but also in nuclear weapons of all types. The latter now total over fifty thousand and their combined explosive power is *one million times greater* than the bomb dropped on Hiroshima. A single missile can carry over *two hundred times* the destructive capacity of a 1945 atom bomb, and can travel six thousand miles in less than thirty minutes, landing within a few hundred feet of its target.[5]

As you might expect, most of these expenditures are found in a handful of countries. The United States and the Soviet Union alone have accounted for 51 percent of the total spent since 1973, and when you add each side's major allies, the figure rises to 73 percent of the total. The Western and Soviet blocs spent $40.8 billion and $8.6 billion, respectively, during the 1972–82 period, while the remainder of the developed world allocated $307 billion and the developing nations $739 billion for the same period.[6]

But it is misleading to assume that the military imperative has affected only the superpowers. In fact, the developing or "have-not" nations have actually increased their percentage of global expenditures from 9 percent in 1960 to almost 23 percent today.[7] It can be argued that a spiraling effect is at work here that accounts for a large part of the increased spending levels for both developed and developing countries. Over $60 billion a year is channeled into military research programs as the "haves"—particularly the United States, the Soviet Union, and Western Europe—operate under a "technological imperative" to upgrade weapons systems.[8] This, in turn, leads to the abandoning of "last year's model," which is sold to the highest bidder (through arms transfers) so that new funds can be acquired to help recover the tremendous research and development costs. Governments often engage in the almost indiscriminate selling of last year's weapons, using tactics that have been likened to those of a used car salesman, with little thought to the consequences of such actions for world peace. (Only recently, for example, has the issue ever been raised seriously in the United States.) An arms trade of $36 billion occurred in 1982, a dramatic increase since 1970 when the United States and the Soviet Union were clearly the predominant exporters.[9] These two countries continue to be the largest dealers, as they have been since 1955, but more countries are now joining the arms sales business as exporters, thus increasing the spread of military capability.

The effects of this military imperative have been demonstrated in some sixty-five major nonnuclear wars (involving at least one thousand deaths each) since 1960.[10] Most of these did not involve the superpowers, or if the Soviet Union or the United States was a participant, the other was not. The reluctance of the two leading world powers to meet directly on the battlefield is an example of the constraints that both sides experience in their dealings with one another and in their efforts to secure other foreign policy goals. In addition, no nuclear weapon has been detonated in any of these wars. By

1981, however, 115 "serious" incidents had been reported involving nuclear weapons.[11]

Traditional warfare has been minimized in favor of alternative, but often equally less cooperative, methods of resolving conflicts. The Korean conflict of the early 1950s ushered in a new approach to military hostilities. For the first time in history neither side in physical combat chose to use all of its military capability—nuclear weapons on the part of the United States and the great mass of humanity on the part of the Chinese supporters of the North Koreans. Although few observers took notice at the time, warfare had changed, and probably never again would we witness the kind of total and global commitment of personnel and resources that occurred during World War II. Today's limited wars take many forms but one common feature is the exercise of restraint in terms of the political objectives, the means employed, the sites targeted, and the geographic area desired. Moreover, major attacks against the enemy's civilian population and attempts to eliminate completely its armed forces are avoided. In addition, terrorism and covert intelligence activities may be used. Even nuclear blackmail is used as a deterrent and often conflict is thereby avoided entirely.

There are other strategies for domination that do not include military objectives. Threats to withhold a vital resource such as oil are commonly employed by those nations fortunate enough to possess such a commodity. This action, termed a boycott, is unilaterally withheld if the resource-rich nations enjoy a near monopoly; or, alternatively, international bodies such as the United Nations are urged to invoke a worldwide boycott as in the typical global response to South Africa's domestic policies.

The shrinking globe

Science and technology have given humankind the capacity to travel great distances quickly and to move goods, information, and finances rapidly across the world. As a consequence the scope of foreign policy has greatly expanded in the twentieth century. Just as important, and occurring simultaneously with this dramatic increase in the *scope* of activity, is a tremendous growth in the *number* of actors that now perform on the global stage.

Since 1945 over one hundred new countries have been created and most of these are concentrated in a few regions of the globe (Africa and Asia). Moreover, the number and magnitude of interactions among these countries (and across them by global partici-

Governmental	Nongovernmental
Nation-State Subcentral Governments	Subnational or National Nongovernmental organizations
Nation-State Central Governments	Multinational Corporations
	International Nongovernmental Organizations
International Governmental Organizations	Individuals and Informal Groups

Figure 1.1   Types of global actors

pants who do not represent countries but operate within them) have been growing rapidly. World exports, for example, rose from $127 billion in 1960 to $1,853 billion in 1982.[12] World grain trade among various regions of the globe increased from 26 million metric tons in 1948–52 to 65 million metric tons in 1969–71 and to 209 million metric tons in 1983–84. The list of examples is endless, all clearly demonstrating that interaction among global actors is growing at a rapid pace.[13]

Moreover, the variety of actors and their interactions is growing. Before World War II, foreign policy actions were undertaken by one primary group: clearly designated officials of the central governments of countries. One scholar, John Burton, has termed this type of behavior the "billiard ball" phenomenon, where nation-states were virtually immune from intervention from the outside except through an overt act of war, while at the same time only formal representatives of the government acted as foreign policy agents in dealing with other governments.[14]

The new types of global actors can be divided into two distinct groups, those composed of *official governmental representatives* and those organized *outside government.* (See figure 1.1.) Each of these types—particularly international governmental organizations, international nongovernmental organizations, and multinational corporations—plays an important role alongside the central governments of nation-states. One major reason for this increase in the role of nonstate actors is the frustration experienced by individuals around the globe because of the inability or unwillingness of national governments to solve fundamental problems of contemporary society. Thus citizens are no longer viewing their governments as primary problem-solvers but are turning instead to a variety of alternative governmental and nongovernmental organizations, and formal and informal groups in order to address society's ills. Many new actors have emerged in order to deal with specific problems or areas of concern. These functional organizations are seen as better equipped to deal with this plethora of problems and to provide increased opportunities for individuals to participate in global problem-solving.

In addition to new types of participants in world politics, new kinds of behavior have emerged as well. No longer is the interaction between two actors the routinized, diplomatic, political behavior of the past—whether it be formal conflict such as declared war or simple cooperative behavior. Participants now use a variety of means to exert influence. In addition to more conventional methods, there are also less conventional techniques such as the manipulation of marketing and financial facilities, pricing controls, technology and expertise, clandestine military activities, and many other mechanisms used in pursuit of foreign policy goals.

Global interdependence

Another important phenomenon of today's world is the increasing linkages that bind countries together. An intricate network of political, economic, and social connections—both formal and informal—has emerged. The comparison of total world trade from 1960 to 1982 cited above is sufficient to present the magnitude of this increasing interdependence. It is important, also, to recognize that economic interdependencies, although a major kind of link, represent only one type of network. Military security arrangements and political or social linkages are other types that must be considered as we examine interdependence.

Resource dependencies.   One particular type of dependency in the world today is the every-increasing need for raw materials, particularly by the developed nations, which can be met only by a few supplier countries. Figure 1.2 lists the extent to which the United States is dependent upon imports in order to meets its needs in twenty basic materials.

Among those nations that possess a high percentage of these desired materials, South Africa is particularly well-provided. Its percentage of the world's total for a number of raw materials demonstrates why many developed countries are reluctant to exert too much pressure for change in its domestic policies: platinum group (95 percent), chrome ore (75 percent), vanadium (74 percent), dia-

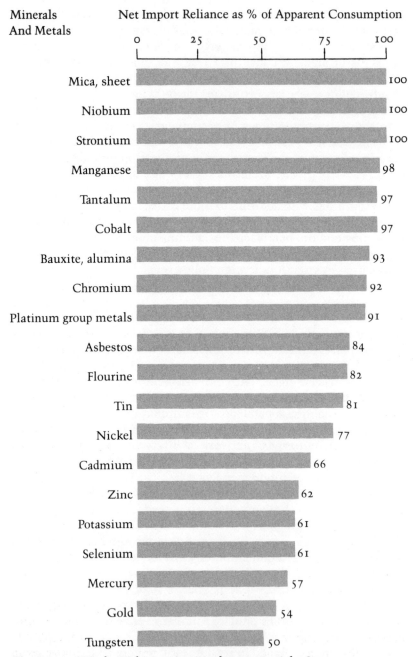

Figure 1.2   U.S. dependency on critical raw materials. Source: U.S. Bureau of Mines

monds (60 percent), gold (70 percent), manganese ore (73 percent), uranium (30 percent), and iron ore (8 percent).

Unmet basic human needs

One final characteristic which bears upon this study of global issues is the extent to which basic human needs go unmet throughout the world, particularly in the developing countries. Governments are typically given a general set of responsibilities that must be met if its citizens are to survive and flourish. The preamble to the U.S. Constitution, for example, enjoins the American government, among other things, to promote the general welfare and ensure the blessings of liberty. Translated, this implies that governments must strive to guarantee basic human needs for food, water, clothing, shelter, education, health, and even employment. Obviously societies vary according to their ability to serve these human needs, but most often the poorer and newly created countries have the greatest difficulty. This fact is relevant to contemporary world politics because these nations have turned outward for help, arguing that the "haves" of the world are obligated to address these problems in the short run and to transform the structure of the global system in the long run so that the poorer nations can become self-reliant and thus fulfill their obligations to their citizenry. The most pronounced effort in this regard is clearly the drive for a "New International Economic Order" that has been promoted by most developing countries and some organs of the United Nations.

Although it is difficult to state precisely the level of unmet human needs, we can document the extent to which meeting a population's social and economic needs is a priority of a government or society. Table 1.1 shows expenditures and other measures for two kinds of nations: the richest fifth and the poorest fifth of the world's population.

As can be observed, the rates for the richest countries are much higher. Not only do those governments spend more to advance the quality of life of their citizens, but the evidence suggests that the citizens do, in fact, benefit. Budget is policy, and in this case the expenditures tend to achieve the desired results.

It is true that in the last decade, developing societies have grown economically at a faster *rate* than those of the developed world. However, this percentage of growth has occurred on a much lower base. Thus, the developed countries' advance as measured by gross national product per capita has been close enough to the developing

Table 1.1   Gap between rich and poor.

	Richest fifth of world population	Poorest fifth of world population
GNP per capita ($)	9,469	206
Government education expenses per capita ($)	497	6
Teachers per 1,000 school-age population	40	12
Women in total university enrollment	43	27
Adult literacy (%)	97	42
Government health expenses per capita ($)	432	2
Physicians per 10,000 people	21	3
Life expectancy (years)	74	53
Infant deaths per 100 births	2	12
Calories per capita as % of requirements	134	90
Protein supply per capita (grams)	99	48
Population with safe water (%)	96	39

Source: Ruth Lever Sivard, *World Military and Social Expenditures, 1983.* (Washington, D.C.: World Priorities, 1983), p. 25.

world that, as a consequence, the gap between the rich and poor nations continues to widen rather than shrink. Knowledge of this fact has been one of the primary reasons why most nations of the globe—rich and poor alike—have made the solution of basic global problems a high priority.

A Framework for Understanding Issues

The world has undergone significant changes, both long-term and short-term, as the above discussion suggests. All of these forces combine to create problems (or to redefine existing ones) that are global in scope and that occupy the minds of the world's leaders. The traditional agenda of a nation seeking the trappings of power (armies and navies) in order to pursue traditional measures of power (wealth, territory, and people) has been replaced by a concern that appears to present an even greater threat. In short, while the traditional agenda still is in place, it exists side by side with a new global agenda that seeks to address these far-reaching sets of problems head on. This new set of problems is characterized by five basic features: (1) the transcendence of national boundaries; (2) an incapacity for autonomous action; (3) a present imperative; (4) a requirement for policy action; and (5) persistence.

Transcending national boundaries

The first basic characteristic of the issues on the global agenda is that they transcend national boundaries. The effects of the problems go far beyond the borders of a single nation. Environmental pollution knows no national boundary. The principle of comparative advantage (one country produces what it can produce most efficiently and purchases from other countries those goods that can be made more efficiently elsewhere) has taken hold on a global scale, and with it have appeared global food and energy problems. Population problems no longer are confined to individual nations and a variety of spillover effects are observed. Boats arrive in Key West from countries with overflowing populations and limited opportunities. No longer are such issues confined to a single nation or even to a single region.

Such issues also become global in nature because the world community has placed them on the global agenda. In 1972 the United Nations Conference on the Human Environment was held in Stockholm. Though typically thought of as the beginning of a concerted global effort to deal with environmental issues, in reality the Stockholm conference represented a culmination of efforts in the post–World War II era to bring together key actors of the globe to address the issue. The conference was, in the words of one observer, "the successor to the great voyages of discovery and exploration that made people aware of the shape of the world and the diversity of its lands and waters, rocks, vegetation, faunas and cultures."[15] International cooperation during the 1957–58 International Geophysical Year (IGY) demonstrated that coordinated effort could work and, moreover, that it is essential if the global community is to acquire knowledge about the far corners of the earth necessary to address its problems. The IGY, in turn, spawned a number of joint ventures that have sought to unlock the secrets of the environment, including the Upper Mantle Project (1964–70), which examined the lithosphere (the outer portion of the surface of the globe, that is, its mantle); the Global Atmospheric Research Program (1970–80); the various projects of SCOPE (Scientific Committee on Problems of the Environment sponsored by the International Council of Scientific Unions); the UNESCO program on Man and the Biosphere, and programs of the United Nations Food and Agricultural Organization (FAO); the World Health Organization (WHO); the World Meteorological Organization (WMO); and the International Union for the Conservation of Nature and Natural Resources (IUCN).

The Stockholm Conference on the Human Environment was the culmination of a number of major developments. First, the scientific community was joined by active environmentalists. Second, the concern for the environment spread beyond the developed Western industrialized nations to both the socialist and the developing worlds. Finally, the approach began to embrace a much broader conception of the term *environment*. All aspects of the natural environment became matters of concern: "Land, water, minerals, all living organisms and life processes, the atmosphere and climate, the polar icecaps and remote ocean deeps, . . . space, . . . the human situation, . . . and the relationship between man-made and natural environments."[16] Perhaps the most important manifestation of this commitment to the environment is the official organization created for implementing the precepts of the Stockholm Conference, the United Nations Environment Programme (UNEP). This organization represented the synthesis of ideas that emerged at Stockholm. It became, in short, a coordinating body that operated under the fundamental principle that responsibility for addressing environmental issues rests with every individual actor, not with a specialized agency. UNEP, in turn, could then become a creative body, an idea generator, a coordinator, and an evaluator. Thus this strategy takes cognizance of the global dimensions of environmental issues.

In 1974 a World Food Conference first turned global attention to a set of food problems, and to the nature of the world's food system and its role in the creation of such problems. The conference adopted a wide range of resolutions designed to alleviate many of the world's food problems and created the World Food Council to deal with these resolutions. Five broad areas of concern have been addressed as a consequence of the conference. These include production inputs, food trade, food aid, nutrition, and global food security.

The world has also placed population issues on its agenda by holding the 1974 World Population Conference at Bucharest. The developed and developing worlds came to this conference, each with its own solution to the problems of population growth. The developed world viewed the high birthrates throughout Asia, Africa, and Latin America as a consequence of the failures of governments to create programs reducing birthrates. The developing world, on the other hand, recognized a link betweeen lower birthrates and economic development, and thus saw the solution of high fertility as lying in economic advancement and advocated the active help of the developed world. Each side compromised and the final plan of action called for both national governmental intervention to reduce fertility and increased first-world aid to assist the third world in its development goals.

Incapacity for autonomous action

A second characteristic of these issues is the incapacity of autonomous action to secure the resolution of an issue. No single actor, or corporate group of actors, is capable of resolving the persistent problems associated with global environment-climatic change; atmospheric and water pollution; the loss of cropland, rangeland, and forests; species and habitat loss; and the effects and potential effects of conventional and nuclear war. Because environmental problems know no national boundaries, resolutions of such issues require (and will continue to require) the cooperation of a wide range of actors, including nation-states throughout the world, as well as a host of others, both governmental and nongovernmental, that operate at the international, national, and subnational levels. While national governments have stepped up their efforts to address environmental ills (witness the proliferation of environmental agencies within the United States), there has also been a dramatic increase in both the number and activity of institutions organized from the grass roots to the international levels. Grass-roots organizations have emerged primarily as a consequence of frustrations expressed by citizens as they perceive, rightly or wrongly, that national governments are unwilling and/or unable to address environmental concerns successfully.

International institutions arose because national governments themselves recognized that cooperation among countries could be enhanced if formal mechanisms were created to deal with environmental issues on a global basis. Thus structures were created for the purpose of trying to understand better the parameters of an environmental problem, or of seeking transnational cooperative ventures to address one concern or another. The United Nations Environment Programme (UNEP) represents the current pinnacle of such activity. Simultaneously, international organizations designed for other purposes have undertaken an environmental role as part of their agendas, approaching environmental concerns from the perspective of their own areas of responsibility. Thus, for example, the Food and Agricultural Organization (FAO) undertakes forest and soil management practices, while the World Health Organization (WHO) uses satellites to monitor soil erosion. One can get a sense of the activity of transnational groups by looking at their participation at global conferences. For example, they were well represented at Stockholm as some 237 such organizations representing twenty-one different fields of interest played vital roles. Three particularly influential organizations were the International Council of Scientific Unions, the International Union for the Conservation of Nature and Natural Resources, and the Friends of the Earth.

In the area of food issues, a variety of actors participate at all levels. At the subnational level, farms and farm organizations possess important direct control over much of what is produced and thereby affect consumption patterns. Other subnational groups, such as those representing consumers or independent (and sometimes less than independent) research groups, may also influence production and consumption patterns. The most powerful actors in the global food system, however, remain the national governments whose overall economic policies, specific agricultural policies, and general trade policies all determine the scope of participation in the food system. The quantity of food people eat in any given country, for example, is more a consequence of governmental choice than of the action of any other actor. Even then, governments themselves may have competing interests. For example, in Japan the Ministry of Agriculture and Forestry continues to seek trade restrictions to protect farmers despite the fact that the government has decided it is cheaper to import food than to grow it. Above the national level, there are still other important food actors. Some, like multinational corporations, operate transnationally (that is, in more than one nation). Multinational corporations may invest in food or agricultural production or sell food or agricultural products overseas. Other transnational actors, like the Catholic Relief Service, may provide food aid through private avenues. There are also international actors, who draw their positions from the representation of component national governments. For example, the European Economic Community (the Common Market) coordinates food and food trade policies for its ten member nations, though not without great and often intractable controversy. Under the auspices of the United Nations, the thirty-six member World Food Council was formed to mobilize support for the objectives of the 1974 World Food Conference. Despite such efforts, these organizations ultimately have no capacity to transcend the individual actions of the governments who compose them. A final type of actor, however, does tend to have such capacity. These are supranational agencies, such as the World Bank, which acquire autonomy to establish and pursue separate (though generally limited) institutional missions. For example, on its own initiative and under its own guidelines, the World Bank issues loans to nations for agricultural development. And finally, food actors engage in the vital transfer of food itself, or the resources necessary to produce food and the information that may improve or otherwise alter the global food system.

A similar situation exists in the area of population issues. It takes but a moment's reflection to recognize that the dimensions of the earth's population are the result of action by individuals and couples throughout the world. Those individuals and couples become the object of the actions, seldom concerted and often competitive, of a wide variety of governmental and nongovernmental actors at all levels. While a large number of nations may agree—as they did at the 1974 World Population Conference—that population issues should be addressed at the national level, other actors such as the Catholic Church or the International Planned Parenthood Federation may not support such a position. And the various sets of actors may hold widely differing views of what action should be taken. Some may prefer a growing population in order to provide employment or military manpower; others may wish to limit population size in order to protect apparently scarce resources. The developing nations may consider it an obligation of the developed countries to aid in relieving the effects of population growth; the developed world, in turn, may demand population control as a prerequisite to aid.

In the same way, no single actor, or corporate group of actors, is capable of resolving the issues associated with energy-dependence on oil, limitations in the quantity and distribution of petroleum reserves, constraints on alternative energy sources, or inaccessibility of nonrenewable options for large-scale use. Energy is an area that exemplifies the worldwide trend toward proliferating numbers and types of actors. The recent energy crisis and its aftermath demonstrated the impact that new actors can have. It was not until 1960 that the Organization of Petroleum Exporting Countries (OPEC) itself was formed for the purpose of redressing what was felt to be an artifically low pricing structure for oil. In little more than ten years, by 1973, OPEC was able to accomplish its objective. But in increasing the price of oil OPEC also gave rise to the formation of other institutions, such as the International Energy Agency (IEA). This organization was instituted by the industrialized nations of Western Europe and North America together with Japan as a means of countering OPEC's control over the international petroleum market. Within another ten years, by 1983, events in the marketplace—largely through the interaction of supply and demand—seemed again to restore some relative balance to the respective levels of influence between these organizations of producing and consuming nations. But in the meantime other actors had entered the arena as well, with new producers such as Mexico challenging OPEC's control of the market by discovering and exploiting new oil fields.

There also have been actors, from individuals to international organizations, who have entered the energy arena in order to advocate a wide variety of resources and approaches intended to replace the worldwide dependence on oil that contributed to a recent energy crisis. All of these actors have different agendas, different points of view, and different stakes in the outcome. What is more, the energy arena in which they struggle is highly interdependent, with complex linkages with other issues (such as economic development or food production). The decisions and actions of any one of these actors or of several of them in combination have a clear impact on the actions and positions of all of the others. Thus the issue of energy cannot be resolved by any single actor, but will instead be resolved in the larger global arena through the combined interaction of many different actors (some of which may be outside of the energy field altogether).

A present imperative

A third characteristic of global issues is that each one possesses a present imperative, which not only impels various actors to press for resolution, but which encompasses the varied and often competing views on how that resolution ought to proceed. For example, most actors for the environment agree upon four objectives: controlling pollution, preserving genetic diversity, conserving resources, and limiting population growth. Support for controlling pollution in the air, in water, or on land came early in the environmental movement and has developed a broad base among wide segments of the global society. The reasons for this development are obvious. Much (but not all) pollution is readily observable, easily documented, and a clearly defined nuisance. The Industrial Revolution brought with it a capacity for widespread pollution and the human race, concentrated in the urban centers of developed societies, learned to live with its consequences for over two hundred years. In the post–World War II era, as population exploded in the developing world, these societies increasingly often suffered from their inability to prevent pollution as a normal by-product of living. Actors also seek resolution of the remaining three problems, although with respect to population a small number of countries believe that their interests are best served by encouraging growth rather than limiting it. Just because most actors support these goals in the abstract does not mean that there is broad agreement over the relative importance of each and the extent to which each should prevail when it comes up against a nonenvironmental value (such as the need for more food or energy). Actors assign differing degrees of importance to various ecological issues as they weigh the need for concern about the environment against the opportunity costs (the cost of giving up one goal in exchange for another) of such concern. It would be misleading to conclude that there is a consensus on how the global community ought to respond to the problem even where there is wide agreement that an undesirable condition exists.

With regard to food, three value objectives typically prevail: efficiency, security, and equity. These values tend to be inherently competitive and the emergent food system reflects the trade-offs achieved among them. A desire for efficiency, for example, concentrates on the optimal production of food. In optimal production, because of comparative advantage a few nations would end up producing the bulk of the world's food, which would then be distributed through open trade channels. Such emphasis would not, however, provide security, since the bulk of the world's nations —the inefficient producers—would necessarily rely on the relative benevolence of the few producers. In contrast, true security would have each nation producing enough food to meet its own needs. Neither efficiency nor security necessarily provides for equity, which would require some standard to ensure an equal distribution of all global food resources. Climate and geological fortune, among other factors, make equity unattainable. Hence, if equity is to be realized in the global food system, the value objectives of both efficiency and security must be superceded. The effort to reach some balance among these values, if indeed an effort is to be made, is one of the major dilemmas within the global issue of food. There may also be a number of nonfood values that compete directly with one or more of the three prevailing food values. Income security in the agricultural sector, through stable pricing in the United States, for example, is a domestic political and economic value that competes with food security from a global perspective. In other countries, such as India, economic growth may take precedence over food equity. In yet others, such as the

Soviet Union, ideological considerations may reduce prospects for food efficiency.

The present imperative can also be illustrated clearly in the field of energy where oil, the prevailing worldwide energy resource, is a finite commodity; that is, the total amount of oil available is known with reasonable accuracy. As we will see, the only questions are how fast it is used and, as it becomes scarcer, what energy resource will replace it. This situation creates differing roles for energy actors. Clearly an oil producer such as Saudi Arabia, which possesses 27 percent of the known oil reserves in the noncommunist world, operates with a set of objectives that differ from those held by most other actors. For example, there are other producer states that have far fewer oil reserves and a far greater need for the profits to be made from the international marketplace than Saudi Arabia. Such nations —and there are several third-world states both inside and outside of OPEC that share those characteristics—would want to maximize the short-term advantage of the current state of oil dependency, therefore preferring to keep prices high and responding to a drop in price by increasing production to maintain a constant share of the market. Saudi Arabia, on the other hand, would benefit instead by preserving the long-term value of its resource rather than responding to short-term fluctuations. Oil is expected to increase in value as it becomes scarcer (barring some breakthrough to a new alternative). As this scenario has unfolded in the 1980s, Saudi Arabia has so far sought to keep production low in the face of declining prices, waiting for demand to increase once again. Other OPEC nations, with greater need for short-term earnings, have resisted (which has caused dissension in OPEC). Consumer nations may seek different outcomes altogether. For them, what may be most important is the lowest possible cost for oil in order to maintain commitments to continued or restored levels of economic growth. Those countries therefore strive to conserve. There also are energy actors who challenge the dominance of petroleum by supporting alternative sources of energy ranging from other fossil fuels, such as coal and nuclear energy, to renewable resources, such as wind or solar power. Still other actors may enter the energy arena with goals not relating to energy. It is quite likely that these actors will challenge many of the values that govern the actions of others. Environmental groups seek to ensure that the choices made in energy will safeguard the environment. Those advocating coal, for example, may be challenged by environmental groups who want laws to ensure that the landscape is not permanently scarred by strip-mining techniques or that the burning of coal will not pollute the atmosphere. All of this points to the fact that much is at stake in the energy arena today and that the issues are still very much unresolved. The outcome will depend on which values, or combination of values, prevail.

With regard to population growth, disagreements again exist over value objectives. For some time now there has been an expression of alarm in the developed nations, particularly the United States, concerning the threat to international peace due to rapid population growth (expressed dramatically in the phrase "the population bomb"). This view has lent a growing sense of urgency to the adoption of vigorous advocacy of population control in the developing world. That position, however, challenges a number of countervailing values in the target areas where the rate of population growth has been high. As noted above, some see national survival as meaning sustained population growth. The efforts from already developed countries to limit such growth are thus viewed suspiciously as a device to keep poorer nations in a state of overall dependency. On the other hand, some developing nations have perceived national survival in precisely the opposite terms and now lead the way toward population control. While an imperative is present due to population trends regardless of competing views, the outcome of those trends will depend on which values, or combination of values, will prevail.

Requirement for policy action

A fourth characteristic of global issues, not peculiar to them but nonetheless integral to the sequence already defined by actors and values, is that their resolution requires policy action. It is evident that action—the process that combines actors with values—implies policy, whether it is formal policy articulated by governments and organizations, or relatively undefined policy that guides individuals in their everyday life. Environmental policies tend to reflect several different approaches to the problem. At one end of the policy continuum, decision-makers urge voluntary restraint or inaction, although its success depends on widespread, even universal, agreement on the costs of failure to comply. This, of course, is a highly unusual situation. For example, the Limited Nuclear Test Ban Treaty of 1963—which banned the testing of nuclear weapons in the atmosphere, in space, under the ocean, and even underground (if the damage spilled over to a neighboring country)—underscores this point. This treaty reflects a kind of voluntary restraint in that nations choose to subscribe or not to subscribe to its provisions and thus make their own decision about compliance. Even though the environmentally related damage level of such blasts is well documented, many nations, most notably France and China, have not signed the treaty and refuse to abide by it. At the other end of this policy continuum is the notion of public (that is, global) responsibility for the resources, actions, and consequences that constitute the environmental problem. This is difficult to achieve because there is no global public enterprise that would assume and enforce the provisions of public ownership even if this strategy were a desirable one. The recent attempt to establish an International Seabed Authority through the new Law of the Sea Treaty to control the resources of the ocean floor demonstrates that, although possible, even a relatively minor effort at public ownership is not without major difficulty. Between the extremes of voluntary restraint and public ownership lie a number of general types of policy options. All require that global actors be bound by some prescription, whether the strategy takes the form of enforced behavior, regulatory or other legal restraints, enforced contributions or support (such as taxation), making identifiable violators completely responsible for actions affecting the environment, or some other mechanism. Without the intervention of comprehensive policy action, it is unlikely that these problems will be resolved.

Policy action is required in the food issue area as well. Food policies revolve around the cycles of the global food system involving production, distribution, and consumption. Production policies affect the growth of food to the moment it leaves the farm itself. Distribution policies encompass the complex set of relationships that move food products from the farm to the consumer: processing, supply, marketing, information, investment, aid, trade, etc. Finally, consumption policy addresses the way food is used by the consumer (including nutritional standards). It is apparent that such food policies are neither easily separable nor necessarily compatible. The policy areas are all part of competing and often conflicting political interests. The term food policy is then something of a misnomer. Food policy is actually an aggregate of all the efforts at a variety of levels to respond to and resolve the myriad problems that define the global food issue. Food policies may even pursue nonfood objectives in either the domestic or foreign sectors, as was evident in the considerations surrounding the United States embargo of grain shipments to the Soviet Union, initially imposed in 1980 by President Carter as punishment for that nation's invasion of Afghanistan and subsequently lifted in 1981 by President Reagan because of its impact on American farm income. There have been other references in a variety of contexts (for example, as a response to oil policies of OPEC) to the use of food "as a weapon." What is more, food policy is linked inextricably to policies arising in other areas such as energy and population. In fact, food policy may be the effective consequence of policies arising in those other areas and not in the food sector at all. In sum, global food policy is a complex system of intersecting actions. It is complex because the system is global; because the problems are vast; because production, supply, and nutrition are not necessarily compatible; and finally because food policy is often either directed at, or the consequence of, a number of nonfood issues.

With the population issue, policies have increasingly often been required to effect appropriate change. The targets of such policies remain those many couples who must make individual daily choices that affect world population growth. But other actors may make choices that are more clearly relevant to policy. Nation-states, for instance, may set and enforce policies that govern the movement of people in and out of borders (immigration and emigration) and therefore help determine population distribution. By the same token, because of the nature of the target actors, the prospects for other policy choices may be less effective and less predictable. Efforts to reduce fertility may, for example, have limited impact because there are other, competing policies that create constraints upon enforcement. Couples tend to make their population decisions in private and without reference to policy pronouncements. What is more, as is the case with many other issues, policies tend to cluster and their impact must be assessed in conjunction with other sets of policies. Thus population policies of fertility reduction may prove to be closely linked with those relating to food, energy, the environment, or other more specific areas. These statements about the reasons for birth control policies are just as likely to apply to policies affecting migration.

The energy issue has also required policy action, and energy policies adopt several different approaches to the problem. The short-term energy problem has been dominated by economic and political considerations. This domination has been evident not only in the emergence of the energy crisis, which was motivated by OPEC's effort to alter the prevailing pricing structure to its advantage, but also in the efforts to resolve that crisis. The formation of the International Energy Agency (IEA) was intended by the industrialized consuming nations of the West in part to establish a more integrated response to actions of the OPEC nations. IEA sought to establish petroleum reserves, for example, so that the effects of a sharp cutoff of oil would not have the same devastating impact as the OPEC oil embargo of 1973. IEA also has sought to coordinate the domestic policies of its members with regard to long-term conservation measures adopted. Indeed, these policy approaches seem to have been successful as oil consumption dropped markedly in the industrialized countries after the peak of the energy crisis of 1979. But in fact it appears that the sheer weight of the high cost of oil had as much impact as various policy approaches designed to provide conservation incentives.

As is the case in so many areas involving multiple actors with differing and competing values, energy policy thus tends to be the cumulative outcome of a number of different factors. The success or failure of those policies seems to be less the product of design than the consequence of complex interactions among the wide variety of actors seeking short-term economic or political gain. Long-term energy policy is more problematic. In the transition that is taking place from a global system dependent on oil to a system that will rely on other sources, setting clear policy objectives is difficult. The competition for short-term gain tends to retard long-term resolution. The ultimate policy choice will probably be affected most by technological developments that have yet to be fully explored. But initiating those developments is a difficult and demanding task. For each of the several alternatives—nuclear power, coal, solar power, etc.—there will be serious trade-offs for the contending actors in the energy arena and for the society as a whole. Addressing production, distribution, and consumption on a global scale is in itself an impossible task. Trying to integrate the competing interests of the many actors on the scene and to accommodate the many issues affected by energy decisions—such as continued levels of economic growth or means to increase food production to meet the rising demand of increased population—makes the effort to develop a comprehensive global energy policy even more challenging.

Persistence

A final element that characterizes global issues is their persistence through time. These global issues force us to examine the future, to look to individuals, groups, and institutions who make it their business to forecast what lies ahead. Although humans have adapted more or less to their current environment, the future is of far greater concern because of existing trends. However, prognosticators disagree about the prospects for and the magnitude of conditions in the future. Both individual analyses and major collaborative reports on the future display this lack of consensus. All do agree that if the human race is to have any chance of surviving on this increasingly fragile planet, the problems must be addressed squarely in a comprehensive analytical manner. The human race has demonstrated its capacity to use science and technology to achieve both good and ill. But future strategies require not only that we use science to create physical opportunities for change, but also that we reevaluate political, social, and economic processes of the past and present in order to determine how alternative structures can aid in effecting a better environment. To achieve this goal six different strategies, discussed in this text, are typically advanced: (1) the creation of new international regimes; (2) reliance on steady-state systems; (3) centralized political authority; (4) a return to more manageable institutional arrangements ("small is beautiful"); (5) a concerted effort to redistribute wealth and resources from the "haves" to the "have-nots," whether individuals or nations; and (6) complete reliance on technology (the "technological fix").[17] The trends and consequences of forecasts and alternatives for global environment are addressed in the final perspective of this volume: the "future" perspective. In the concluding chapter we step back and reflect once again on progress recently made and draw hope for the future.

Food is an essential element of human existence and therefore of global survival. In any discussion of the food issue, three alternative scenarios tend to be sketched for the future. The first, a pessimistic view, projects chronic scarcity. In this scenario the food available is substantially inadequate to meet the existing demand. Severe malnutrition on a global scale thus becomes an expected (and accepted) aspect of the human condition. A second scenario optimistically projects world abundance and focuses in contrast on a world food supply above demand, allowing hunger and lingering malnutrition to be overcome. Finally, a third scenario extends the present pattern with chronic, though not severe, malnutrition based on pockets of poverty in the less-developed world. Food supply remains a function of world harvests and the impact of policies adopted by national governments.

In the present pattern governments of the developed world have tended to treat food as a problem peculiar to the less-developed world. In all of the future scenarios, however, the food system is treated as a global entity. Hence, part of the prescriptive thrust of these scenarios suggests that the developed world must recognize that poverty and malnutrition are problems that ultimately (and increasingly often) affect the economic prosperity, political stability, and general quality of life for all. As projections are advanced for the global food system, one central element therefore is the status of the less-developed countries. Optimists tend to favor the impact of technological factors in improving prospects for self-sufficiency for these countries (for example, nuclear fusion as a power source, as yet undeveloped, releasing fossil fuels for agricultural use). Pessimists tend, on the other hand, to muster arguments against self-sufficiency. They point to the continuing presence of major climatic and environmental forces and to the limitations of technology, which has often fallen short of expectation, sometimes leaving cultural confusion and disruption in its wake. The three future scenarios discussed here—optimistic, pessimistic, and the extension of the present pattern—were examined in a comprehensive study conducted under the auspices of the U.S. Government and published as *The Global 2000 Report*.[18] In all three, there was a set of common conclusions: (1) that the world has the physical and economic capacity to meet a substantial increase in demand for food through the year 2000, though with some qualifications; (2) that the near-record growth in food demand is driven by a combination of population increases in the less-developed countries and growing affluence in the industrialized countries; and (3) that growth in food supply is characterized by increases in both the resources committed to food production and to gains in productivity. How these factors will affect the world beyond the year 2000 is still uncertain. But the trends and consequences of such projections are critical to understanding the global future of food.

The future of global population is also a critical element in trying to deal with the wide range of global issues. Population projections have emerged with regularity from the United Nations, the World Bank, the U.S. Bureau of the Census, and other governmental and nongovernmental agencies. From such projections policy prescriptions emerge, and against these predictions competing values are ranked. Projections on mortality, for example, show a continuing rate of decline based upon the diffusion of modern health procedures throughout the developing nations. Barring major medical breakthroughs, the same projections for developed nations show relatively little potential for change. However, when such projections are linked with analyses of fertility, a view of the prospects for global population emerges. Here the tolerances for interpretation are wider, but the results tend to point to a reasonable consensus. The developed world will tend to remain constant; in the developing world the rate of population growth will begin to decline. But in the latter case the present population configuration—women now in or emerging into their childbearing years—promises a continuing high absolute growth in population. The trends and consequences of such projections are critical to understanding the global future.

Energy has proven to be an essential component of human development and human existence. It is therefore also an essential component of global survival. As in the case of food issues, there is no clear agreement among experts about the global energy future. Optimists argue that the past decade has proven the capacity to extend the timeline for the transition from oil. That is, instead of using up the oil reserves available to us early in the twenty-first century, forecasts now focus on a period closer to the middle of that century. In the short term this view is reinforced by the recent reductions in the level of consumption, the exploitation of new fields, and the accompanying decline in the price of oil. Some analysts contend that the principle of demand and supply has shown that energy will be produced as long as demand remains. Other analysts take a more pessimistic view, arguing that regardless of the short-term adjustments that have taken place recently in the petroleum marketplace, the long-term energy problem remains and little has been done to resolve it. They perceive changes over the past decade as retarding the effort to take a clear stand on the energy future. The drop in the price of oil that occurred at the beginning of the 1980s is seen as having an ultimately negative effect. Because of the high price of oil during the energy crisis, a number of initiatives were undertaken in the energy field to find alternative forms of energy. Techniques began to be developed that would enable energy to be extracted from nontraditional sources. In the end of the dominance of oil the established energy institutions saw the need to find other bases in order to play a continuing role in the energy picture. The large oil corporations began to diversify their operations into other areas —nuclear power, synthetic fuels, and renewable energy sources, for example—and began to invest in research efforts to seek even newer and more innovative solutions to the energy problem. But as oil declined in price and its prevalence as an energy resource seemed to extend further into the future, such investment became more costly relative to the development and marketing of petroleum. As a consequence, corporations began to reduce their alternative efforts. In all, there is no clear sense of the energy future. Many possible alternatives to oil will have to pass the crucial test of commercial feasibility, and for those energy resources that are not ultimately exhaustible—the "renewable" resources—that feasibility seems a long time away. How the energy picture will look after the year 2000 is still uncertain. It is evident that oil cannot continue to play the role that it has played; experts agree generally on that point. But there is no agreement about what will replace oil as the dominant energy resource for the world.

Finally, we need to observe that all of these issues are characterized by being linked to one another. Factors affecting one issue also have an impact on other issues. Increases in population mean that more food must be grown, but to grow more food requires additional energy consumption which may have adverse affects on the environment. Thus not only do characteristics of each issue itself mitigate against ready solutions, but the potential for impact from and toward other issues increases the difficulty of solution. Figure 1 in the series preface shows a schematic representation of these characteristics of global issues.

Part II
Essential Elements of Global Issues

In Part II we select four global issues: food, energy, population, and environment. While most individuals have some sense of what these problems look like, our purpose in Part II is to demonstrate that each of the issues is infinitely more complex, involving a much wider variety of elements, than popularly thought. While the focus is on the discrete nature of each of the issues, nonetheless there is some implicit discussion of linkages across these issues. Each of the four chapters focuses on one specific issue.

2 The Food Issue

The role of food in the global arena is often difficult to comprehend even when it seems to have grown more visible on nightly television and in our daily newspapers. Evidence of world hunger appears again and again in the international news. For a period in the early 1970s, in the Sahel region of Africa, drought became so severe that we were shown scenes of inhabitants with barely enough energy to function, let alone to be a productive part of society. In 1979, in the refugee camps in war-torn Kampuchea, we saw children with distended bellies and empty eyes touchingly confirming that hunger was a human reality and not just a statistical condition. Most recently it is Ethiopia, struck once before by widespread drought, that has become the object of widespread national and international attention. Reports indicate that the drought-induced famine could ultimately claim 200,000 lives. Often, however, what we see on broadcast news or read about in newspapers shows only dramatic instances of hunger. As the examples suggest, these occurrences often arise from man-made disasters, such as the war that brought famine to Kampuchea, or from natural disasters, such as the droughts in the Sahel and Ethiopia, or the cataclysmic storms and earthquakes that have occurred elsewhere in the world. Ironically, because such events capture the world's attention, international agencies and other mechanisms (the most popular of which have been the efforts of recording stars in Britain—"Band-aid"—and the United States—"We Are the World"—who came together in 1985 for the "Live Aid" concert) are usually able to provide emergency food supplies to meet immediate needs in the stricken areas.

Aside from such events, reports seem to contradict the images on television and in the newspaper. It is a fact that food production has increased continually in absolute terms in the past three decades (although the rate of increase is now slowing). The years of the

1950s and 1960s in particular witnessed record rates of growth as new resources and new techniques increased agricultural production. Based on total output of grain alone, converted into its nutritional value for individuals, there are more nutrients available in the world today than are needed to feed its population adequately.[1] And that statement does not reflect all of the earth's resources. Some potentially productive land is not used to grow food crops because of economic or political choices made within individual nations. In the United States, the world's largest grain exporter, cropland has actually been taken out of production for domestic policy reasons. The grain that could have been produced on that land in 1983 was estimated at 92 million metric tons.[2] World grain stocks carried over (that is, held from trade as reserve stocks) in that same year totaled 191 million metric tons. In other words, there seem to be adequate sources of food available not only to provide for the emergency needs of those whose tragedies appear before us from time to time on the nightly news, but also to meet the fundamental nutritional needs of a far wider population. Why then are we told that there is a problem with world hunger? Can we not prepare ourselves for the broader food requirements of the globe in the same way that we can provide short-term emergency relief?

Unfortunately the dimensions of the global food problem are systemic and severe, extending beyond disaster-induced famine and the simple calculation of gross production figures in relation to nutritional values. Indeed, hunger itself is complex. It is a condition where individuals suffer from inadequate nutrition caused by deficiencies in the quantity or quality of food. This condition, commonly referred to as malnutrition (although that too is an imprecise term with a variety of meanings and manifestations) severely affects both the physical and mental capacities of humans. Reliable estimates place the number of severely malnourished people at from 100 to 200 million, mostly found in Southeast Asia and sub-Saharan Africa. In fact, two-thirds of those suffering from serious deficiencies exist in nine countries—India, Bangladesh, Indonesia, Pakistan, Philippines, Cambodia, Zaire, Ethiopia, and Brazil.[3] But even these figures do not account for those who suffer from lesser forms of debilitation—simple energy deficits, for example—from the inadequacy of their diets. Projecting hunger in the broadest perspective, the World Bank has estimated that malnutrition could affect as many as 1.3 billion people by the year 2000.[4] That is, as much as one-sixth of the world's population or more may not be able to satisfy minimal nutritional needs.

The structure of this problem is shaped by a number of conditions related to the availability of food. We can begin to understand those conditions by considering natural resources that support food production. In the first place, we should understand that the earth is not especially well-endowed for purposes of agricultural production. Only about one-third of it is land, and most of that is too hot or too cold or too wet or too dry to support cultivation. Of all of the land available, just 3 percent is arable, that is, conducive to agricultural production. The problem begins here because these agricultural resources are not distributed evenly. There are relatively few areas that have soils that are rich enough and climatic conditions that are good enough for sustained and reliable crop production. Much of this condition does depend of course on the nature of the crops to be produced. What is more, food production has become increasingly dependent on the availability of other kinds of resources, such as technology, advanced scientific knowledge, and management skills.

As we will see in more detail, overall food output is a function of two factors: area—land that can be used for agricultural output—and yield—the amount of agricultural output from any given area. In the case of area, virtually all of the globe's arable land today is already devoted to that purpose. This means that, insofar as the record growth in food production has been related to expanding area, that expansion has nearly ended; further projected increases in production will probably have to come almost exclusively from expanded yield—that is, getting more food from the land now in use. The prospects for expanding yield, however, are heavily reliant on scientific knowledge and modern industrial capacity. Increased yield has come through the application of energy-intensive implements (such as tractors, harvesters, processors, etc.), fertilizers, and other factors commonly found in developed societies. For both area and yield, only a few nations, uniquely blessed with both abundant agricultural resources and advanced technological capacities, account for the bulk of the world's food production. Moreover, because of the conditions that now support production in these nations, they will likely continue to do so. All of these nations are in the developed world; most of them are in North America.

The importance of this last observation is due to another, more pressing condition governing contemporary world hunger: the rapid growth in population since World War II. The world's population nearly doubled between 1950 and 1975, growing from 2.51 billion to 4.03 billion, and it is expected to slightly exceed six billion by the year 2000. The number of people on earth of course directly affects the food problem. We often use the metaphor of a "slice of the pie" when talking about resources. If the "pie" we speak of is of a fixed size, any increase in the number of persons eating it will mean a smaller slice for some, or, assuming an equal distribution, for all. Because humans must eat to live, the relationship between food and population can be stated almost that simply. The addition of one person into the population increases the demand for food by one (that is, technically, the population elasticity of food is one).[5] As a consequence, worldwide population growth must place a commensurate burden on the world's capacity to feed the additional populace. The size of the pie and how it is divided will determine how much is available to those who will be able to get a piece of it.

In the real world, the size of the "pie" is not really fixed, as we have already seen. Food production has increased, so the pie has grown larger. However, the news is not good: not only has food production not increased at the same pace as population growth overall, but the rate of increase in food production has been declining (in the 1950s agricultural output rose at the rate of 3.1 percent per year; in the 1960s it was 2.6 percent per year; and in the 1970s it was 2.2 percent per year).[6] This trend can be expressed more clearly in terms of the annual rate of growth in world grain production per person; it has declined from 1.2 percent in the 1950s to .8 percent in the 1960s and to .5 percent in the 1970s.[7] When one adds to these observations the growing scarcity of arable land mentioned above, the news becomes even less heartening. With this increase in population, the amount of land available for farming (which is, remember, relatively fixed and nearly all of it already being used) is projected to decline steadily on a per capita basis as we approach the year 2000. For each person on earth there will be less land available to provide food. More important, perhaps, the rapid increase in population, just like the availability of agricultural resources, has not been evenly distributed among the nations of the earth. In fact, there has been an inverse relationship between resource availability and the distribution of population increases. The bulk of the rapid growth in population has occurred in the less-developed countries concentrated in Asia, Africa, and Latin America. As indicated above, moreover, those are precisely the areas of the world least blessed with natural agricultural resources and least equipped with technical and managerial resources to improve food production.

Looking at these two conditions makes the solution to the food problem appear simple. We should move the food produced in places where resources are abundant to those areas where the need is greatest. However, the simplicity of that notion raises a further condition that helps us to gain understanding of the global food problem: food is both a nutrient and a commodity. The nutrient characteristics of food seem self-evident: one must eat to live. Food is therefore a resource of a special kind, for to deny food is to deny or impair life. The question, however, is not always whether there is something to eat, but whether there is enough to eat based on the adequacies or inadequacies of the individual diet. Healthy people can be hungry. People with enough to eat can be unhealthy because of the nature of their diet. Yet even with individual idiosyncracies there are calculable minimal nutritional requirements, based on the biological functioning of the human body, that set the standard for food as a nutrient.

But food is also a commodity. It is bought and sold. The commodity characteristics of food therefore make it subject to the economic forces of the marketplace. Farmers—at least in the prevailing system of market economies—produce food for profit. They therefore respond to market conditions in determining what they will plant and how much. As food enters the market its price, like that of any other commodity, will be determined by the interaction of demand and supply. The marketplace for food, though closely interrelated with domestic markets, is now international. In the period of rapid population growth and increased food production, both the scope and the volume of international food trade have also expanded tremendously. For example, since the 1970s the share of world food production entering international markets has increased from 10 percent to 17 percent.[8]

Clearly these market factors shape the global food problem. As we will see, the market tends to vary because food supplies are unstable, affected by such things as the weather and what farmers believe will yield the best return on their investment in any given crop year. Market fluctuations—changes in supply and demand —affect the prevailing price of food so that it too fluctuates. The availability of food, barring intervention by other agencies, becomes predominantly a function of income rather than of nutritional need. And the dynamic force in the market is purchasing power. For this reason, the prevalence of world hunger and various levels of malnutrition are seen to be closely associated with poverty. If sufficient funds were available to each and every one of the earth's inhabitants, it is argued, then hunger would not be a problem. Since enough food is produced to provide each individual with three thousand calories a day, there is more than enough to sustain healthy life. With sufficient funds, the global food system could be used to produce the right kinds of foods and the people of the world taught to eat the right kinds of food. Unmet basic nutritional requirements could then be satisfied. One calculation suggests that, disregarding the cultural elements that also determine what is food, one pound of grain could supply most of a person's daily nutritional needs and this grain could be purchased for less than a quarter.[9] The problem is that most of the world's hungry people do not have a quarter.

The Global Food System

We can return then to the dramatic instances of the world hunger problem, as seen most recently in Ethiopia, and understand why it has been possible for recording stars to respond to such emergencies by donating the sales from a hit song or the proceeds from a benefit concert. The money is used to buy food and to pay for its shipment to the needy areas. But we can also see that these occurrences do not begin to capture the true dimensions of the global food problem.

To expand our understanding of this problem, we must turn to the global food system. This system can be addressed in terms of three simple functional categories—*production, distribution,* and *consumption.* The interaction among these components—on both a domestic and an international scale—determines the movement and availability of food worldwide. Food *production* accounts for all of the forces that drive the output of food and the selection of what kinds of food get produced and marketed. Production issues therefore apply to whatever happens to food up to the point when it leaves the farm for market. At that point food enters the *distribution* system. While there are extensive domestic components that affect the distribution of food—for example, agriculture in general is characterized by direct government intervention ranging from overall control over trade policies to specific political action such as the U.S. embargo of grain shipments to the Soviet Union in 1980 in protest against that country's invasion of Afghanistan—it is the international movement of food that is of concern here. Again the commodity characteristics of food provide the driving force. Food products are bought and sold in the international marketplace. To a lesser extent, food has moved in the postwar period by means of aid, including loans, concessional sales (that is, sales under special advantageous conditions) and outright transfers (aid). The final category, *consumption*, encompasses all those factors relating to the ultimate destination of food, the individual consumer. Although centered on the problems of undernutrition and hunger, consumption is not restricted to these problems alone. A companion to the malnutrition prevalent in those nations with an insufficient supply of food, for example, is overnutrition prevalent in the developed world. Like malnutrition, overnutrition can contribute to the incidence of disease. There is a clear correlation between the high incidence of heart disease in the West and diet—overweight, high cholesterol levels, and so forth. When viewed analytically, production, distribution, and consumption are interrelated; they give us categories into which we can place various food activities. But when they are viewed from the perspective of actual global practice, they tend to be far less coherent. We will see that much of the problem with the global food system arises from the often disjointed relationships between the mechanisms of production, distribution, and consumption.

Production problems

The production of food has been plagued globally by serious and recurring shortfalls. These shortfalls have resulted from several factors—both physical and procedural—that have acted singly or in combination. Among the physical constraints the most important are those relating to the availability of natural conditions and resources conducive to agricultural production. Climate, for example, has been in large part responsible for a series of bad crop years in the Soviet Union. As a consequence, grain production fell well below planned goals and that in turn produced a kind of ripple effect throughout the system. Anticipation of insufficient stocks of feed grain meant that livestock would need to be slaughtered before they were fully developed, which then promised to create a meat shortage, and so on. To try to counteract those projections, the Soviet Union has regularly turned to the world grain marketplace to supplement its lagging production, buying grain principally from the United States. Since the Soviet Union is itself the largest grain producer in the world, shortfalls in Soviet production and sales from the world grain market mean less grain available for other consumers. Moreover, the negotiated sales agreement between the United States and the Soviet Union sets a price standard for grain that affects the overall world price. The less-developed countries with less to trade and a lesser individual share of the expected market, are not parties in the process. Thus, although this example is greatly oversimplified, a series of climate-related grain shortfalls on the territory of a major producer have meant an overall world shortfall for all prospective consumers, regardless of national affiliation.

Shortages or changes in other kinds of resources can also affect production. To appreciate this factor, one must recognize again how important are the commodity characteristics of food. In simplest terms, farmers in market economies grow food in order to make a profit by producing at the lowest possible cost and selling at the highest possible price. The income from a bushel of wheat, measured by its market price, will indicate a profit insofar as it exceeds all of the costs of producing it. Those costs must include the "opportunity cost" of not producing some other commodity—corn, soybeans, sugar beets, or whatever—that might yield a larger margin of profit. When, at some point, some added unit of cost put into the land—for example, more chemical fertilizer —will not produce a commensurate increase in what the farmer gets from the land in return—such as a measurable increase in the yield from his wheat fields—then there will be no added profit and thus no incentive to produce more. Consequently, if the cost of some important resource such as energy increases (which it will no doubt do, especially in the event that any given resource becomes scarcer), the farmer will no longer seek to increase production and may in fact cut back or shift to another crop in order to reduce the cost relative to output.

The applicability of this behavior to current food production issues arises from the fact that in the decade of the 1970s the cost of a number of farm resources, energy in particular, increased. In fact, the increase in the cost of energy beginning with the 1973 "energy crisis" had a multiple effect. Cheap energy had allowed agriculture to overcome several difficulties and therefore to maintain the unprecendented rates of growth in production in the 1950s and '6os. Through the use of petrochemical fertilizers (fertilizers drawn from petroleum) and of fuel to run farm equipment—which allowed more extensive tillage and irrigation—it was possible to overcome such obstacles as the loss of topsoil and the scarcity of water. But in 1973 the oil price increases imposed by OPEC put an end to cheap energy. By that time the application of other technologies—for example, new varieties of seeds and pesticides—had also reached the peak of its potential to increase crop yields. In the end, there emerged a new environment of production marked by sharp declines in the rate of increase that had characterized the 1950s and '6os. In addition, because of the increased costs of energy-related resources, the farmer's return on the investment of additional inputs no longer showed increases in profit commensurate with the increases in cost. Farmers began to produce less or to grow other crops to maximize current gains. The whole environment of global food production thus became less stable, prices fluctuated sharply, and it became difficult for either producers or consumers to establish a reliable pattern of trade.

These conditions refer largely to the developed world, those advanced industrial countries which account for the greatest portion of world food production and the bulk of all food exports. It does not refer to production issues in the less-developed countries, most of which—characterized again by rapidly growing populations —are food-deficit nations, nations with a more or less constant shortage of domestic food production (requiring them to import food to make up the shortfall). During the decades of growth in food production and the shifts of the early 1970s, there was a concentration on the physical problems of food production in these nations. Some of the problems are similar, having to do with the economic basis of producing commodities for trade. In fact, food production in these countries tends to be local or regional in scope rather than national, let alone international. For example, world price fluctuations generally have little direct bearing on farming in small villages in Africa. Most of the food-deficit countries not only experience the need to provide resources to make farm land productive (irrigation, erosion control, knowledge of proper crop rotation, etc.), but they also lack adequate facilities for the transportation and storage of food once it has been produced.

In addition to the physical constraints, food production is also affected by procedural constraints. One characteristic of world agriculture in general is low productivity. This is a function of the physical constraints introduced above as well as of issues of management. Many of the economic conditions that motivate farmers in market economies, for example, are not present in nonmarket or socialist economies like that of the Soviet Union. It has been estimated that while one U.S. farmer feeds forty-nine people, one Soviet farmer feeds four people. Similar comparisons can be found. In 1982, 24.8 million cows in the European Economic Community produced 111 million tons of milk, while in the Soviet Union 43 million cows produced only 90 million tons of milk. Agriculture has been a constant problem in the Soviet Union, which organizes its agricultural production through a system of collective and state farms. Farmers are either employees of the state or they are a part of the collective that shares the income from the output of the farm. Testimony to the role of economic incentives in this system is found in the private plots that each collective farmer is entitled to hold. Goods produced on such farms may be sold in separate local markets. The output from these farms appears to show a much higher level of productivity (and quality) than that produced on the collective farm itself. There are additional management problems in less-developed countries that restrict agricultural output, including the handling of resources, the treatment of the harvest, and the access to distribution networks. Where production facilities do exist, the object of production is often not the domestic market, where there may be pressing needs, but the export market through which food production becomes an instrument for the larger goals of development that these countries pursue. Agricultural resources are thus devoted to cash crops, such as coffee, bananas, or sugar, rather than food crops for the domestic market.

Distribution problems

The same forces affecting production also affect the global distribution of food, since the bulk of the distribution function is accounted for by trade. Thus, in simplest terms, the profit-motivated farmer entering the international marketplace looks for a buyer who will pay the best price. Of course there is really no single international marketplace in the literal sense where food is traded. The overall distribution of food throughout the world takes place in a variety of different markets at different levels. There are numerous local markets throughout the world to which farmers do come with their produce and sell or trade, and there are larger, often government-controlled national markets where entire crops may be traded (sometimes before they have been produced, with investors basing their actions on expected future production, the so-called "futures" market). Regarding the global food system, however, it is the international market that most concerns us here. While no literal marketplace exists, there is a real analytical structure through which food moves around the world today.

The structure of international food trade is in fact complex. First, it is important to understand that it involves a variety of different actors, not just farmers and consumers but many "middlemen" —shippers, traders, multinational corporations, and the governments of both exporting and importing nations. National governments now tend to play the most influential role. Because food is an international commodity, it is subject not only to the economic forces of farmers and traders wishing to make a profit, but also to all of the constraints and problems of trade policies with which national governments seek to protect both producers and consumers from market shifts. Both trade and agricultural policies are areas in which national governments tend to intervene actively.

The volume of international trade in food—largely grain—has grown steadily in recent decades. That growth means that more food is being exported, and those exports represent a greater share of the output of producing countries. It also means that there are other nations that have commensurately increased their food imports so that imports occupy a greater share of their food consumption (the paradox is that many food-deficit nations still export food as limited cash crops and use their earnings to purchase food for domestic consumption). With this growth in international food trade, all those taking part have become increasingly sensitive to any changes in the market. We have already seen some of the factors that may bring about those changes—for example, climate (which has greater long-term implications than the year-to-year impact in one or another region would indicate), production decisions by farmers in food-producing countries, fluctuations in price resulting from the interplay of demand and supply in the market, efforts by individual governments to control that interplay, etc. The consequence of increasing international food trade has been to make the entire global food system more unreliable, a process we have already seen in the production function. This unreliability results in the problem of food security, that is, assuring a reliable supply of food. Instability in supply and fluctuations in price make it extremely difficult for food-deficit nations to count on the availability of imported food.

This instability is one of the causes of the unevenness of international food distribution that in turn also has an impact on consumption. Operating within the distribution function, consumption must be understood in terms of demand, not need. The distinction is important: demand is an economic force related to the ability of an actor to purchase a commodity; on the other hand, need refers to nutritional requirements, the amount and type of food necessary to sustain life. This distinction highlights the difficulty with the mechanisms for global distribution of food and returns us to the separation between developed and less-developed countries. Any commodity, without intervention of some sort, will flow to the consumer willing and able to pay the going market rate. As a result, those best able to pay will be best able to obtain the commodity. The greater the demand, generally speaking, the higher the price. Similarly, scarcity, no matter how it is induced, will result in an increase in market price. Those with limited resources tend to have little impact on the market and must compete at the price that emerges from interaction among the major traders. The major traders in international food tend to be developed countries. For food this means once again that the less-developed countries—having experienced rapid population growth in recent decades, having little international purchasing power, and having generally inadequate food production of their own—have a difficult time finding food security in the import market. The problem manifested itself acutely in the 1970s because of sharp increases in the price of food. Because of a combination of factors—weather, Soviet grain purchases, greater market demand for livestock production, and national policies of major grain producers—food prices on international markets tripled betweeen 1972 and 1974. These price increases severely constrained access to the market for the less-developed, food-deficit nations (which had come to rely on imports). Purchasing power then carries over from production to distribution as a principal force in the global food system. Two prestigious commissions—the Independent Commission on International Development Issues (the Brandt Commission) and the U.S. Presidential Commission on World Hunger—in separate reports have focused directly on the consequences of this fact, citing poverty as the major condition to be overcome in order to alleviate hunger.[10]

However, there are mechanisms that can circumvent the determinative forces of the market by counteracting the advantage that the developed, food-producing nations have over the less-developed, food-deficit nations. The foremost of these mechanisms is food aid —provided directly or indirectly—although its patterns are somewhat uneven. Emergency relief, for example, is a form of food aid, and there are a number of international and independent agencies established to provide such relief. Broader programs also exist to provide food aid to nations in need. The United Nations established the World Food Program in 1962 to help coordinate aid efforts by securing commitments of support from member nations. Not all nations have met the goals set by this program, and its resources are not adequate to meet the range of emergency food needs that have arisen over the years.

In addition, individual nations also have provided food aid. The United States in particular has been a prominent actor in international food aid. This role, however, provides a good illustration of how food aid is related to the overall system of food distribution. U.S. food aid developed in large part because of the agricultural surpluses of the 1950s. In order to dispose of these surpluses, it was important to develop domestic policies that would maintain farm income. At the same time, with intensifying political competition from the Soviet Union in the third world, it seemed politically expeditious for foreign policy objectives to extend this support to these emerging nations as a mechanism to demonstrate both American goodwill and the advantages of democracy in a free enterprise capitalist economic system. Accordingly, the United States provided large quantities of food for newly emerging nations in the 1950s and '60s, providing the largest share of the world's food aid. Since the 1970s the United States has become more reluctant to play such a role because of price increases and the growth of international food trade (and some domestic political sentiment that the food "giveaways" had not created the anticipated level of political support for the United States from the third world).

Food aid is also provided indirectly in the form of funding for agricultural activities. Aid in this form is generally given through international financial institutions that have come to play an increasing role in the overall international economy. Again, note the association with the commodity characteristics of food. There are public sources of funding for agricultural activity in the less-developed countries. International organizations like the World Bank seek to provide support for the national development of agricultural production capacity. The World Bank finances agricultural projects through loans provided at market rates. Many of these international agencies are in turn supported by the major developed countries of the world who have a prominent role in determining overall policies (for example, in the case of the World Bank, the funds come primarily from selling bonds on Wall Street). More recently there has been an increase in the role of private investment in development in the less-developed countries. These efforts are financial, however, and not necessarily directed at food per se. The international lenders or investors seek a favorable return on their investment. While not necessarily negative, insofar as such investment encourages these nations to grow their own food, this effort has brought its own share of problems. In a similar way, the international debt crisis that has surfaced in the current decade is related to the food problem. Since the debtor nations, in order to service the debts they have incurred, continue to focus on cash crops for export, the imbalance between the developed and less-developed worlds has been perpetuated. Other investors encourage the export of food commodities and thereby impede whatever efforts might otherwise be made to approach self-sufficient domestic production. In its prevailing forms—emergency relief, grants of food, the transfer of financial resources, etc.—food aid has not yet provided the solution to the commodity-based inequities of global food distribution. Many believe that it will be unlikely to do so.

Consumption problems

The consumption function is difficult to address for it is the least structured component of the global food system. Consumption can be understood either in terms of demand, as we considered it above, or in terms of need. We must, in the latter case, address the issue of nutrition, especially undernutrition (including, as an acute form, malnutrition), which is where the problem arises. Humans derive fundamental nutrition from protein, an absolute requirement for sustained health. Beyond that fact the issue becomes increasingly less certain. Specific nutritional requirements vary for individuals and are affected by a number of nonfood conditions such as culture or religion that often define what is and what is not considered to be a desirable food. Food itself—the same food—varies sometimes in energy and nutrient content. Even the body's capacity to process food varies; illness, for example, reduces that capacity, thereby creating a vicious cycle in which hunger impedes the ability to use whatever food is available and hence makes the nutritional deficiency more difficult to overcome. For example, of those who die of malnutrition, most die of the associated diseases, not of starvation. Thus although there is no question that there are minimum nutritional requirements that determine mental and physical functioning in human beings, questions are raised about efforts to generalize those requirements and use them to assess world consumption levels. Overall, such assessments must use imprecise measures, because it is difficult to translate individual requirements and individual food intake into populationwide measures of food sufficiency.[11] Most assessments look at caloric intake—the number of calories a person consumes in a given day—as a rough measure of nutritional status. Caloric intake, however, is only a crude approximation of actual nutrition. While it is important to recognize the difficulties with these measures, which may lead to imprecise statements of the scope of the problem of undernutrition, there is little doubt that severe food deficits exist worldwide.

These deficits reflect the same disproportions between agricultural output and purchasing power that separate the developed and developing nations in the production and distribution function. Undernutrition is overwhelmingly a third-world condition (although there are also poverty-induced pockets of hunger in nations of the developed world, demonstrating again the relationship between income and hunger). In looking at that condition, we must keep in mind that food production has increased worldwide so that global statistics show an increase in per capita food consumption, with a steady improvement in the 1960s and 1970s (except for sub-Saharan Africa, per capita consumption of calories increased by 4.1 percent and per capita consumption of protein increased by 2.8 percent from 1961 to 1977).[12] However, the result of this increase has largely been that the affluent—those able to pay—have benefited by eating better, rather than an improvement in overall global nutrition. It appears, for all of the reasons stated in discussing production and distribution above, that diets have even deteriorated in some countries, especially among the poorest sectors of the population. Using as a standard the "average daily food supply as a percentage of minimum daily requirement to sustain normal activity" (observing the caution with regard to the imprecision of such measures), we can get some sense of the nature of the problem of undernutrition (see figure 2.1). The United States, for example, meets 135 percent of this requirement. Note by this measure that the Soviet Union has an identical figure and that several East European countries exceed both nations. But the important observation that arises from these data is that food deficiencies are concentrated in the less-developed world. The principal food-deficit nations, most of which are located in central Africa, show figures below 90 percent. That is, on the average, people in these countries do not meet their daily nutritional needs. Moreover, these figures do not mean that every citizen in these countries has available even the percentage of food indicated. The figures are averages. Some people are far better off and, consequently, some people are far worse off.

Consumption is affected by socioeconomic status and taste. As people become more affluent, their tastes change. They are able to acquire not only more food but "better" food. Most of the developing world derives its nutrition from basic foods, termed *staples*—rice, wheat, and other coarse grains—which provide necessary protein. In

Figure 2.1   Where the world's hungry live. Source: *New York Times*, 16 August 1981.

Average daily food supply as a percentage of minimum daily requirement to sustain normal activity. Data are for 1977, the latest available.

North America					
Canada	127	Spain	128	Kenya	88
United States	135	Italy	136	Angola	91
Mexico	114	Greece	136	Zambia	87
		Turkey	115	Malawi	90
Latin America		Bulgaria	144	Mozambique	81
and Caribbean		Albania	113	Zimbabwe	108
Cuba	118	Yugoslavia	136	South Africa	116
Jamaica	119	Rumania	130	Lesotho	99
Haiti	93	Hungary	134	Madagascar	115
Dominican Rep.	93	Czechoslovakia	139		
Guatemala	98	U.S.S.R.	135	**Asia and Pacific**	
El Salvador	90	Poland	140	Syria	108
Honduras	89	East Germany	139	Lebanon	101
Nicaragua	109			Israel	122
Costa Rica	114	**Africa**		Jordan	62
Panama	101	Morocco	105	Saudi Arabia	88
		Algeria	99	Yemen	91
South America		Tunisia	112	Southern Yemen	81
Colombia	102	Libya	126	Iraq	89
Venezuela	99	Egypt	109	Iran	130
Trinidad and Tobago	111	Mauritania	86	Afghanistan	110
Brazil	107	Mali	90	Pakistan	99
Ecuador	92	Niger	91	India	91
Peru	97	Chad	74	Sri Lanka	96
Bolivia	83	Sudan	93	Bangladesh	91
Chile	109	Ethiopia	75	Nepal	91
Argentina	126	Somalia	88	Bhutan	88
Paraguay	122	Senegal	95	Burma	106
Uruguay	114	Guinea	84	Thailand	105
		Sierra Leone	93	Malaysia	117
		Liberia	104	Singapore	134
Europe		Ivory Coast	105	Indonesia	105
Norway	118	Upper Volta	79	Phillipines	108
Sweden	120	Ghana	86	Vietnam	83
Finland	114	Togo	90	Cambodia	85
Ireland	141	Benin	98	Laos	94
Britain	132	Nigeria	83	China	104
Denmark	127	Cameroon	89	Mongolia	104
Netherlands	124	Cen. African Rep.	99	North Korea	121
Belgium	136	Congo	103	South Korea	119
West Germany	127	Zaire	104	Japan	126
France	136	Rwanda	98	Hong Kong	126
Switzerland	130	Burundi	97	Papua New Guinea	85
Austria	134	Uganda	91	Australia	129
Portugal	126	Tanzania	89	New Zealand	127

these instances the protein intake is direct, derived from eating the grain. In the developed world the predominant source of protein is meat, which is protein converted from grain consumed by livestock. In the process of conversion, however, both calories and protein found in the original grain are lost (used in the process of growing the animals). Grain converted to meat loses 75 to 90 percent of its calories and 65 to 90 percent of its protein value.[13] Beef, the most popular (and prestigious) form of meat, requires eight calories of grain protein to produce one calorie of meat protein. When viewed from the perspective of global nutrition, this is not an efficient way to use available protein. But as nations grow more affluent, or, more precisely, as some sectors of the developing world grow more affluent, consumption of protein in the form of meat grows apace. World meat consumption is indeed increasing. This trend affects both domestic and international food patterns. Much of the world grain trade is composed of grains used for feeding livestock, which in turn drives up the domestic price of grain for all purposes. Overall, more grain is now fed to animals than is consumed directly by one-quarter of the world population living in the low-income, food-deficit countries of the developing world. More important, the proportion of grain now being consumed by livestock has doubled, from 20 percent to 40 percent in the last two decades. Trends in consumption patterns do not therefore favor improvement of the lot of those people in the developing world who now suffer from undernutrition.

Food Policies

The outcome of the food issue will be shaped by the capacity of the three functional components of the global food system—production, distribution, and consumption—to respond to the difficulties it poses. Thus there are just three ways to address the problem: to increase the production of food, to change the prevailing framework for the distribution of food, or to alter the present patterns of consumption.[14] It is evident that these approaches are not mutually exclusive, but each carries its own constraints in contributing to the outcome of the global food problem. Moreover, we need to begin once more with a caution. The policies that shape actions in the production, distribution, and consumption of food are not a set of coordinated, coherent efforts. They involve a wide variety of actors and conditions many of which are not designed to deal with food at all. What we discuss as global food policies are therefore the aggregate of the various local, national, and international actions taken in the food area. It should also be recognized that the distinction between each of these policy areas is imposed, not natural, especially with regard to production and distribution. Often the two are not as clearly differentiated as the discussion here would indicate. In the discussion we will change the order used so far, beginning with the consumption function and ending with distribution, because this represents an ascending order of effectiveness in attempting to resolve the food dilemma.

Altering consumption patterns

One direct way to shift the food consumption trends of the past two decades is to reduce population growth. We have seen that the food problem as it exists today, in both scope and location, is to a large extent the outcome of two decades of population increases concentrated in the food-deficit nations of the third world. Among those nations, the most significant food problems are in Africa, which also possesses the highest birthrates in the world today. There food consumption per capita has over the last decade fallen far below minimum requirements for a large proportion of its population. Estimates of the proportions of undernourished people range from some 8 percent in the Ivory Coast and Morocco to 50 percent or more in nations like Mali, Chad, and Mauritania (not including the recent drought-induced famines in Ethiopia).[15] If the population growth rates of these African countries are not reduced (and other contributing conditions remain the same), then the demand for food will continue to outstrip supply. Thus population control offers an instrument to reduce demand, and policies aimed at reducing the growth rates of world population may in this sense be interpreted as food policy—remember that the population elasticity of food is one.

This approach, as we have learned, however, is a "good news, bad news" effort. The "good news" is that population growth rates, linked directly to the increased demand for food, are already declining. The "bad news" is that regardless of the impact of positive steps to reduce population growth rates, there are already too many people to feed within the prevailing patterns of the global food system. In contrast to Africa, for example, where the rate of population *growth* is a problem, in Asia, where growth rates are declining, it is the *size* of the existing population that creates the problem. Population control is a mechanism for long-term management of the food problem, but it will provide no relief for the immediate needs of today's population and the growth which that population will produce. In addition, the less-developed countries are not very receptive to suggestions from the developed world presenting population control as the solution to the problem. As will be discussed in a later chapter, population control has been advanced repeatedly by the developed countries, especially the United States, as a way of managing the challenges of development. The less-developed countries, while acknowledging that population growth exacerbates the issue and accepting that the food problem is part of a larger set of issues, insist nontheless that concentration on population control is an evasion of the responsibility that the developed world must assume in third-world development.

Another way of approaching prevailing consumption patterns is to focus on the way the affluent consume food. The reasoning in this approach is superficially attractive. If the affluent, many of whom are "overnourished" (consuming more than the minimal requirements for proper nutrition), were to change their consumption patterns, it would be possible to make additional food available for distribution to the needy. Translated to the scale of global hunger, two things would need to occur: the rich nations of the developed world would need to change their eating habits, and the additional food would need to reach the developing world. How would the developed world's eating habits need to be altered? One way would simply be to eat less; as we have seen, the caloric intake of the North exceeds minimal requirements. Another would be to eat less meat. If the affluent were to reduce their meat consumption, particularly the consumption of beef, then (the argument proceeds) grain used to feed livestock could be used to provide protein to humans directly. This would mean more grain on the marketplace (and presumably the price of grain, driven up by the competitive demand for feed grains, would also decline). Some people have therefore suggested "meatless" days as a way to begin the process of change in consumption patterns. This then is a "redistributive" approach in terms of nutritional needs; it seeks to solve both the problems of overnourishment in the developed world and undernourishment in the developing world by decreasing consumption in the former and redistributing the food to the latter.

While superficially attractive, there are a number of problems with this approach when it is tested against the world food problem. First, it is not easy to persuade the affluent to alter their eating habits. Because of the commodity characteristics of food, those habits are linked more closely to socioeconomic patterns than they are to nutritional concerns. As the populace, or portions of it, gain greater economic choice, they tend to increase their intake and to choose different diets. Because such dietary improvement is associated with status, domestic political policy may be at work as well. The Soviet Union's entry into the international grain market in the 1970s, which we noted earlier, is a case in point. The Soviet leadership made a commitment as far back as the 1950s to increase meat consumption as a way of improving the nation's diet. Due to a combination of poor management and poor harvests, that commitment proved difficult to keep. In an effort to do so, the Soviet Union became an active feed grain importer in the 1970s, contributing to the growing instability of grain imports to food-deficit nations. The same pattern of using meat consumption as a measure of improved diet is now emerging in the developing world. It seems difficult, therefore, to find an incentive that would alter the eating habits of the well-to-do on a scale sufficient to affect the global food problem. The issue is similar at both ends of the spectrum—that is, the seemingly unbreakable link between income and food consumption. Experience suggests that the well-to-do would rather contribute money directly through some charitable institution (or buy a record for "a good cause") than change their eating habits.

Another difficulty comes when we think about how the food would get into the hands of those who need it. This difficulty may be characterized as the "pipeline problem." Assuming that the affluent do change their eating habits (health trends in the developed countries are in fact shifting attention away from such heavy reliance on red meat), would that trend result in more grain being made available for the needy in low-income, food-deficit nations? This seems unlikely, barring some significant change in production or distribution. Impediments exist at each end of the pipeline. The constraints are again human and not material. Remember that the farmers are going to make decisions based upon an assessment of highest return on their investment. A reduction in meat consumption in the developed world would not necessarily impel farmers to continue to grow grain for sale to the third world, but might more likely cause them to shift from growing feed grain to growing some other product that will gain profit in a market that has been altered by the new patterns of grain sales. Price dictated by demand and supply will determine what is most profitable. The low-income nations will not necessarily be more competitive in the international marketplace just because the affluent have stopped eating meat (unless there is intervention by some other institution). At the other end of the pipeline there are problems as well. The exchange of food is to a large extent controlled by national governments. Those governments have not always proven to be reliable conduits for getting food into the hands of the needy, sometimes using the food to their own ends whether for political, economic, or personal gain. A further handicap in these countries, which has contributed to food deficits in the first place, is lack of domestic structures that will permit the efficient distribution of food internally, whether it is locally grown or imported. What is more, even where food is available in the developed countries it may not be culturally acceptable in third-world countries that often have tastes that differ from those of European cultures. Thus, even if some success is achieved in altering the consumption patterns of the affluent, it may have little impact when the result ripples out to the poor in the less-developed countries that are undernourished. The problem is persistent: the neediest nutritionally are also the neediest economically whether measured internationally or domestically, and therefore they are not part of the system that determines how their nutritional needs will be met.

Increasing food production

There are two sets of approaches—institutional and technological —that address the issue of food production. The first set focuses on the political and economic structures that govern the world's food supply. Remember that demand is an economic variable, not a nutritional one. As we have seen, the increases in food production in response to demand have not yet resulted in improved diets for the undernourished. From a production perspective that outcome is not solely attributable to international food patterns. Food production worldwide is largely dictated by domestic policy. Not only are the developed nations, with food surpluses for their own populations, motivated by food's commodity value, but so also are the less-developed countries. Thus a number of the impediments to production arise in the very nations that are experiencing the greatest deficiencies. Many of these countries have more potential to influence the production process within their own borders, through control of pricing, tax policies, domestic investment programs, and the like, than do the various international structures of the global food network. However, like so much of the food problem, this is not a simple issue. National control over agricultural policies in the less-developed countries is part of a complex set of development strategies.

The bulk of the developing countries have sought to follow the path of rapid industrialization as a means to develop. The intent of this strategy is to translate overall industrial development into economic gains that will stimulate demand within the domestic economy. The increase in demand will in turn stimulate the agricultural sector to produce more goods to meet the demand and thereby provide income and jobs in the rural areas. In practice, this choice has meant for the most part that the industrial sector has usually received the bulk of attention at the expense of the agricultural sector. Thus economic growth has been accompanied by a reduction in the role of agricultural production in the developing economies, with the rural sector receiving a declining share of national resources, jobs, and income. Insofar as demand has been stimulated, the proportion of the increase affecting agricultural production has not been significant.[16] Thus the rural poor have tended to remain so, regardless of overall development gains.

This strategy also begins to explain the paradox of food-deficit nations engaging significant portions of their populations and agricultural resources to produce crops for export, and in some cases importing food for domestic consumption. Using 1979 figures for ninety less-developed countries, estimates report that agricultural exports account for 50 percent or more of overall agricultural output in ten of the nations, more than 20 percent in thirty others, and more than 10 percent in the remaining fifty. At the same time, 8 percent of food eaten in these countries overall is supplied by imports.[17] The exported foods are predominantly cash crops designed to earn foreign currencies from trade. The earnings received are then used to promote overall development objectives. As it turns out, they are also used to pay for the imported food necessary to meet domestic demand that was not satisfied by national production, particularly in the growing urban, industrial areas. Such trends indicate that the most important actor in agricultural production in developing countries, the small farmer, has little influence on the process of food production beyond the immediate rural area in which he operates his farm. Land tenure, the policies of the national government, and the attractions of the international market all tend to favor the large landowner. Meanwhile national policy attracts more and more people to industrial areas where the inadequacies of domestic food production are more acutely felt and where imported food becomes a short-term solution.

Based on this experience and in the face of widespread undernourishment in the developing nations, some observers recommend an alternative strategy that concentrates on food production as the foundation for economic development. This *food first* or *self-provisioning* approach takes a stance virtually opposite to that just described. Here it is argued that development should begin with food production. Instead of large-scale efforts to build a competitive industrial base, the developing nations should take the necessary steps to improve their own food supply by encouraging farmers, especially the small rural landholders, to produce for domestic consumption. This approach places a premium on nutritional over developmental needs, and it seeks to alter the international structures that perpetuate the dependency of the South on the North for its development.

Food first is therefore advanced as an independent path to economic development. Proponents argue that in this approach, over the long run, the agricultural products entering the national economy would have the effect of producing income for the agricultural sector. That income would then generate demand for industrial products, which would in turn stimulate industry that utilizes local resources, allowing the nation to move away from dependence on relatively unstable and inequitable foreign markets. At the same time, the need to trade food products internally would require more diversified food production (as opposed to "monocropping," the concentration on a single commodity dictated by its export value). Domestic industries would need to develop in order to provide the consumer products to trade in return for food. The industrial sector would thus also be encouraged to produce more, with the farm income providing the jobs and capital that industry needs. As agriculture developed, it would still be possible to sell any excess crops on the world market, but that market would no longer drive the availability of food within the nation.

This use of agriculture as the driving force for development would require far greater attentiveness to the agricultural sector on the part of the national governments of these countries than has been the case so far. In most cases, there are serious difficulties in the support structures for agriculture—the infrastructures of cultivation, transportation, storage facilities, and marketing—that would need to be overcome if a *food first* strategy is to work. Much of the agricultural production that exists remains subsistence farming that never becomes a part of the national economy (yet it may account for as much as three-quarters of employment in some of the low-income, less-developed countries). That sector in particular must be modernized. Additionally, however, the solutions to many of these difficulties are technological. That is, they require support of a kind that is already available in the developed world. Acquisition of the necessary technology will still involve trading with the developed countries, which will require something to trade. It may not be easy therefore to break the dependence on the developed North simply by shifting development strategies to concentrate on meeting national food needs from within. In addition, a strategy that relies on agriculture to stimulate industry is a slow way to pursue economic development objectives, still based on the rapid achievement of Western standards of modernization. Few of those in positions of influence in the developing world have been willing to abandon those standards of development for the sake of feeding the poor. Those who control domestic power in most of the less-developed world have stood to gain more from rapid economic development than from a gradual *food first* approach. Consequently few developing nations have thus far chosen to follow this path.

Technological approaches

A second set of approaches aimed at increasing world food production have been technological. At the beginning we observed that an increase in food production could come by either increasing the area in production or by increasing the yield—the agricultural output —of the land already under cultivation. There still remains a large area of arable land that is potentially productive. However, it cannot be made profitably productive. There are many factors which enter into the calculation of profitability, including climatological limitations, the cost of reclamation (in rain forests or deserts), and the unavailability of adequate water supply. Under these conditions, arable land is actually being lost worldwide to natural phenomena such as encroaching deserts and salinization, or to human influences such as housing, industrial development, or recreation. Some of this loss has been a consequence of unsuccessful efforts to place marginal land into cultivation. As a result of these actions, much of the recent effort to increase production has concentrated on improving the yield of the land currently under cultivation. The technological advances of the postwar years have taken several forms, usually manipulating inputs such as fertilizers to enrich the soil or pesticides to control insects or herbicides to control weeds. Other technology has focused on farm implements allowing more extensive cultivation of the land; these include tractors, combine harvesters, or processors of various sorts that reduce post-harvest loss.

Much of the increase in global food production in the 1950s and 1960s was attributable to such technological gains. Many of the techniques used, ranging from petrochemical fertilizers and pesticides to mechanized cultivation, proved to be energy-intensive. Even the expansion of irrigation, reclaiming water-poor land, consumed more and more energy. This is one of the reasons that agricultural production was so seriously affected by the energy crises of the 1970s. The increase in energy prices contributed directly to the rise in food prices and to food shortages as farmers found diminishing returns from more costly inputs. Because of their technological orientation, these approaches have originated largely in the developed world, but their apparent success led to their being exported to the developing world as a solution to agricultural problems there. With the exportation of the advanced technology, there was also an exportation of the limitations of technology-based agriculture. Insofar as they had adopted these technologies, the less-developed countries thus found themselves both directly and indirectly caught up in the energy crises affecting the developed nations.

The most dramatic and celebrated of the technological efforts made in recent years has been the so-called Green Revolution. The Green Revolution applied genetic and other forms of research to develop new high-yield varieties of staple grains. The objective, the "miracle," of this process was to increase significantly the agricultural output of the third world without requiring any expansion of cultivated land. The Green Revolution was much heralded when it began, and indeed it seemed to achieve its intended purposes. For nearly two decades, between 1961 and 1980, the yields of staple grains (cereals) increased at a rate of 2 percent per year. However, as more experience was accumulated, the promise of the Revolution began to be questioned. The high-yield seeds turned out, like many other products of advanced technological societies, to require large amounts of similarly technologically advanced inputs—fertilizers, pesticides, agricultural implements, irrigation, and a number of other facilities lacking in the countries that were to benefit from the miracle grains. The technological advances of the Green Revolution disregarded the institutional characteristics of the less-developed nations. Thus the low-income farmers who most needed the increased outputs had limited opportunity to take advantage of the benefits provided. The more affluent farmers who could afford the additional inputs benefited, as did the industrialized countries that became the suppliers of the technology needed to support the success of the Revolution.

Other criticisms of the Green Revolution have focused on the consequences of the genetic changes induced to cause the higher yields, including reduced resistance to plant disease, increased susceptibility to climatic effects, and in some cases lowered nutritional value. In addition, acceptance of the promise of the high-yield seeds led to the disregard of traditional, regionally based varieties that some feared would become extinct, replaced by poorer alternatives designed and tested in a different environment. Even if these problems did not materialize, the increases in yield would be limited by the resource base upon which they too must rest. In short, the technological promise of the Green Revolution, though lingering, seems now to represent less of a miracle solution and to have become another factor defining the limitations of the global food system.

A final technological approach that deserves mention is the quest for alternative food sources. One proposal that has gained in popularity, for example, is to make better use of the ocean as a food source. Fish are a rich source of concentrated protein. Under present techniques, fishing is gathering, not cultivation. As overall food demand has increased in recent years, fishing has become more and more competitive, and technology and more extensive fishing have combined to deplete fish stocks. It has been suggested (and such research and development are under way) that the oceans be cultivated to gain maximum benefit from their resources. This proposal sounds easier than in fact it is. The oceans, like the land, are largely infertile. Only a few unevenly distributed areas of the sea actually are conducive to fishing, and therefore to cultivation. While there may be some potential in farming the oceans or other aquatic environments, probably no quick technological fix can be found here for the global food problem.

Other approaches have examined novel food sources, to make potential foods more attractive or to expand humans' relatively limited tastes (every year there is a contest in the United States for the best recipe using earthworms, an easily grown protein-rich creature; thus far, the earthworm has not been marketed for human consumption). Some of these food sources are designed to replace the staple grains now used to feed livestock (thereby freeing grain for human consumption). Others take some of the other foods used to feed livestock and try to make them attractive to humans. Another effort seeks to fortify foods that are both recognized and available but are nutritionally inadequate in their natural state. These various approaches and others are efforts to expand food production within the constraints that now prevail. The more pressing question is whether those constraints can themselves be altered.

Changing the Framework for Distribution

Whatever the conditions, it is the pattern of food distribution that links agricultural production to human consumption. Most observers agree that there are deficiencies and inequities in that pattern, although they do not agree on either the sources or the solution of those problems. The general objective in trying to rectify the distribution patterns is to establish a system that will provide global food security, that is, assurance of access to food sufficient to meet minimal nutritional requirements. At the World Food Conference held in Rome in 1974, in the wake of the food "crisis" of 1972–74, there was overall agreement that a more stable and secure global food system needed to be developed. There, however, the agreement stopped and the prescriptions began to differ radically. The conference produced a number of resolutions, some highly rhetorical, some potentially operational, but none with any regulatory oversight to assure accomplishment. The overall goal of providing food security worldwide is still short of realization regardless of improvements. Most of the shortfall can be found in distribution problems.[18] We will focus on three areas of concern with regard to food distribution. The first addresses international food trade as the predominant form of world food distribution. The second area addresses food aid as a supplemental (though changing) mechanism. Finally, the third area focuses on the much more difficult question of the relationship between income and food, for under prevailing conditions adequate income will allow access to available food and participation in the process of making the decisions that affect food futures.

Food trade

Trade has of course long served as a means to move products from areas where they are most efficiently produced to areas where they may be more costly to produce in exchange for other products with similar characteristics. There is nothing inherently amiss in such a system. But because the partners in a trading relationship operate within national settings, international trade turns out to be a system that functions through complex mechanisms. As we have already noted, government intervention is commonplace as national leadership seeks to promote and protect the economic well-being of the country. Trade is competitive and market-oriented. Goods are traded in the interest of maximizing gain, that is, making a profit. Government intervention, serving the interests of individual nations, also interrupts the free operation of the market, trying to assure national benefits from trade. Governments set taxes, tariffs, and other nontariff barriers in order to control trade. In the postwar period, international trade has been dominated economically by the developed nations. This dominance has characterized the international food trade as well as the extensive trade in manufactured goods. In fact, the bulk of the world's food trade, like trade in industrial products, actually takes place between developed countries and other developed countries. In contrast, the less-developed countries conduct nearly 80 percent of their trade (nonagricultural as well as agricultural) with developed countries and only the smaller remainder among themselves. As a consequence, the less-developed countries, minor partners in the overall trading enterprise, have little influence. As in any market setting the international market for food favors the most powerful economic actors.

For the international food trade this condition has placed the third world at a distinct disadvantage. The prices for goods that the less-developed countries must import, including food, are set by exchanges between the more affluent developed countries. At the same time the prices for goods that the developing nations export to gain foreign earnings, including food exports, have fallen. This phenomenon in the international marketplace, called the terms of trade, has thus worsened the distribution of food through trade. The less-developed countries must trade more at a lower price, and will receive less at a higher price. Under conditions of scarcity, such as the food crisis of the 1970s, the burdens of the international food trade were most acutely felt among the low-income, food-deficit nations. One can recognize from this phenomenon, together with our discussion of the difficulties in food production, the circularity of the problem. Trade must be adjusted through some mechanism if the low-income, less-developed nations are to gain access and not be economically and institutionally excluded. However, to make such adjustments—known as trade liberalization —requires willingness on the part of the dominant actors to change their policies. Those policies, however, are designed to protect against disadvantage in trade. In short, the less-developed countries are asking the developed world to alter the very foundation of the whole complex structure of the trading system that they have established. There has been a reluctance to do so.

Now the strategy prevalent in the developing nations of concentrating agricultural resources on cash crops seems more comprehensible. In many cases, such crops are among the few resources that these countries possess for purposes of trade. The objective of such trade is to acquire sufficient foreign exchange earnings to allow the developing nations to become active participants in the international market. But here too there are difficulties. Many of those cash crops—sugar, bananas, or coffee, for example—are subject to alternating gluts of supply and shifts in demand, often resulting in low prices. These food products are not vital resources for which demand remains relatively constant. This has not been the case with petroleum, which permitted the Organization of Petroleum Exporting Countries to form a powerful cartel that could control supply and therefore the price of their product. Efforts to form sugar and coffee cartels were attempted, but the consumers for these products were willing to go without or were able to find some alternative supplier. What the less-developed countries need in return for their exported agricultural goods makes the imbalance worse. These food-deficit nations (remember that parts of the developing world, the so-called "newly industrialized countries," have been able to make progress in selling manufactured goods, though in the face of growing trade barriers) need staple grains to feed their own populations. The developed nations, trading principally among themselves, set the market terms for those products and dominate the marketplace. Just four countries—Canada, France, Australia, and the United States—accounted for 90 percent of wheat exports in 1982. In that year, the United States alone provided almost half of the wheat exported worldwide. Demand for such grains, remember, is in large measure set by the increased world demand for meat. Without some intervention, economically or institutionally, the disadvantageous position of the low-income developing nations is unlikely to change in the foreseeable future.

What forms of intervention have been proposed to help break this apparently circular problem? One approach, vigorously advocated by third-world countries, is to restructure the entire international economic system that sustains the developed world's advantage. This approach, termed the New International Economic Order (NIEO), seeks to enlist the developed nations in redressing the imbalances that have prevailed over the past few decades by giving preferential treatment to the developing world. That perspective represents not only a radical solution to the problem but a radical interpretation of its causes that is not universally accepted, especially in the affluent nations that would have to make the adjustments.

Another structural approach to this problem has concentrated on building food reserves to use on behalf of the less-developed countries in stabilizing the international market and thereby promoting greater security. Although the specific proposals for food reserves are detailed, they may be divided into two types: reserves intended for emergency relief and reserves intended to stabilize more fundamental aspects of the international market. The first category is relatively simply treated, although there have been lapses and reluctance to build up emergency stocks. The second category has greater potential impact on the imbalances of the international food trade.

These stabilizing reserves would be formed by building up grain stocks from the food-producing nations during good harvest years when prices were low. They would then be used under the direction of an independent international authority to moderate the fluctuations in the international market when food stocks are scarce and prices are high. The objective would be to alter the conditions that make it so difficult for the less-developed countries to compete. These reserves could be used to ensure a steady flow of food preferentially to the neediest nations. They could also be applied to the marketplace to guard against rapid shift in prices due to the kinds of conditions that produced the grain shortages of the 1970s. Some observers argue that adequate reserves of staple grains that form the base of international food trade might also have a positive effect on food production in the developed countries as well because they would add greater predictability. However attractive the notion of food reserves to moderate the market, there has been no agreement on the critical issues needed to implement such a program, such as: who would control the reserves; how much would each of the food-producing nations be required to contribute; what market conditions would be set to determine when and how the reserves would be used, etc. The United States, among other nations, has always vigorously protected domestic farm income, now deeply involved in the international market, and has thus far been unwilling to support such a proposal without a number of safeguards to protect American agriculture.

Food aid

The second major distribution mechanism for food has been food aid. As mentioned earlier, food aid—other than emergency relief, which has been around for many years—began to be an active form of international assistance in the 1950s. U.S. farm surpluses and the commitment to maintaining domestic farm income combined with the foreign policy objectives of competing with expanding Soviet influence in the introduction of a broad foreign aid approach. This direct food assistance (known as the "Food for Peace" or the PL 480 program, after the number of the public law which authorized it) sent an enormous quantity of food to the developing countries, sometimes as outright grants, sometimes in the form of concessional sales (for example, low-cost loans repayable in foreign currency to be used in the recipient country). American food aid was governed by a number of both political and economic conditions that by the 1970s had become less persuasive. Consequently, the United States began to cut back from this direct food assistance program. By that time, however, both the direction and content of food assistance had changed as well. In the 1970s, international economic assistance in general had begun to emphasize agriculture. Additionally this aid, from both national and international agencies, also turned away from direct food assistance and more toward development assistance. In earlier periods, consistent with overall development strategies, food assistance concentrated on "modernization." That concentration sought to provide the less-developed world with the advanced agricultural techniques utilized in the industrialized world. But as we have already seen, although modernization produced expanded agricultural output, it failed to alleviate the problems of undernutrition and malnutrition among the predominantly rural poor in the less-developed countries.

In any case, direct food aid is at best a short-term solution to food problems among the poor. An old aphorism says, appropriately: give a man a fish and you give him a meal; teach him how to fish and you give him food for life. Once food or development assistance has been delivered, governments in the recipient nations have often used it to their own economic and political ends. The beneficiaries of the assistance have proved often to be the large-scale farmers and the products have tended to go into the export market rather than into domestic consumption. Food aid has even produced a disincentive to national production, since the easily available food alters the structure of the local marketplace and may, as a form of "dumping" of the agricultural surpluses of the developed world, also depress markets available to food-producing nations in the third world. The distribution problem has seemed in some cases even to worsen.

In the past decade, both national and international food assistance has adopted a different orientation. It has sought less to support agricultural projects and more to support the development of the missing infrastructures of the food-poor developing nations, concentrating on small-scale rather than on large-scale production. This support has thus focused on building the nonfood support for national distribution—rural roads, rural energy, and even rural industry. In such an approach, termed the "small farmer strategy" one can recognize features of the *food first* orientation to development.[19] Lending agencies providing assistance have also attempted to use that assistance to alter the market conditions in the countries seeking their financial support in order to favor improvement of the domestic food system. It is increasingly difficult to assess the relative success of this approach as opposed to direct food aid or even indirect food assistance, which can be measured in terms of food delivered or food produced. There is also growing attention, after the Brandt Report and the President's Commission Report on World Hunger, on the alleviation of poverty as the root cause of hunger. Considerable controversy remains over the issues of food aid, direct or otherwise. The shifting environment of aid, however, focusing on the small farmer, domestic markets, and development of agricultural infrastructures in the less-developed countries represents the adoption of a much longer-term strategy than has been the case in the past.

Income and food

In the long run, most observers agree, the solution to the global food problem will be found in the commodity characteristics of food. These characteristics now affect most of the obstacles that exist in the global food distribution system. Poverty—the inability to gain access to food—is closely correlated to hunger. We have seen repeatedly that food power is ultimately purchasing power. Thus any change in the global food distribution system will result in, or be preceded by, changes in the commodity structure of the international flow of food. The problem is again a circular one. The key to alleviating poverty is income. The key to income is employment. Employment in the low-income, food-deficit nations will come through development. Development will come through economic growth, the absence of which is where the problem began. Food distribution can be improved if jobs can be provided to the populations of the developing world. But that is an enormous undertaking. In part, we must recognize again that rapid population growth has contributed to the difficulty. Most of the population growth has been recent. The developing countries are characterized by young populations; the real employment problems are yet to come. But if that employment can be provided and the conditions of poverty that persist in the developing world alleviated, then the substantial gains in food production of recent decades can carry over into the distribution system. There are widely differing opinions, among observers in the developed and developing worlds alike, concerning the inequities of the international economic system and how that system might be altered to make it more equitable. But as long as farmers who affect the global food system do produce food for profit, purchasing power will determine access to food.

The Future of Food

Like so many issues in the global arena, the solution to the food problem will be neither easy nor quick. It will require progress across a number of fronts if the nutritional deficiencies projected for the next decades are to be met. In the long term, there must be some moderation of demand. Analysts who concentrate on the impact of population on food are persuasive in showing that the consequences of rapid population increases in the developing world have shaped much of the acute discrepancy between supply and demand that perpetuates and even increases undernutrition in low-income countries. Most who approach the problem also recognize that more research and development are needed to increase both the quantity and quality of agricultural production. It appears that the hopes for some technological quick fix, as promised by the Green Revolution, will not be realized. By the same token, the Green Revolution did have dramatic impact in increasing food production in a number of countries, such as India. Whatever the outcome in the areas of consumption and production, virtually all who have looked at the food problem agree that the most immediate constraint on the global food system today lies in the distribution systems that currently operate. That constraint is largely economic; it requires some means to overcome the poverty of the food-deficit nations, whether through self-development, external intervention, or, more likely, through some combination of both.

While many observers can agree on the contours of the food problem—population growth, poverty, instability of supply, low productivity—less agreement exists on the proper course of action to alleviate it. Each course has its own limitations. Technology, which offers radical solutions, also has tended to mean increased use of increasingly expensive energy inputs. Even if these inputs were economically feasible, there are still technological limits to production, dictated by available water and climate. Technology that relies on depletable resources will simply refocus the basis of the problem. Similarly, while institutional changes in political and economic systems seem unavoidable, there are significant obstacles to such change, for it strikes at the heart of the structures that built and maintain the prevailing system in the first place. It may be more prudent and potentially more effective to try to adapt the areas that are deficient in food to the commodity norms of the system than to reorient that system. The most feasible approach is probably one which recognizes all of the components of the system and addresses them on a variety of issues. Such an approach will be incremental, neither offering a radical breakthrough nor accepting the inevitability of failure. In any case, it is vitally important that the food issue remain at the forefront of efforts within the international community, for in a literal sense the fate of mankind is at stake.

3 The Energy Issue

The global nature of the energy issue can be introduced by examining several characteristics of the contemporary energy system. To begin with, at the present time and for the foreseeable future, the bulk of the productive energy in the world is drawn from nonrenewable sources. These are known as fossil fuels because they are the result of the accumulation of centuries of geological activity on earth. In particular, although it is not the sole energy resource, the global energy system in recent years has been dominated by one particular form of fossil fuel, oil. The presence of oil—petroleum and petroleum products—in our daily lives is so pervasive that we are sometimes not even aware of it. Petroleum powers our automobiles, heats our houses, cultivates our farms, energizes our industry, provides us with fertilizers and pesticides, and does countless other things to make our lives as citizens living in an advanced Western society convenient. Because of this convenience, petroleum has become the driving force for modernization and development worldwide. In particular, in the aftermath of World War II, the availability of relatively inexpensive oil made possible the economic recovery of the war-torn countries of Europe and the resurgence of Japan as an industrial power. Later, the less-developed countries also began pursuit of modernization through industrial development. The global economic growth of the 1960s reached an all-time high as more and more actors began to lay claim to the world's petroleum resources.

There are, however, inherent limitations to those resources. First, the fossil fuels of the world are finite. Only a fixed quantity is available and that quantity is not renewable. Once extracted from the ground and transformed into their many by-products, these energy resources cannot be re-created; they are exhaustible. Consequently, the increasing demand for oil in recent decades has

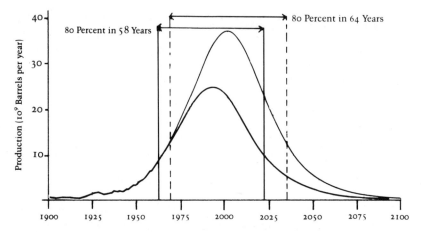

Figure 3.1   Hubbert's curve. Cycle of world oil production. Note: Cycle of world oil production is plotted on the basis of two estimates of the amount of oil that will ultimately be produced. The higher curve reflects Ryman's estimate of $2,100 \times 10^9$ barrels, and the lower curve represents an estimate of $1,350 \times 10^9$ barrels. Source: M. King Hubbert, "Energy Resources of the Earth," *Scientific American* (September 1971):69.

meant that energy has been continuously used up and not replaced. The extent of the finiteness of petroleum has been calculated by an American geologist, who estimated the amount of oil that would be produced based upon a projection of all of the oil that has been, is being, or ever will be recovered in the world. Named Hubbert's curve (figure 3.1) after its author, this estimate (and further research updating it) suggests that the production cycle for the world's petroleum will reach its peak close to the year 2000 and then begin a steady decline, falling below the point at which the recent increase in demand began by about the year 2030. We will see that other intervening factors, economic and political, have "flattened" Hubbert's curve with regard to rate of consumption so that the peak may not be reached as early as projected and the slope of decline may be more gradual. However, the basic point of Hubbert's curve remains. Oil is an exhaustible resource and within a reasonably determinable time it will no longer be available for use as the principal energy source on earth. The energy needs associated with the expanded demand that has emerged and is likely to continue will have to be met by some other energy source. It is not yet certain what that source or sources will be.

There is a second limitation on the world's energy resources that shapes the energy issue in its immediate form: those resources are not evenly distributed. The geological conditions that created the oil fields being tapped for today's energy existed only in limited areas of the world. Those areas, however, are now defined not by geology but by the contemporary international political system, which is based on the concept of territorially defined sovereign states. Sovereignty means, among other things, that states hold legal possession of all the resources which fall within their borders (for coastal nations, defining those borders becomes critical because many oil resources lie offshore along the continental shelf). Given the nature of the formation of fossil fuels, political and economic control over global energy resources today is therefore largely a consequence of the accident of geological history. Some nations are blessed with the possession of rich energy resources; others are not. Most important, especially in the high-demand energy environment that emerged in the 1960s and 1970s, an imbalance has existed internationally between access to energy and its use. This has been particularly true for today's dominant fuel, petroleum. Most petroleum use—consumption—occurs in the industrialized states of North America, Western Europe, and Japan. However, the greatest concentrations of petroleum resources —production and production potential—are found in the Middle East and in a few other countries in Latin America, Africa, and Southeast Asia that are not industrially advanced. (The Soviet Union is also a major consumer and a major producer of petroleum, but as we will see it has not as yet become a major actor in the international energy system beyond its own needs and those of its East European client states.) The imbalance between the production and the consumption of oil has both economic and political ramifications. Nations that consume oil must purchase it from the nations that produce it. The interaction between demand and supply—and control over the resource —will determine its price. Thus the flow of oil is conditioned by an international market.

In addition, insofar as there are differences in political orientation between the oil-consuming, developed nations and the oil-producing, less-developed nations, economic interactions have the potential of being colored by political interactions. To understand some of those interactions it is useful to look at how oil developed as the dominant energy resource. Oil has always been closely related to American enterprise. It was in fact discovered in the United States in 1859 and, tellingly, is closely associated with the rise of American big business. The oil industry typified the high concentration of capital and technology that led to virtual control over the market by one or a few corporations, the so-called trusts such as Standard Oil owned by John D. Rockefeller. These trusts were eventually broken up by federal action, but the U.S. oil corporations continued to be powerful economic forces. Oil was an attractive and efficient fuel and its use expanded quickly. At the same time, so did exploration for additional sources (in the face of predictions of shortages that never materialized). That process of exploration began the globalization of oil, for the geologically rich petroleum basins were found overseas, in Mexico, Venezuela, and the Middle East. American and to a lesser extent British and Dutch corporations led this movement into overseas oil fields. The large American oil corporations, the "majors" such as Texaco, Mobil, Standard Oil (of California), and others dominated the effort.

After World War II, the process of exploration accelerated, particularly in the Middle East where the oil was especially plentiful and rich, and more and more oil was produced. But even as the United States discovered and exploited foreign oil, it also "protected" its domestic oil industry through import quotas, restricting the amount of oil that could be imported from abroad. With the United States, the world's largest consumer, restricting its imports and therefore not competing in the international market, the international price of oil remained artificially low. In this respect the United States contributed to the postwar recovery of Europe and Japan, for those regions were able to take full advantage of the inexpensive oil to fuel their economic "miracles." As the postwar era progressed, the international political environment began to change. New nations emerged and they, together with many of the established less-developed countries, began to assert their independence, embarking on economic development through industrialization. Much of that effort concentrated on the raw materials such as petroleum that these nations possessed. Gradually, the impact of global economic growth was felt in the upward pressure of demand. Oil had become a more valuable resource. The oil-producing countries reacted to the prevailing pricing structure for oil, which they considered to be too low because of the dominance of the developed countries in the market, and began to seek ways to increase the price. In 1960 they had formed an association called the Organization of Petroleum Exporting Countries (OPEC) to try to coordinate their efforts to control the market. In the meantime, the United States too had become a major oil importer and by 1970 was competing with all the other consumers.

Much of the contemporary character of the energy issue is determined by these conditions. World energy is dependent on oil. Oil is a finite resource and is therefore exhaustible and potentially scarce. But scarcity does not arise solely from the finiteness of a resource. It is an economically determined condition, arising from the interaction between supply and demand in the marketplace. Hence, as we will see in more detail, the scarcity of oil has developed over the past two decades not simply because of the finiteness of oil reserves but also because of the action of the combination of political and economic factors that intersected in the 1970s to produce a world-wide "energy crisis." That "crisis" arose in the marketplace and not in the subterranean oil beds of the world. The reliance on oil had risen to a point at which the world's consumers could not easily or quickly find an alternative energy resource (economists call this market condition "inelasticity of demand"). The supply of oil to meet this demand was drawn to a great extent from a few producer nations that formed OPEC, who were now determined to control the price of their valuable commodity. At the same time, consumers had no alternative supplier of petroleum (economists call this market condition "inelasticity of supply"). After 1970 the market conditions of inelastic demand and inelastic supply prevailed in the international petroleum market. The developed consumer nations of the North, especially the United States, had grown dependent on imported oil and had nowhere else to turn but to the major oil suppliers of OPEC. For economic reasons, then, OPEC was in a position to control the market for oil. By 1970 the OPEC nations began to take steps to do so.

All that was needed was a catalyst to bring all of these conditions to bear. That catalyst came in 1973 when yet another Middle Eastern war, the Yom Kippur War, broke out between several Arab states and Israel. The United States and some West European countries had provided material and diplomatic support to Israel in this conflict. The Arab members of OPEC (who formed themselves into the Organization of Arab Petroleum Exporting Countries—OAPEC) decided to express their solidarity with the Arab states warring with Israel by placing an embargo on oil shipped to those countries supporting Israel. These included not only the United States, the world's largest energy consumer, but a number of West European countries as well. At the same time, already galvanized by the economic conditions of the market, the OPEC countries chose to exercise their newfound control over the market and raise the price of oil by 70 percent (eventually the price of a barrel of crude—that is, unrefined—oil would increase by 1,000 percent). Within a matter of months the world was thrust into an "energy crisis." Global dependence on petroleum had become so great that the entire international economic structure was shaken. Prices for all goods went up because of the high input of energy they required (including agricultural goods that had become heavily energy-intensive), economic growth everywhere slowed, and the world as a whole entered a recession from which it did not begin to recover for over a decade.

The energy crisis was both uncomfortable and serious. The discomfort came because for the first time the developed world was inconvenienced by the petroleum-based energy system upon which it had grown to rely. Supplies of gasoline and home-heating oil, essentials of daily living in industrialized countries, were limited (people had to wait in long lines at service stations to receive limited amounts of fuel) and the prices of that which was available began to soar. But the energy crisis itself was a short-term phenomenon. There was in fact plenty of petroleum to meet the world's needs. OPEC was simply manipulating the market by setting the price of oil as high as possible, and its members did so by cutting back on production in order to assure that the supply would be low enough to continue to support the high prices. They were also using their control over the market to assert a political position regarding the controversial Arab-Israeli dispute over Palestine.

The short-term economic and political factors that had induced the crisis, however, focused attention on the long-term consequences of the global energy system's dependency on fuels that were ultimately exhaustible. The immediate alternatives to oil were other nonrenewable resources—coal, natural gas, and nuclear power. For the long term, these would eventually create the same kinds of problems that dependency on oil had created (although the distribution patterns for each of these fuels would change the economic and political balance that characterizes petroleum). The energy crisis demonstrated that the energy needs of the future would have to be met in some different way than those of the past. Oil had emerged as the basic energy resource because of its inherent properties. Now a new energy source was being sought, not because it was more attractive than oil but because oil would not last. It had become clear that the solution to the energy problem would be neither quick nor free of cost to society.

The Global Energy System

It is evident from this description that today's world energy problem is a product of both the long-term technical characteristics of energy resources and the short-term economic and political conditions of the energy market. Energy, like many of the other vital resources of the earth, is a commodity. Its scarcity and its value are expressed commercially through the market forces of demand and supply. Much of the development of the energy issue—past, present, and future—is shaped by the structural characteristics and operations of the energy market both domestically and internationally. We have already taken note of the imbalance between these forces in the production and consumption components of petroleum. The interconnection between these components is distribution, the complex of systems used to move energy from where it is produced to where it is consumed. Using those components, we will address the global energy system in more detail, first examining its structural characteristics and then turning to its operational patterns.

Structural characteristics

One of the immediate consequences of the energy crises of the 1970s was the restructuring of the global energy system. Since the short-term causes of these crises were related to the political and economic structures that prevailed at the time, the short-term responses were also political and economic. While many circumstances had come into play, the immediate focus of attention was necessarily OPEC, a relatively new actor in the global energy system. Moreover, it was collectively representative of a whole set of countries that were recent entrants into international politics (its members are Algeria, Ecuador, Gabon, Indonesia, Iran, Iraq, Kuwait, Libya, Nigeria, Qatar, Saudi Arabia, the United Arab Emirates, and Venezuela). Beyond the market conditions of low elasticity of demand and supply, a number of other factors contributed to the immediate success of OPEC. Although the bulk of the OPEC members are Arab, there exists within OPEC the Organization of Arab Petroleum Exporting Countries (OAPEC), formed to coordinate regional interests among the Arab producers, who at the time of the crisis controlled some 60 percent of world oil trade. All of the OAPEC nations are developing nations that had come to share a growing solidarity around economic issues which divided them from the developed, industrialized nations. While these factors were not themselves sufficient to weld together a stable alliance (and contained the ingredients that would eventually challenge the political and economic stability of OPEC), they formed a strong foundation for a common posture toward the oil-consuming nations. The OPEC members achieved success by collaborating in the areas of price and production. They met to negotiate a common price to be set for their oil, and, based on their past production patterns and production potential, they agreed to restrict their production in order to maintain economic conditions necessary to keep that price high. Initially price proved to be easy to fix, and by 1981 it had been raised to $35 for a barrel of crude oil from its 1973 price of just under $3 a barrel.

The immediate response to OPEC action was also political and economic. The most urgent task for the oil-consuming industrialized nations of the North, especially the United States, was to address the market conditions that empowered OPEC. Thus it would be necessary to regain influence over the shaping of demand and supply in an effort to restore some greater elasticity to the energy market. Internationally the developed nations formed the International Energy Agency (IEA) from essentially the same membership as the Organization for Economic Cooperation and Development (OECD). OECD is an international organization of the major industrialized states of North America, Western Europe, and Japan. Like the OPEC members, these nations also shared common orientations. The energy crisis they now faced caused them to examine the individual and collective energy policies they had pursued. As was also characteristic of OPEC, the degree of consensus in OECD was fragile (France, for example, was unwilling even to join IEA), built largely on the sense of urgency that the oil shortages and increased energy costs had caused. IEA sought to shape the demand side of the market by adopting a set of coordinated policies with regard to consumption. In addition, IEA nations developed planning guidelines for cooperation on sharing oil reserves in order to dampen the effects of any further sudden shortfalls like those imposed by the Arab embargo.

Although to this point we have emphasized the roles of OPEC and IEA—two intergovernmental organizations—the principal instruments of the global energy system are nation-states. The functional and regional organizations that played a role leading up to and following the energy crisis of the 1970s were vehicles for expressing the interests of individual nations. By consuming nearly one-third of all the world's energy output, the United States is of course a major energy actor (though a substantial portion of consumption continues to come from domestic production). The high consumption profile in the United States was accompanied by a set of energy practices and a complex of domestic political and economic structures (the "energy syndrome") that created and sustained dependence on oil, the one energy resource least available domestically.[1] As a consequence, reliance on imported oil increased until by the 1970s the United States was vulnerable to manipulation, whether for political or economic reasons. During this time the United States also shifted the focus of its importation from Latin America to the Middle East. Immediate American response to the energy crisis arose in the context of these structures. In the aftermath of the crisis, then-President Nixon established *Project Independence* by which the United States was supposed to free itself of reliance on foreign oil by the year 1980. To do this the pattern of consumption and the control of national producers over the domestic market had to change. Over successive administrations, as the seriousness of the problem became more apparent, the United States sought to limit American consumption through conservation measures (such as the 55-mile-per-hour speed limit and energy tax incentives). In a series of institutional responses, a cabinet-level Department of Energy was created to coordinate and administer U.S. energy programs. Eventually, in what President Carter called the "moral equivalent of war," control over natural gas and oil prices was deregulated, removing the constraints on the economic forces of the market so that price would be determined in the free flow of demand and supply.

Another strategy followed by the United States had been to try to influence the supply side of the equation through relations with major oil producers. This effort was initially concentrated on Iran, a non-Arab Islamic nation that under its Shah was dedicated to an intensive modernization program. Iran's posture in the Middle East was generally moderate and broadly supportive of American interests. Iran was also strategically important to the United States because of its location adjacent to the Soviet Union. Iran was moreover an OPEC member and a major oil producer. The United States thus invested a large amount of diplomatic and economic effort into maintaining good relations with Iran, while seeking Iran's help in dealing with OPEC policies. However, a fundamentalist religious revolution in Iran in 1979 deposed the Shah and simultaneously introduced an anti-American government and interrupted oil flows further (as did the subsequent lengthy Iran-Iraq war). These events brought an additional shock to the already troubled energy system.

The United States then turned its diplomatic attention to building better relations with Saudi Arabia, a nation with several attributes important to American policy. First, Saudi Arabia possessed 23 percent of the world's known petroleum reserves. Second, Saudi Arabia had a high production capacity, allowing it great flexibility in petroleum output. For these first two reasons, Saudi Arabia played a definitive role in the price and production negotiations of OPEC. Finally, like Iran before the revolution, Saudi Arabia had a conservative monarchical regime that generally assumed a moderating position in the volatile Middle Eastern political scene, though staunchly supportive of the Palestinian cause. American foreign policy now turned its attention to U.S.-Saudi relations, seeking an instrument to influence OPEC in order to moderate the effects of pricing and production decisions on U.S. energy supplies. Observers have cautioned, however, that Saudi Arabia has some of the same potential for disruption that Iran had—threats from revolutionary regimes on the border, pockets of extremist fundamentalism, and the Palestinian issue that continues to be an irritant. In fact, with regard to the latter, part of the U.S. approach to the Middle East in general has been to try to reduce the disruptive potential in the Middle East. The United States was the major catalyst in the Camp David accords between Egypt and Israel and has continually sought to moderate the conflict in the area.

Although the focus on the energy problem is necessarily concentrated on the major Middle East producers, it is also important to recognize the roles of other nations. First, within OPEC, a number of lesser producers have economic development objectives that breed a different approach to the energy market. These countries are termed "high absorbers" because of their interest in obtaining maximum gain from control over petroleum; they wanted to absorb as much as possible of the foreign earnings from oil sales as quickly as possible in order to accelerate their industrial development. These nations were generally less well endowed with oil resources and had more immediate development needs. Nigeria, for example, reformulated development plans around the windfall gains of the energy crisis.[2] This approach would eventually create difficulties for OPEC in the face of the larger producers who were generally "low absorbers," willing to take gains from the market steadily over a longer period of time.

Another category of nations that has responded to the energy system are new producers who are not OPEC members. Mexico, for example, has a significant oil reserve that it has cautiously integrated into its development plans, with careful attention to its own projected energy needs. Nevertheless, Mexico's potential as an oil supplier would over time dampen the effects of the OPEC cartel (although the OPEC price structure of course works to Mexico's advantage and Mexico has attended OPEC meetings as an observer). Within a little over a decade after the energy crisis, the United States was importing more oil from Mexico than it was from Saudi Arabia.[3] Induced by OPEC dominance, these new producers were part of a general effort to find other suppliers (and new fields) for petroleum.

Finally, mention should be made of those nations that were simply bypassed in the events precipitating the energy crisis. The less-developed countries that do not possess petroleum resources (the so-called "no-pec" countries) were excluded from virtually all of the political and economic forces that led to the crystallization of the energy problem. These countries need energy resources for their development efforts but are in no position to compete in a market in which the price is set by the interaction between the world's major consumers and the world's major producers. For them the energy problem is even more severe, but for the most part they lack any of the political or economic resources to participate in resolution of the issue. Their only alternative has been to seek financial assistance to redress the imbalance created by soaring energy costs.

Throughout the development of the energy issue the large oil corporations, headquartered in the industrialized states, have also played important roles. Recall that these multinational corporations were a major part of the overseas exploration and exploitation of petroleum from the beginning of the development of this resource. They represent some of the largest business enterprises in the world, with sales that exceed the gross national products of many less-developed countries. These corporations are highly "vertically integrated," that is, they control the full range of petroleum operations from exploration and extraction in the oil fields to refining and retailing in the national marketplaces in the consuming nations. Many also operate their own distribution networks, moving the oil from overseas to domestic refineries and then marketing the product through service station chains. Thus from wellhead to gas pump, the multinationals exercise great economic power of their own. As integral parts of the global energy system the multinationals were necessarily affected by the factors governing the energy crisis. In the period preceding the crisis, the multinationals were subject to the actions of national governments, first in establishing national control over oil assets and then in asserting controls over oil production. As the major oil corporations were removed from the pricing structure by the rise of OPEC, they still were able to retain influence because of their mastery of the distribution and marketing phases of the operation (termed "downstream operations").

The onset of the energy crisis brought additional problems for the multinationals. Domestic efforts to regulate the international oil industry placed constraints on their operations and exposed them to greater public scrutiny concerning issues such as the environment and the equity of their overall profit policies. In response to these pressures, the multinationals began to restructure their operations. Facing projections of decreasing rates of domestic production and high-priced foreign petroleum, they began to diversify, seeking alternative energy sources. Thus, "vertical integration" was supplemented by "horizontal integration." The major oil corporations became major energy corporations, exploring and investing in such options as nuclear power, shale oil, and synthetic fuels. The corporations also began to expand their domestic exploration efforts in order to provide alternatives to buying at the inflated OPEC prices. Throughout the process, which was accompanied by great instability and change, the multinationals still sustained their economic dominance of the energy industry.

Operational Characteristics of the Global Energy System

We can begin to understand the operational characteristics of the global energy system by reviewing the functional components of that system. The various energy actors who take part in energy developments do so from the perspective of their roles as producers, consumers, or distributors. Within those functional roles are inherently competing or conflicting interests. We have already seen that there are significant differences, for example, between the major oil producers and the major oil consumers. These have been manifested in the changing dynamics of the market. The producers wanted to gain the highest possible price for their product; the consumers sought the lowest possible price. However, at the time of the energy crisis in the 1970s, having a reliable source of supply usually transcended price in importance, at least in the richer countries that could afford the higher price. Moreover, consumers in the developed world were in a more advantageous position than consumers in the developing world, who had not yet achieved sought-after levels of industrialization. Similarly, although demand and supply both had low elasticity in the 1970s, the ensuing decade and a half has altered those patterns so that more competition now exists in the market among producers, which has tested the integrity of OPEC.

Beyond these economic concerns, political considerations also shape interests. Energy actors exist in a rich political environment that has measurable influence on energy outcomes. It is not possible to remove current developments in the energy system from such political events as the conflict over the Palestinian issue between Israel—supported by a major energy consumer (the United States)—and the Arab states, including many major oil producers. The Iran-Iraq War, which began in 1980, affected oil distribution because of the threat to the flow of petroleum through the Persian Gulf that supplies the bulk of the Western European states and Japan with imported oil. Political objectives often color or even transcend economic considerations in the global energy arena.

One area where competing political and economic interests have become more pressing is in North-South relations. The contention between the developed North and the developing South over the distribution of scarce resources has led to a realignment of more traditional East-West political divisions. The South holds two positions. One is that the income distribution between the developed and developing regions is inequitable and acts virtually to close out access for the less-developed countries to resources vital to their development. In a second and related position, the South holds that there should be a more equitable relative distribution of all the earth's resources based on need and a sense of common heritage rather than economic or technological advantage. These concerns are particularly applicable to energy, but with a twist. We have seen that the pricing structure and therefore the availability of energy is determined in the interaction between demand and supply. But with regard to energy, the bulk of suppliers are in fact developing nations. Their profits and increased influence have come as a benefit of this income imbalance. Thus the South itself is divided. Petroleum nonproducers are excluded from both the profits from sales of energy resources and access to the product needed to meet their development needs. The South, with more land and people, wants to counteract the economic and political leverage that the North has been able to bring to bear because of its greater development. One clear way that the less-developed countries could achieve that objective has been to assert control over national resources needed in the North. Over the early years of development the nationalization of these resources, including petroleum, seemed to serve that purpose. However, the raw materials that constitute these resources require applied technology in order to be useful, technology that is still in the hands of the North. Hence, even in intensely nationalistic countries such as Libya, oil production is supervised under contract by representatives of the major oil corporations. Nationalization in itself is not sufficient to counter-act the imbalance. More broadly, therefore, the less-developed countries, operating in as coordinated a fashion as their inherent regional and political differences permit, have claimed the right of preferential treatment through resource allocations and financial assistance.

There are also competing interests among the oil producers regard-ing how best to exploit the advantages they hold. This conflict can be illustrated by returning to the different development needs that divide the "high absorbers" from the "low absorbers." Saudi Arabia possesses 27 percent of the known petroleum reserves outside the communist world. With a relatively small population and a monar-chical government, it has different objectives for its use of resources than do oil producers with fewer reserves and greater immediate need for earnings from the international marketplace. A number of nations fall into the latter category, but because of Saudi Arabia's unique resource position, none has the degree of leverage it exerts. These differences now plague OPEC in its efforts to sustain coordi-nated pricing and production control. Saudi Arabia has kept produc-tion low, willing to reap the long-term benefits for its oil. But it has done so also to maintain the integrity of OPEC. Now the market has shifted. There is greater elasticity of demand and supply. The price is steadily declining as consumption has decreased and other sup-pliers have entered the market. The high absorbers want to get as much as possible as quickly as possible from this declining market. But they can only do so for as long as the low absorbers are willing to go along. There is less willingness to do so as market projections indicate that the long-term value of the resource will decline as the world turns to alternative resources. Some OPEC nations have begun to cheat on agreed-upon production quotas as well as on pricing. The discipline of OPEC is thus being severely tested. Should Saudi Arabia choose to do so it could unleash its great production capac-ity and drive the price of oil down while still reaping great eco-nomic gain. The high absorbers with fewer reserves would see the value of their commodity plummet and would lose even the short-term benefits that they have had.

Concerns arising from outside the energy arena are also influential in addressing operation of the global energy system. Perhaps the foremost of these are security concerns. Energy is recognized as a vital resource for national development, but it also serves military functions. The Defense Department is far and away the largest consumer of energy within the U.S. government. Dependency on overseas oil, especially when linked to as volatile an area as the Middle East, associates American and Western security interests closely with overall energy policies. The energy needs of the United States and those of its closest allies are critical to maintaining their defense requirements.

At the same time the United States has maintained a long-standing commitment to Israel, a policy that has contributed to the instability of the political setting of the energy problem because of the unresolved Palestinian issue. Beyond that the United States also concerns itself with the proximity of the Soviet Union to the Middle East, a concern heightened by the Soviet invasion of Afghanistan. At one point in the 1970s the U.S. secretary of state warned that the United States would not be "strangulated" by the interruption of oil flows and implied that military intervention was a consideration (a congressional study explored the feasibility of seizing the oil fields in an emergency). When the Soviet Union invaded Afghanistan, the American response was immediately attuned to secure threats to energy flows to the West. President Carter pledged to keep Persian Gulf oil distribution open with the use of military force if necessary (the "Carter Doctrine") and a special command structure was implemented in order to do so. The Iran-Iraq War has evoked similar concerns. And when the Soviet Union began to develop plans for a natural gas pipeline to Western Europe, the U.S. considered the possibility that the Soviet Union would then be able to interrupt energy flows and, at one point, sought to prevent its completion.

With these concerns in mind, many nations have also turned to "strategic" stockpiling of energy resources. Principally this effort is insurance against future disruptions in oil supplies. But stockpiling has the further capacity to provide a means to compensate for damaging fluctuations in price. Stockpiling has limitations because it is expensive (without a direct return on the investment) and because it is truly a short-term measure, inadequate for any serious interruption.

Despite such concerns, the predominant factor that determines the operation of the global energy system has proven to be cost. Cost as a function of the low elasticity of demand and supply in the market precipitated the energy "crisis" of the 1970s. Now the market dynamics have changed and observers are talking about an oil "glut" that will make oil far less costly and have a series of effects on political and economic development worldwide that may be as profound as those during the 1970s. Some speak of the "twilight of the oil age." The changes that have taken place in the relative characteristics of demand and supply have shifted the character of the energy problem. We have already seen how OPEC has lost its previously tight hold over the petroleum market. Within five years, from 1977 at the height of the energy crisis to 1982, the OPEC share of the production of oil went from 67 percent to 48 percent.[4] The obvious conclusion from this drop in percentage is that alternative (non-OPEC) suppliers had entered the production market and that some level of competitiveness had returned to the market. Indeed, the data show that non-OPEC suppliers controlled a larger share of the market. Some of these suppliers, such as Mexico, already existed, but required some time before production and entry into the market could be accomplished. Other suppliers, including those who increased production within nations like the United States that had previously relied upon imported oil, also entered the market. Finally, new supplies were introduced both domestically and internationally as a consequence of the inducement that the crisis provided for new exploration.

Much of this increased production and the entry of new suppliers was bolstered by direct governmental intervention. The most common form of this intervention was through artificial supports to encourage production activity or through the removal of artificial constraints that had held down domestic prices and therefore economic incentive. A number of these governmental interventions were also directed at the development of energy sources other than petroleum. Nonetheless, some observers have concluded that the result of these dynamics in production and pricing will mean that oil will retain its importance in the energy market for some time to come.

Action in the consumption component also has suggested a prolongation of the role of petroleum in the global energy system, at least for a period until the long-term prospects of the system can be treated. The energy crisis produced a relatively rapid reduction in demand as a consequence of the policies adopted by consuming states. There were a number of circumstances influencing this reduction—slowing economic growth, shifts to domestic supplies, imposed conservation (such as the 55-mile-per-hour speed limit), etc.—but the major incentive to cut back on consumption was the increase in cost.

Consumers—individuals, corporations, and governments—preferred not to pay the high prices imposed by the crisis and thus began to adopt their own conservation measures. For individuals, these measures ranged from doing less recreational driving and purchasing more fuel-efficient automobiles to adding insulation to their homes. Corporate policies responded to these trends, concentrating on products that were low-energy users. The automobile industry in the United States, for example, completely changed its marketing and production criteria to emphasize fuel efficiency. At the governmental level, policies also emphasized efficiency—lowering speed limits, providing investment tax credit for efforts to reduce energy usage, enacting mandatory standards for energy-related elements of new residential and commercial construction, statements of fuel economy for new cars, etc. While there was neither universal acceptance of these measures nor clear evidence that any one effort was more or less effective than the others, an overall decline in consumption did take place.

Other domestic and international factors have affected the operation of the energy system. One such factor has to do with the role of the multinational corporation. We mentioned above that as a result of the attention caused by the energy crisis the multinationals were exposed to greater public scrutiny. As we have seen, these corporations are powerful actors in virtually every aspect of the global energy system—production, distribution, and consumption—at virtually every level. In the face of efforts to force divestiture of some of their vertically integrated holdings and place constraints on their activities, the multinationals still have operated to seek higher prices for oil and to search for alternative energy sources as long as it was economically attractive to do so. As the market began to change, the multinationals backed away from some of the investment in alternative sources. And as the demand has declined they have moved to acquisition of other oil companies as an alternative to developing new production facilities. In the latter case many of the multinationals are merging to become "super-multinationals."

Contributing internationally to this overall picture has been a further dynamic. The enormous rise in the price of oil was instrumental in the onset of a worldwide recession that took hold in the late 1970s and early 1980s. This costly reduction in economic growth had a paradoxical effect; it became part of the corrective to the factors that caused it. Thus the slowdown in the world economy contributed to the reduction in world demand for oil, which has in turn contributed to the oil glut and the pressures that have now been created for the reduction in oil prices. The unanticipated reduction in demand has left the entire oil industry off balance. In the wake of the crisis, much of the industry began to gear itself up to respond to increased demand. But as it did so the demand actually leveled and began to decline. Hence, production facilities were left idle and distribution and marketing plans were unrealized (the move to giant supertankers has created maritime parking lots where these giant ships now lie at anchor empty and unused). This drop in demand has been costly in and of itself and has driven energy industries away from efforts to develop alternatives to oil.

In addressing these observations we must separate the short-term effects and responses from the long-term characteristics of the energy issue. Thus there is concern that the shift in the market, in postponing a confrontation with the exhaustibility of oil (and of fossil fuels in general), will weaken efforts to consider long-term approaches to the energy problem. Just as we have seen that the "energy crisis" was a relatively short-lived phenomenon, so it is argued that concepts such as "glut" and "twilight of the oil era" will also be transient phenomena. This argument is supported by the contention that if there is to be continued economic growth, then demand for energy must grow as well. The contribution of the energy crisis to the world recession and forecasts of another phase of rapid growth if energy costs go down (as it is predicted they will; some forecasts suggest prices below $20 per barrel) are cited to underscore the point that the foundation for energy demand has not really fallen. Economic recovery could then put the issue right back into a cycle of energy shortfalls and rising prices. Indeed, this concern seems to be valid. As noted, the decline in prices and the increase in the availability of petroleum have changed the conduct of the major energy corporations that have retreated from their pursuit of alternative energy sources (which were well-advertised when allegations were being made that the multinational oil corporations were raking in windfall profits from the rising price of oil) and even from exploration for new sources of petroleum. The International Energy Agency has become an outspoken advocate of this position, warning about renewed demand in an environment of continuing energy dependency. Also, in contrast to many short-term forecasters, the U.S. Department of Energy has forecast a sharp increase in price in the 1990s and beyond, reaching $60 per barrel by the year 2000.[5] Among other things, the range in the forecasts demonstrates the uncertainties with which the energy system must operate.

There are a number of such uncertainties. For example, most calculations of energy trends exclude the Soviet Union. The Soviet Union is, however, the largest single producer of oil in the world. Its production in 1982 was 11.8 million barrels per day, in contrast to Saudi production of 6.3 million and U.S. production of 8.7 million.[6] Analyses that do look at the Soviet Union compare its production capacity with the projections of demand (and here again there is a considerable range of disagreement among the specialists). But the Soviet Union has not been a major participant in the international energy market. Almost all of Soviet production is used for domestic needs or for the needs of its East European and other communist client states. However, the Soviet Union has recently increased its efforts to export oil in order to gain the foreign hard currency earnings that it needs to purchase high technology and other goods from the West. If oil prices do drop, the Soviet Union will need to increase its total exports just to maintain the same level of hard currency earnings. This requirement comes in the face of projected increases in Soviet demand (although their economy as a whole is lagging) that have already kept the Soviets trying to increase production while other major oil producers have cut back. Some experts have raised doubts about the ability of the Soviet Union to continue to increase production because of limited facilities (although it is well-endowed with natural gas). If this is so, then the question becomes, what happens to market projections if the Soviet Union were to become a net importer (which would of course worsen the Soviet hard currency problem)? That prospect is not an immediate one, but it illustrates the kind of uncertainty that prevails in this area.

The Future of the Global Energy System

We have seen that energy outcomes have developed less by design than by the complex interactions of a number of factors. In the short term, these factors seem to relate principally to cost with the various actors in the global energy arena seeking to maximize economic or political gain. In the long term, however, looking forward to the year 2000 and beyond, these considerations are more problematical. There are still economic and political interests to promote and protect, but the outcomes are less certain. The transition now under way will take the energy system from its dependency on oil to a system that will rely on one or more new energy sources. Setting a clear policy direction is difficult. What is more, the competition for short-term gain has a tendency to retard the search for long-term resolution. The choice is likely to be the result of technological development produced by research. But even that process is affected by institutional structures (will it be socially acceptable?) and by the ultimate test of commercialization (will it be profitable in the market?). For each of the available alternatives —coal, nuclear power, solar power, or some other renewable energy source—there will be trade-offs between contending interests and both costs and benefits for society. While it may be desirable to address the resolution of these issues from a global perspective, that is a foreboding and probably unrealizable objective. At the present time, even the national energy environment is difficult and controversial. It is unlikely that the integration and accommodation that have been only partially achievable on the domestic scene could be achieved on the global level. The further into the future one attempts to project issues, the more speculative they become. The range of differences among the experts and decision-makers is much broader than that in the short term. We have already seen the disagreement over forecasting in the next decade, let alone the next century. It is much more difficult to extract an immediate sacrifice in the interest of the future than it is to resolve contentious issues in the present.

The factors determining the global energy future are many of the same ones that have affected short-term outcomes. The first relates to available sources of supply. These sources can take the form either of existing energy sources or potential undeveloped sources. The former include the fossil fuels in various forms not presently being exploited (largely because it is not cost effective to do so at current prices; were oil prices to rise again, the profit at the margin may be great enough to warrant the additional input). The latter lie virtually at the limits of scientifically feasible imagination, but for the present are focused on such things as solar radiation, geothermal sources (steam heated by the core of the earth and tappable through drilling), and fusion reactors (thereby reducing the problem of nuclear waste). A second set of factors relates to projected level of demand. Demand is based on the complex linkages between energy and society. For example, economic growth in general and industrial development in particular will determine how much energy will be needed in the future. In the past there has been a one-to-one relationship between energy usage and economic growth. A 1 percent increase in economic growth requires a 1 percent increase in energy usage. More recently, with closer attention to consumption, the developed countries have been able to reduce this ratio. But it is uncertain whether the developing countries will be able to do so. Similar questions arise with regard to the increased demand for food. Past food production increases and anticipated efforts to expand present production levels have been associated with energy-intensive programs. It is not clear how these requirements will be met. Conservation programs will also be able to affect these outcomes, although once again there is a high degree of speculation because of uncertainty over energy sources.

In anticipating the choices to be made, cost is again likely to predominate, with supply and demand operating as the strongest influences on energy developments at all levels. Efforts by individuals and national governments to become more energy-efficient, for example, have been induced largely by cost. So too have actions at the international level to find alternative suppliers and alternative sources. These incremental adjustments, rather than long-term energy policies, have brought about the fluctuations of the world petroleum market. Many of the actions taken were focused on the characteristics of the forces of demand and supply. The most successful energy programs over the past decade have been those most closely aligned with such market forces, sometimes unconsciously. International initiatives to deal with energy as a problem have tended to be expressed in the same economic terms with which that problem was framed, again expressing the forces of the market. And proposed resolutions have tended to revolve around the same set of energy resources that have existed since the onset of the crisis and in the same proportions relative to the overall energy system. Thus the initiatives have tended to produce only incremental changes in the overall balance of the problem. The next decade seems still to revolve around the automaticity of the market. Whatever the future outcomes may be, these are the considerations that seem likely to prevail.

The long-term resolution of the problem may, however, prove more challenging. So long as the market prevails as the main incentive for action, long-term policy needs to offer a favorable return on commercial investment. But the uncertainties in long-term energy projections make those incentives difficult to establish. Differing projections call for differing forms of action, so that even the process of forecasting is competitive. Hence, there are at present competing arguments concerning whether the "oil glut" is real and will last, or whether, as some contend, the 1990s will promise another period of energy pressures toward a search for alternatives.

While most energy experts do agree that the production cycle for oil is finite and that both conservation and a search for alternative sources are necessary, few agree on what operational means should be pursued to accomplish these objectives. The trade-offs forced by the short-term pressures of the market are much more difficult to obtain in the abstract framework of the future. Whatever form the transition to a future energy system may take, several of its characteristics seem clear. First, it will be a lengthy process. The extension of reliance on oil through various measures in the production and consumption sectors has prolonged the need to confront the issue, regardless of fluctuations in oil pricing that may come in the 1990s. Second, commercial feasibility rather than institutionalized reform is likely to be the determining factor in the final choice or choices of future energy resources; this includes not only the cost of the resource but also the cost of the entire system needed to support it. Although the global energy system is being pushed away from oil as the prime energy resource, there is no reason to believe that economic considerations among the various alternatives will not continue to pull it back.

Energy is an essential component of human existence and of global development and it will continue to be an essential component of the maintenance of productive life on this planet. The era of reliance on petroleum is drawing to a close; it will end in the reasonably forseeable future. Many possible alternatives exist. The actual successor will need to pass the test of commercial feasibility. But we have seen that it will also be tested in a dynamic economic and political environment with ever-changing and competing interests. How the energy picture will look after the year 2000 is uncertain. The choices that lie ahead promise to be more deliberate and comprehensive than those taken in the past. The issues are complex and the stakes are high.

4 The Population Issue

Consider the following information on population for the year 1982. In every single second the world population increased by 2.5 people, the consequence of 4.15 births and 1.65 deaths. Every second! This adds up to an increase throughout the globe of 150 people per minute, 9,038 people per hour, 216,916 people per day, 6,597,858 people per month for a total of 79,174,297 people per year. As you read this page 150 additional people have been added to the global rolls. That means 150 additional mouths to feed, 150 bodies to shelter and to care for, 150 minds to educate, and 150 future jobs to be provided. This daily increase is equal to the approximate size of Dayton, Ohio. And those figures are for 1982; one year later the gain was 82,077,000, and the absolute figure continues to grow each year.[1]

Most of this population growth occurred in the developing or third-world nations, where the population is increasing at the rate of 2.3 per second, as opposed to the developed world where the net growth is only 0.2 people per second. The biggest contributors have been the populous nations of India, China, Indonesia, Brazil, and Bangladesh. From that information, one might immediately conclude that the contemporary population problem is not really a global but rather a regional issue, confined primarily to those societies that have not yet acquired a high level of development. There is some truth to this view. The existence of high population growth rates is largely confined to the developing world. But such a conclusion would be in error for two reasons. First, regardless of whether the growth rates are in the developing or developed world, the problems affect the advanced industrialized nations because it is they who must provide the necessary capital and supplies to overcome underdevelopment, and increased numbers of people translate into increased costs worldwide. Moreover, if present trends continue, the developed or first-world nations will likely have to absorb excess population from the disadvantaged parts of the globe in the not-too-distant future. We have already seen evidence of this movement in the migration to the developed world in the "boat people" of South-east Asia and the Caribbean. Second, high population growth rates and the resultant large size are only part of the global population issue. Growth rates that are too small are also a problem to some societies. Too many young people or too many old people create another set of problems for society. Too much or too little urbanization, or relocation of population within a society, may gen-erate still other difficulties. And so it goes.

In this chapter we want to identify those population situations which together constitute the global population issue. Much of the discussion will distinguish between the developed and developing worlds because each group appears to face a separate kind of concern. We will describe the nature of three basic population processes at work—fertility, mortality, and migration—and their resultant consequences. We will place the numbers into the framework of theories about population dynamics, particularly as they relate to future predictions about population. We will also examine the nonpopulation consequences of a number of population character-istics. Finally, we will touch on the story of sub-Saharan Africa, the region of the world with the highest growth levels.

The reasons why population is a global issue were introduced in chapter 1. So let us begin our discussion by first examining our own situation in the United States. We do this for two reasons. First, when speaking about population issues, Americans tend not to think of problems within our borders. Rather they immediately conjure up a visual image of teeming masses in some faraway coun-try in Asia, Africa, or Latin America, usually wallowing in abject poverty. That is, as we will see, a narrow-minded view. Second, the United States has a number of adverse conditions that have grown out of the work of certain population dynamics, none of which relates to a high growth rate. These conditions have required the attention of governmental and other institutions for some time now and will continue to do so. Although they pale in compari-son to population problems of the third world, these new popula-tion configurations have had a major impact on the demographics of American life. The point to be made is that population problems, whether in the developed or developing world, are not necessarily related directly (or even indirectly) to large size. Population prob-lems emerge because of changes taking place among people (the official phrase is demographic trends). These changes might be decreases in the birthrate, changes in the age composition (for example, more of one age, such as old people, as opposed to others), or movements of people from one location to another. Here are some examples that illustrate the effect of demographic trends:[2]

> In the 1960s and 1970s, there was tremendous growth and prosperity of industries dealing with baby foods and products; now there is a need for products, facilities, and services geared to the aged.

> During the 1960s there was a shortage of schoolrooms and teachers at all levels; today there is a drastic decline in school enrollments and a surplus in schoolrooms and teachers.

> During the recent economic slowdown there has nonetheless been a continuing growth in the labor force, resulting in high rates of unemployment, especially among teenagers and young adults, and in increased pressures for early retirement.

> There has been a major increase in women's participation in the work force, from 31 percent of all women in 1950 to over 50 percent today; fewer than one American family in six now fit the traditional stereotype of a breadwinner husband and a homemaker wife caring for dependent children.

> There has been a heavy migration of Americans from the North and Northeast to the South and West of the country, and a growing concentration of minorities within decaying central cities. These trends affect tax bases and economic vitality across the country, thereby altering the distribution of federal funds to the states and the distribution of political power nationwide. For example, many seats in the House of Representatives were reapportioned after the 1980 census, and the northeastern and north central states were the big losers (New York alone lost four seats, while the South gained seven seats and the West four). As a result, the South and West together have a majority of House seats for the first time. Similarly, at the local and municipal levels, there is an ongoing redistribution of political power from central cities to the suburbs and rural areas as a result of these population movements.

> There is a steady aging trend in the American population as a whole that affects federal-state fiscal relations as well as the overall economy. Most public expenditures for the

country's young, primarily for education, are financed by state and local taxes. Most public expenditures for the elderly, in contrast, are for health and social security programs that are financed by the federal government. Spending for the elderly at the present time amounts to nearly 25 percent of the federal budget. By 2025, because of increased numbers of old people, 40 percent of the federal budget will be needed to support these same services. Our Social Security system is financed by payroll taxes paid by the currently employed. As the proportion of older people grows, they will have to be supported by a relatively smaller work force. Current projections are that Social Security expenditures will start to exceed payroll tax revenues in about thirty years, when the baby boom generation begins to retire. But general tax revenues at the federal level will probably be needed even before that time both to keep payroll taxes below a politically tolerable upper limit and to make up the difference between income and expenditures.

Each of these statements describes a situation in the United States created by a characteristic of the population. These conditions emerged primarily because of the impact of the post–World War II baby boom (high birthrates immediately after World War II) followed in recent years by a very low birthrate in the United States.

We can see that these characteristics of population in the United States lead to important social, political, cultural, and economic consequences. The point to note, however, is that they seem quite minor when compared to the problems created by changing population characteristics or demographic trends in Asia and Africa.

Population Factors

Before we address population problems throughout the world, we need to develop a clearer picture of the factors that are important in determining demographic trends such as those mentioned above. Figure 4.1 shows the various population factors that are important for understanding world population problems.

As we can observe, three of the factors (or variables as they are called because their values tend to vary) are labeled *process* and three are called *structural.* The reason for such labeling is clear. Those on the left are dynamic conditions; they are actions that are occurring. People are being born *(fertility)*, they are dying *(mortality)*,

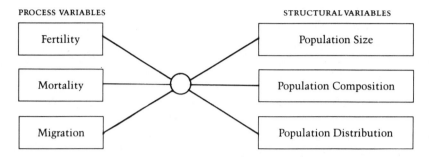

PROCESS VARIABLES   STRUCTURAL VARIABLES

| Fertility |

| Mortality |

| Migration |

| Population Size |

| Population Composition |

| Population Distribution |

Figure 4.1   Population factors. Source: Marden, Parker et al., *Population in the Global Arena.* (New York: Holt, Rinehart and Winston, 1982), p. 18.

or they are moving from one place to another *(migration)*. As a consequence of these three actions and the interactions among them, three characteristics of the population emerge. The population reaches a certain numerical level *(population size)*, each age group of the population—infants, youngsters, teenagers, middle-aged adults, older individuals—has a certain percentage of the total population *(population age composition)*, and each sector of a country—inner city, suburb, county, state, province, and region —finds these people living in different numbers *(population distribution)*.

Population problems occur because the dynamic processes of fertility, mortality, and migration change and interact in such a manner that the resultant population conditions of size, age composition, and distribution (or location) will lead to some identifiable problem. There is not enough arable land, there is inadequate housing, more schools must be built (or closed), additional jobs must be found, and so forth.

Trends in World Population

Before one begins to analyze these population-related problems, one must first have an appreciation of the present conditions and trends of the dynamic population process. Our concern in this chapter is with the global nature of population. Let us examine, therefore, the total picture of population size in the world—how fast its population is growing, where it is growing, and why it is growing. Once one has this picture one can move into the problems created by these patterns; again, the problems will not

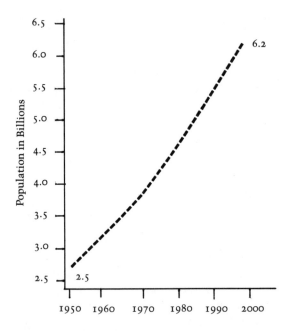

Figure 4.2   World population trends, 1950–2000. Source: Barnett F. Baron, "Population, Development, and Multinational Corporations." Speech presented in San Diego, 12 December 1979.

be just those of size but of age composition and distribution as well.

Figure 4.2 presents the amount of world population from 1950 to the present, and shows projections of the year 2000. These figures represent future estimates by the United Nations. As you can observe, current world population is approximately 4.4 billion. This contrasts with a 1950 figure of 2.4 billion and a projection of 6.2 billion by 2000. The figure shows the tremendous recent growth and the high projections for the latter part of the twentieth century.[3]

If you were to extend the figure back in time, you would find that for most of human history population grew very slowly. In fact, the major population problem throughout history was not too many but too few people. More specifically, the number of deaths in a given year was close to the number of births and in some years even surpassed it (meaning a net drop in the total population for that year). Survival of the human race was the principal goal as death from disease, famine, and war constantly took its toll. Figure 4.3 charts the size of world population back to ancient times. It

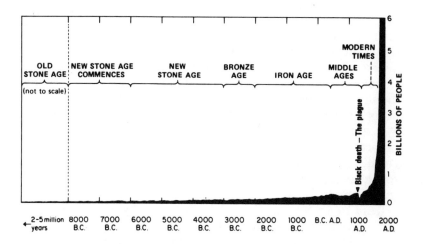

Figure 4.3   World population trends, 8000 B.C. to A.D. 2000. Source: Population Reference Bureau, *Our Population Predicament: A New Look* (1979).

shows a remarkably slow (but steady) increase for hundreds of years until recent decades, when there is a dramatic acceleration of increase.

Of course, population is not growing at the same rate for each country (the same number being added each year for each thousand currently in the population). Figure 4.4 divides world population totals for two types of countries—developed societies (essentially Western Europe, North America, and Japan) and developing countries (mostly Latin America, Asia and Africa). One can observe the significant differences in population trends between the developed and developing nations. Most babies born into the world will continue to be born in the latter group of countries, not the developed nations.

If one separates the data further into the growth rates for different regions of the globe, it is possible to acquire a better sense of where the greatest growth has been occurring. Figure 4.5 reveals that Africa, with a growth rate of 136 percent between the years 1970 and 2000, will experience the largest jump, followed by Latin America with 99 percent.

Rates of Growth

The reason for the differing growth rates is, of course, not only that the developing countries have more people to begin with—and therefore have a larger base from which the population "takes off" —but also that the rate of growth is much larger in these societies. The annual rate of growth, usually expressed as a percentage, reveals the increase in the population from one year to the next. Thus a rate of growth of 2 percent in a given year means that 2 percent of this year's population will be added to the present level in order to give next year's total number. Notice the trends in the rates of growth (as opposed to the total increase in population) displayed in figures 4.2 to 4.5.

Figure 4.6 reveals the changes in the rates of growth for both the developing and developed world for the period between 1950 and 2000. Examine this information carefully in order to understand

Figure 4.4   Population growth in developed and developing countries. Source: Baron, "Population, Development, and Multinational Corporations."

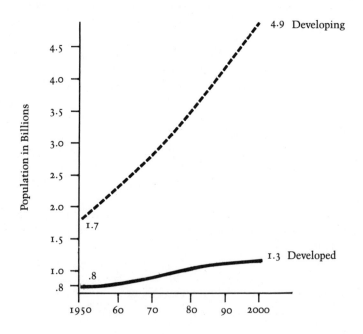

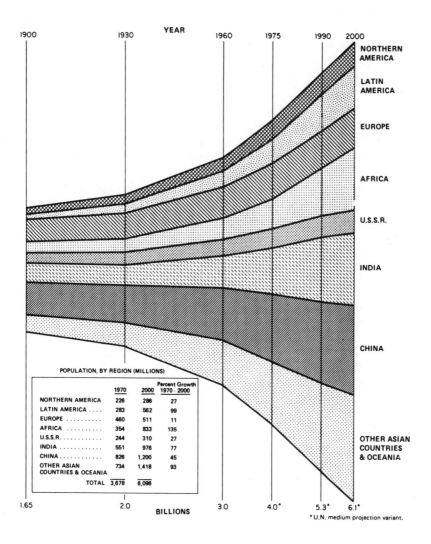

Figure 4.5   Regional growth, 1900–2000. Source: Mary Barberis,
"The Global Population Predicament: Policy Implications," *Population Bulletin* 34, 5 (1981): 2.

what is happening, and then we will try to draw out the implications of this information. In 1955 developing countries were growing at a rate of 2 percent per year. That means that there was an increase (births minus deaths) of twenty people for every thousand in the population. This trend reached a high of 2.35 percent (23.5 people per thousand) in the early 1960s but is projected to drop to 1.84 percent (18.4 per thousand) by the year 2000. That is the good news! The bad news is that after this success in reducing the growth rate, *even at the 1.84 percent rate of growth, the developing world will double its population every thirty-eight years!* The developed world, on the other hand, will double its population every 137 years if it meets its projected growth rate of .51 percent (about one-half of 1 percent) by the year 2000. The rate of growth, therefore, is an important concept. It is particularly important for the manner in which the world's population will distribute (and redistribute) itself.

Figure 4.6   Rates of growth, 1950–2000. Source: Baron, "Population, Development, and Multinational Corporations."

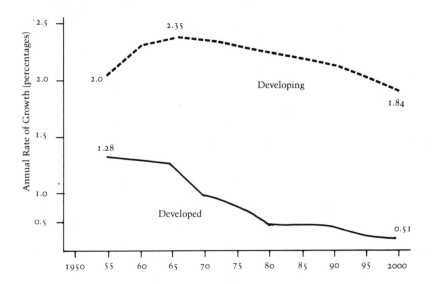

Table 4.1   World birthrates.*

	1950–55	*1980–85*	*1995–2000*
World	35.6	28.1	23.8
Developed	22.7	15.9	14.9
Developing	41.8	32.1	26.2

*per 1,000 population
Source: Baron, "Population, Development, and Multinational Corporations."

Birthrates

If we ignore migration for a moment, the rate of growth is a function, as we suggested earlier, of births minus deaths. Therefore we should study the birth (fertility) and death (mortality) rates because they will shed additional light on what is occurring in the world of population dynamics. Consider birthrates first. Table 4.1 reveals the birthrate for the globe as a whole and for the developed and developing categories of nations.

We should observe that while growth rates are expressed in percentages, birth and death rates are given as a number per thousand. What does the information show? First, for the world as a whole and for both subgroups of nations, it is evident that the birthrate has declined since 1950 and is projected to decline even further by the end of the century. Again, that is a positive finding if one believes that population is growing too rapidly. In the developing world the decline during the last half of the twentieth century is over fifteen babies per thousand (from 41.8 to 26.2). In the past twenty years, there have been substantial declines in many developing countries. These figures contradict a popular myth that births are increasing in the developing world. This is simply not true. Whatever the reason (and we shall discuss this later), developing countries have made great strides in moving away from high birthrates.

Death rates

Since the growth rate is calculated as a combination of birth and death rates, we now turn to the latter rate for the three groups of countries (that is, for all nations, and for the subcategories of developed and developing). This information is found in table 4.2. As you can see, developing countries are experiencing a dramatic drop in

Table 4.2 World death rates.*

	1950–55	1980–85	1995–2000
World	18.3	10.6	8.7
Developed	10.1	9.7	10.1
Developing	22.2	10.9	8.3

*per 1,000 population
Source: Baron, "Population, Development, and Multinational Corporations."

the rates of death that, despite no change in these rates for the developed world, affects the world average downward for the last half of the century.

The reason why the death rate is low for the developing world is twofold: First, since the birthrate has been so high, particularly in the early 1960s, in many of those countries almost half the population is under twenty years of age, which means that—although they will not live as long as we can expect to in the United States —they have not reached the age at which they can be expected statistically to die (their life expectancy). Second, since World War II international agencies such as the World Health Organization and governments of the developed nations have been quite successful in introducing many modern health practices to the countries of Africa, Asia, and Latin America. This has had a particular impact on babies as more and more are now surviving their first year. That is, the infant mortality rate (percentage of babies dying in the first year) has declined dramatically.

Thus, although people are living longer in the countries of Asia, Africa, and Latin America, the impact that increased life expectancy has had on death rates is not nearly as great as the increase in the survival rate of newborn babies. However, despite a major drop in the infant mortality rate, it still remains high at over 150 (that is, 150 out of every thousand babies will *not* live one year) in many countries of Africa, between 135 and 150 in the Middle East and East Asia, and between 65 and 100 in most countries of Latin America. In contrast, the infant mortality rate in the United States is about eleven.[4]

One may ask the question: How do individual fertility decisions affect these rates? Or, can one person make a difference? The answer is obviously no, but a large collection of individuals can do so. Consider the projected difference in the growth rates of the world among three scenarios: 3.8-child family (current fertility), three-child family, and two-child family (replacement fertility). Figure 4.7

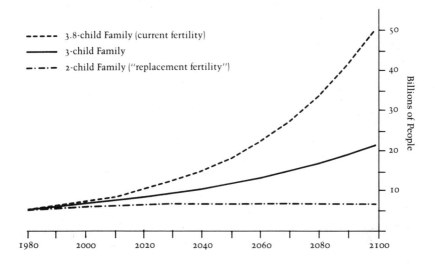

3.8-child Family (current fertility)

3-child Family

2-child Family ("replacement fertility")

Billions of People

50

40

30

20

10

1980   2000   2020   2040   2060   2080   2100

Figure 4.7 Future world population under three assumptions. Source: Population Reference Bureau, *World Population: Fundamentals of Growth* (Washington, D.C., 1984).

shows these projections. By examining this figure you can see that at the two-child family rate, world population would reach slightly above 6 billion in 2100, but at the three-child rate it would reach about 21 billion in about the same year, and at the current 3.8 level it would balloon to over 50 billion. Clearly, the decisions of families will make a difference. These figures should not be surprising. Consider the difference between a two-child average and a three-child average over four generations. As figure 4.8 suggests, in the former there are fourteen direct descendants while in the latter the figure rises to thirty-nine descendants.

This kind of decision-making exists in every family throughout the world and constitutes part of the problem in the third world. Families in many societies live in a culture where many children, particularly boys, are highly valued. Moreover, children provide security for the future as parents must rely on their offspring to care for them in old age. In families of the past, several children would die young and thus women had to produce many if they wanted to make certain that some children would still be alive when needed. Today, although the statistics have changed, cultural influences have

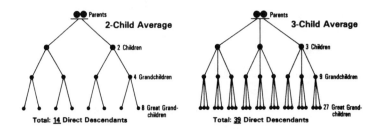

Figure 4.8   Average family size over four generations. Source: Population Reference Bureau, *World Population.*

not. Hence it is difficult to convince parents that they need not have as many children as in the past because a greater percentage of them will now live.

Age composition

In any country, as a consequence of the varying birth and death rates over time, the percentage of the population in different age groups (0–5 years, 6–10 years, and so forth) changes. The relative stability and equality between births and deaths in the developed world create one pattern of age composition characterized by an even balance of age groups (called age cohorts) within the population. On the other hand, the dramatic changes in the birth- and death rates of the developing countries, as well as the vast differences between these two rates at any given moment, create quite a different pattern of age composition. There the base of the population is predominantly young, below the age of fifteen, and there are few old people. Figure 4.9 compares these two patterns by the use of population pyramids. The implications of this pattern are many, and we shall discuss these later in the chapter.

Migration

Migrating is as old as the human race itself. Early fossil remains indicate that early man traveled great distances. The western hemisphere was probably reached first by those who walked across Siberia through Alaska. The story of Moses and the Children of Israel being led out of Egypt is one familiar to readers of the Bible. Later,

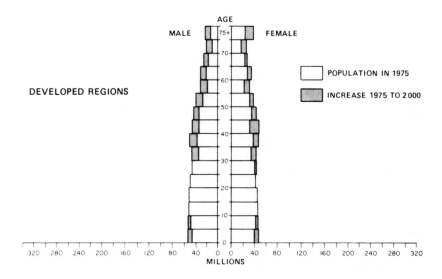

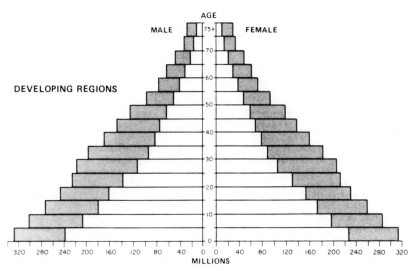

Figure 4.9   Age composition in developed and developing countries.
Source: "World Population: The Silent Explosion," U.S. Department of
State Bulletin, Fall 1978, based on U.S. Bureau of the Census, "Illustrative
Projections of World Population to the 21st Century." Current Population
Reports. Special Studies Series P-23, No. 79, January 1979. The data for
2000 represent the Census Bureau's medium projection.

various conquests resulted in forced migration. During the Roman Empire the population of Rome was composed largely of forced migrants, while at one time 25 to 35 percent of those living in Athens were slaves.[5] Trade throughout the Mediterranean area and later exploration by the major countries of Europe resulted in extensive migration.

This latter migration began in the sixteenth century and continued into this century, with some 60 million Europeans emigrating to the United States, Argentina, Canada, Brazil, Australia, New Zealand, South Africa, and the British West Indies. Most of this migration, around 50 million immigrants, took place between 1845 and 1924. Since World War I the flow has changed from the earlier pattern of movement from East to West toward a pattern of movement from South to North—from Asia, Africa, and Latin America to the developed countries of the North. It is also true that earlier there was substantial forced migration—slavery and indentured labor—from Africa and Asia. One estimate suggests that 9.6 million Africans were imported as slaves to various countries between 1451 and 1870.[6]

Migration from Asia existed before World War I but escalated thereafter, and not just to the United States (though there was a large influx of Chinese to America as cheap labor). Many Asians saw this movement as an "occupational ladder,"[7] while others were principally attracted by trade opportunities.

During and after World War I the movement of refugees in Europe characterized migration involving Russians, Greeks, Bulgarians, Turks, and Armenians. With the rise of dictatorships—Franco in Spain, Hitler in Germany, and Mussolini in Italy—in the 1930s, another wave of refugees emerged, particularly Spanish refugees moving into France and other countries, and German Jews to Western Europe and to the United States.

World War II and its aftermath brought more refugees: some 20 million Eastern and Central Europeans, many of them to North America; some 14 million Indians and Pakistanis within the Indian subcontinent; about five million Japanese from China and other East Asian countries; Koreans from throughout East Asia; citizens of European colonial powers from former colonies (200,000 in number); and from North to South Vietnam. Chinese also fled the mainland in great numbers following the victory of the communists in 1949. African civil wars and struggles of independence beginning in the 1950s had a similar impact on populations, as did the Cuban revolution in 1959. One author, writing in 1969, estimated that in the period between World War I and the mid-sixties some 100 million or more people throughout the globe had been "involuntary migrants."[8]

After World War II voluntary migration from Europe flourished, moving primarily to Australia, Canada, and the United States, and to a lesser extent to Latin America, New Zealand, and South Africa. Australia and South Africa particularly encouraged European immigration. On the other hand, Northern and Western Europe became home to immigrants from elsewhere. Especially affected was Great Britain, which saw an influx of migrants from British Commonwealth countries. South American nations, particularly Brazil and Venezuela, received tens of thousands of immigrants from Europe and Japan, while Israel as a new nation in 1948 grew dramatically as a consequence of new immigrants (in-migration).

The United States continues to receive long-term immigrants, with each decade since World War II showing an increase in the annual average. Asia and Latin America are the chief regions of origin for modern immigrants. Canada is also a net-receiver with about 15 percent of its population being foreign-born, but in the last decade the annual number of immigrants has declined. The majority of migrants arrive from Africa, Asia, Latin America, and the Caribbean, although in a recent year Great Britain and the United States contributed about 30 percent of the total. About 20 percent of the population of both Australia and New Zealand are foreign-born. In each case the mix of countries from which migrants come has increased. Where in the past most came from the present and former British Commonwealth countries, they now arrive from a larger number of countries.

In sum, there have been major changes in the directions of world migration since the 1930s. For almost a hundred years prior to that decade an East-to-West pattern, principally from Europe, dominated. A South-to-North flow, begun in earnest before World War II, accelerated after the war. Now there appears to be a stabilization in the rate of movement to the North or the developed world.

Refugees

The situation with respect to refugees is a different matter. At the beginning of this decade one author estimated that about 16 million refugees were "adrift in the stormy seas of world politics."[9] While this figure may be too high—the United Nations has suggested 14 million and the U. S. Committee for Refugees estimated about half this number in 1983, not including internal migration or border camps[10]—nonetheless, it is clear that the figure is enormous.

Refugee situations fluctuate greatly depending on the extent of economic disruption, physical conflict, and political unrest at a given moment. Most analysts suggest that the number of refugees in Africa passed the six million mark in the early 1980s.[11] Before this time South Asia had the highest number. In eastern Africa the war between Ethiopia and Somalia and subsequent famine in the region have produced countless refugees. But other countries in the area, again because of continuing armed struggle, both produce and receive refugees. Middle Africa and northern Africa share the characteristics of their eastern neighbors, as war, change of government, and famine have created uncertainty for large segments of the population. In southern Africa thousands fled or were removed from Namibia during the 1970s out of fear of South African forces. Western Africa experienced large numbers of refugees in the past—one-quarter of the Guinean population live abroad—but the flow has slowed recently. Nigeria has been the most affected in the last decade. The important point to be made with respect to the refugee situation in Africa is that the root of the problem is not too many people. Rather, it relates to political unrest: upheaval as new governments are created, civil wars, hunger, and other war-related problems.

In Asia, where population size is a real problem, the situation is different. Countries tend to discourage immigration, when they are physically able to do so, particularly of refugees. Conflicts in Vietnam, Laos, and Kampuchea (formerly Cambodia) in the last twenty years have fueled the refugee problem. Thailand became the principal recipient of refugees during the last decade, but it in fact has embarked on a massive campaign of relocation.

In Latin America, Cuba experiences considerable outflow when permitted by the government while Haiti has had a continuous outward stream. Recently fighting in Nicaragua and El Salvador has also resulted in a high number of refugees.

Urbanization

Urban growth refers to increases in the size of cities through any means. Urbanization, however, represents a different concept. It refers to the percentage of the population of a society living in urban areas. As such, urbanization is a major population trend of contemporary society.

Increases in urbanization are a relatively recent phenomenon, for most humans throughout history have lived in rural areas. In 1800 and 1900, for example, the percentages of urban dwellers in the world were only 3 and 14 percent, respectively. By 1984, the figure had risen to 40 percent worldwide although there are dramatic differences among regions and countries of the globe. Latin America and Middle East countries have high levels of urbanization (68 and 58 percent, respectively), particularly when contrasted to African and South Asian levels of 25 to 35 percent.[12]

The ways in which urbanization has occurred and is occurring in the developed and developing societies form a study in contrast. The great wave of urbanization in the developed world took place during the nineteenth and twentieth centuries as a consequence of industrialization. Job opportunities, newly created, convinced people to move from the countryside to the city. In the early days of such internal migration, the death rates in cities were particularly high because of contagious diseases, the lack of sanitation, and other related conditions. So most urban growth occurred through migration.

In the developing world the picture is entirely different. With the diffusion of modern medicine and health care from the developed world to the urban sectors of the third world, mortality declined accordingly, resulting in a rise in the growth rates for city dwellers. People still leave the rural areas for the city in developing societies, but unlike their predecessors a century or so ago they are not likely to find jobs. That fact represents a fundamental problem for governmental leaders as they struggle to assimilate these new arrivals into city life.

In many cases, cities are growing by as much as 7 percent per year, and the largest number of large cities is shifting from the developed to the developing world. While in 1950 only three of the largest ten cities were in the developing world, by 2000 it is estimated that eight will be. Projections for the year 2000 place Mexico City as the world's most populous urban center with 35 million people.

Why Is Growth an Issue?

We must ask ourselves a basic question: why does population growth evoke so much discussion? Why is it a cause for alarm? Why are countries in the developing world now looking for ways to bring about a decline in their rates of population growth? The answers to these questions are not simple but much of the emphasis focuses on *the relationship between economic development and population growth*. These in fact are major goals of most of the countries of Asia, Africa, and Latin America. Researchers who have studied population trends and economic development have discovered a pattern. It is this relationship between these two factors that we shall now discuss.

Demographic transition model

Researchers have labeled the pattern of population growth that occurs within a country as the *demographic transition model*. This suggests the population equation mentioned earlier:

population today = population before + births – deaths + in-migration – out-migration

Ignoring migration, which has little effect today in the total population figures of most of the third world, we are left with births and deaths. If *both* births and deaths are either high or low, population will grow slowly. But, if births remain high (or decline slowly) while deaths decline rapidly, then the result is rapidly increasing population. This is the pattern of population growth that is associated with the last two hundred years in the developed world, as shown in figure 4.10.

Note that on the left side of the diagram, both births and deaths remain high. This was the case when living conditions were difficult and people did not live long. Populations did not grow much despite the high birthrates. In fact, high birthrates were necessary because the survival of the group could be in jeopardy. In the middle period of the model, birthrates decline but death rates drop more rapidly, causing the total population to grow at a high rate. Finally, as the right side of the chart suggests, both birth and death rates eventually even out at a lower rate, meaning that population growth has slowed again. Thus the demographic transition has three stages:

1. High births + high deaths = slow growth
2. Declining births + rapidly declining deaths = rapid growth
3. Low births + low deaths = slow growth

Figure 4.11 reveals the growth pattern for Sweden from 1750 to the present as a case from the developed world. Migration patterns are superimposed on the figures for birth and death rates to indicate the relatively minor impact made by the movement of people in

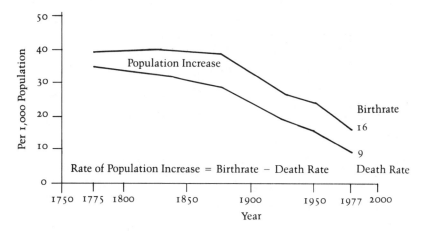

Figure 4.10 Demographic transition model in the developed world.
Source: Population Reference Bureau, *Our Population Predicament.*

and out of the country. As you can see, the period of great growth
was around the turn of the century when the gap between births
and deaths was the greatest. By 1930, both fertility and mortality
were close, meaning no increase in the population. By 1929, the
two were virtually touching. It took Sweden more than a century
to complete its transition from high births–high deaths to low
births–low deaths.

The countries of Western Europe and North America are called
traditional developed countries because their patterns of economic
growth mirror this pattern of population growth. The Industrial
Revolution had not fully taken hold as the nineteenth century was
ushered in; it reached its zenith as the population "took off," that
is, grew rapidly and leveled off as individuals recognized that large
populations were undesirable in an age of mechanization. This pattern typically was followed throughout the developed world. The
countries of the developing world, however, have followed a different pattern of population growth. Birth and death rates remained
high well into this century, but in the post–World War II period, as
we suggested earlier, there was a drop in both figures. However, the
decline in death rates has been much sharper. Figure 4.12 presents
the typical demographic pattern for developing countries.

The key in the developed world is that the pattern of industrialization and economic growth followed precisely the pattern of popula-

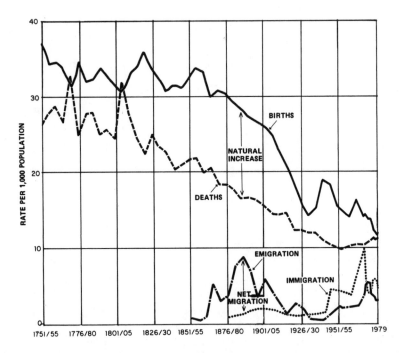

Figure 4.11 Sweden's growth pattern. Source: Population Reference Bureau, *Sweden Faces Zero Population Growth* (1980).

tion growth. It is this fact that has caused alarm in the developing world. Before the early 1970s, the less-developed countries looked with suspicion at suggestions from the developed world that they ought to limit population growth, accusing the latter of trying to commit genocide. But by the time of the World Population Conference in 1974 the less-developed countries had become convinced that the increases in population, so necessary for the traditional Western countries in the early days of industrialization when people were needed to run the machines, might now be a liability. The reason for this is that the great increase in population—due to a decline in death rates attributable to the transfer of modern medical practices—occurred *before* industrialization. As a consequence, needed money that would be used to build factories and roads (which yield economic growth) must, instead, buy food and shelter for the poor masses of people.

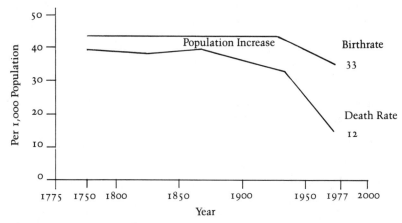

Figure 4.12   Demographic transition in the developing world. Source: Population Reference Bureau, *Our Population Predicament.*

Five Population-Related Growth Problems

We have been suggesting that the poorer countries have recognized that there is a relationship between population characteristics and development. This began following World War II as the death rate declined while birthrates remained high. But the population problem has not simply been one of size; other aspects of population have resulted in a variety of problems for societies. It is this range of problems that we wish to explore now. Let us consider five different kinds of growth problems that have emerged. These problems have evolved historically in the sense that they tended to have been prevalent during successive periods since the 1940s. We will formulate each problem as an equation.[13]

   1. Large Population Size + Limited Arable Land = Food Shortage, Starvation, Malnutrition

In India in the 1940s policy-makers saw an increasing population in conjunction with limited farm (arable) land as *the* population problem of India, and lack of food being the obvious consequence. These policy-makers believed that limiting population would help solve the food problem. This appearance of increasingly large numbers of people and limited food production capability was repeated throughout much of Asia in the 1940s and 1950s. The *world* population problem was therefore known as an *Asiatic* problem rather than a global one. As a consequence, the Asian countries were first among the poorer nations to try to do something about population.

2. Large Population Sizes + Limited Resource Base = Handicap to Improving Living Standard Through Industrialization

Not only were these Asian countries affected by inadequate food production, but they also suffered from a lack of oil, coal, iron ore, and other resources necessary for industrialization.

3. Rapid Population Growth + Low Level of Economic Development = Population "Stumbling Block" to Rapid Development

By the 1950s, the poorer countries were acutely aware of the contribution of declining death rates to high population growth rates. This perception clearly brought home the adverse consequences for economic development that resulted from the high rate of population growth. For example, if a country's population was growing at 3 percent per year, the economy would have to grow at the same rate just to keep even. Even with this economic growth, no development would take place; no significant improvement in the standard of living would occur. There would be no accumulation of capital necessary to build roads and factories that would aid the economy. Because population was growing so fast, any additional money had to be used to feed, clothe, and house people.

4. Very Young Population + Limited Public Funds = Difficulties in Overcoming Illiteracy, Improving Health Conditions, Increasing Economy

By this time, mortality was declining, as we have seen, but it was primarily affecting the younger members of society rather than the old. That is, it was not so much that people were living longer (although life expectancy was inching upward), but that babies and young children were no longer dying in as high percentages. Modern medicine was allowing the infant mortality and childhood mortality rates to decline. As a consequence, by the end of the 1950s almost half the populations of most developing countries were under the age of fifteen. This high proportion of youths placed strains on governments as these children were consumers of public funds rather than producers who paid taxes and contributed to the public treasury. Consequently, scarce funds had to be used to pay for vital services such as education and health care rather than for the building of roads and factories. By the end of the 1950s the perception of the population problem had changed from one of size or density in selected countries to one of high growth and its accompanying high percentage of children in all developing countries.

5. Rapid Population Growth + Low Level of Industrialization = Unemployment and Political Instability

By 1970 all of these children who had created problems ten years earlier were now ready for employment. However, jobs were not available. The young adults moved from the countryside to the city seeking employment, but most fared no better. This placed a tremendous burden on governments that were (and are) being confronted by disenchanted and active people. It is estimated, for example, that 655 million new jobs must be created in the developing countries between now and the year 2000. This represents more jobs than presently exist in all the richer countries of the world combined.

These five basic kinds of problems typify the societal consequences of current population configurations. As a result of problems such as these, governments have begun to try to intervene in the lives of their citizens. We shall discuss governmental efforts to reduce fertility in chapter 8.

Population Growth in Sub-Saharan Africa

We turn now to look at sub-Saharan Africa, a part of the world now experiencing the greatest difficulties associated with population growth. The population of the 42 countries in this region, which lies south of the Sahara desert of North Africa, was estimated at 434 million as of mid-1984 and is likely to triple to 1.4 billion by 2025.[14] The annual growth rate is 3.1 percent, significantly higher than twenty years ago and equal to a doubling of the population every twenty-two years. In Kenya alone the 4.1 percent annual growth rate translates into a doubling of the population every seventeen years. Births average forty-eight per thousand in sub-Saharan Africa while deaths are seventeen per thousand and declining. The birthrate has increased primarily because women are healthier than in the past and therefore more fertile. The 3.1 percent growth is particularly troublesome when contrasted with other birthrates. When Europe was experiencing its heavy population growth in the nineteenth century, the annual growth rate never exceeded 1.6 percent. In Asia, excluding China, and in Latin America the growth rates are currently only 1.8 percent and 2.4 percent, respectively. In West Africa the birthrate in 1984 was forty-nine per thousand, which averages out to 6.9 children for the lifetime of each woman. In Kenya, based on current fertility patterns, the average woman will bear 8.1 children during her reproductive years.

Because of the high birthrates over a period of years, the average age of most African countries' populations is very low. In forty of the forty-two countries (excluding Gabon and South Africa) over 45 percent of the population is under the age of fifteen. There are two implications of this fact. First, in the future substantial capital must be invested in order to feed, clothe, and educate this nonproductive age group. Second, the momentum for future population growth is present as these youngsters are only beginning to enter their fertile period.

Added now to the problem of famine in sub-Saharan Africa are the enormous difficulties created by internal and international migration. Africans have been traditionally migratory people and the search for food and a way out of poverty has increased this pattern. Movement from the rural areas to the towns and cities occurs at an ever-increasing rate. Cities grew an average of about 6 percent per year during the 1970s, although a majority of people still live in the rural areas. Economic factors also result in large movements across national boundaries as people search for jobs. Much international migration is also involuntary, creating a class of refugees fleeing war, political strife, and drought. Over 2.7 million refugees are found throughout sub-Saharan Africa; and the nightly news continues to bring Americans pictures of the plight of these refugees who exist with little food, clothing, shelter, or employment.

Why has high fertility been so prevalent in Africa in the face of the obvious adverse consequences? First, most Africans are low-income, poorly educated farmers with small landholdings. Traditionally, throughout the globe, people in this category have had large families. Second, African women, despite an important role in agriculture, are still viewed primarily as wives and mothers with limited legal rights and few if any outside employment opportunities. As a consequence, childbearing yields status and children can help with house and farm chores. Third, African women marry young and have large extended families who provide both material and psychological support. Fourth, children represent a social security system for the elderly. This influence is complicated further since African women who usually cannot inherit land must therefore make certain that sons are around when their husbands die. Fifth, substantial ethnic diversity in sub-Saharan Africa also contributes in many cases to high fertility. As ethnic groups within a country vie for political control, they view the size of the tribe as an important power dimension. Fifth, disease, famine, and war have historically resulted in high death rates, including high infant mortality. Thus pressure has been ever-present to keep ahead of these mortality-inducing conditions by engaging in high-fertility behavior. Sixth, knowledge about safe, effective birth control is limited and confined mainly to major cities.

Some researchers also believe that two other factors might be related to fertility. Religious tradition may resist government sanctioning of family planning as immoral and against the natural order. The expansion of Christianity, whether or not traditional tribal practices exist alongside it, may also be affecting family size. Moreover, life in rural areas is fraught with danger at times, and large family size means better protection. In short, African women are having large families because they want them, a statement that is supported by the World Fertility Survey undertaken by the World Bank. This survey revealed that the average number of children desired is 7.6 in the ten sub-Saharan African countries included, hardly a positive sign for declining fertility rates.

The Future

In analyzing the future, we must return again to the three processes that shape population—fertility, mortality, and migration. Although all projections are based on a variety of assumptions that may not occur—and this is particularly true of population, given the awakened interest in fertility reduction programs—we can at least acquire a general picture.

Fertility

Crude birthrates are heavily influenced by age composition— the larger the percentage of women in their fertile years, the higher the likelihood of a high birthrate. But in addressing the issue of fertility, it is better to replace this focus with an examination of fertile women themselves. The Gross Reproduction Rate (GRR) measures the relative sizes of future generations of women. Specifically, it measures the average number of daughters that a generation of women in their fertile years is likely to produce. A GRR of 1.0 means that each woman of a generation is likely to produce one daughter; she is simply replacing herself. A GRR of 2.0 implies that the population will likely double each generation, while a value less than 1.0

will lead to a decline of the population in the long run. In policy-making efforts, the GRR rate is much more important for analyzing the future than birthrates because it factors out the age-composition variable over time.

In 1950 the GRR for the developed world was 1.41, suggesting that the population would increase by almost half again as much every generation or almost triple every two generations. By the turn of the century the GRR in the developed world is projected to be 1.04. That is, there will be hardly any increase over time in the populations of these regions.

In the developing world, using the GRR is particularly important since we wish to factor out the reality that a high percentage of the population has only recently entered the fertile period and will remain there for some thirty years. This fact must be taken into account in order to assess the effectiveness of fertility reduction programs. In 1975 the GRR for the developing world was 2.31, meaning that the population more than doubled every generation. Africa's rate was 3.13; during each generation the population would triple.

The United Nations predicts that the consequence of fertility reduction programs throughout the developing world during the last part of this century will result in a drop of the GRR to 1.63 by the year 2000. This represents a dramatic decline from the recent 2.31 figure. At the projected rate for the turn of the century the population will double "only" slightly sooner than every three generations. Africa will remain the major focus with a projected rate of 2.41 by the year 2000.

Mortality

As we suggested earlier, mortality rates have been declining primarily because of decreases in the rate of infant mortality, particularly in the developing or third world. In the developed world, the principal reason for any slight decline in mortality—with most occurring prior to 1965—is due to increased life expectancy created by advances in modern medicine. We use life expectancy here because it is not affected by age composition in the manner that crude death rates are. The life expectancy of males in the developed world is projected by the United Nations to rise from 63.1 years in 1950 to 70.1 years by 2000. Similarly, the life expectancy for women of the same regions will climb from 67.3 to 75.5 years during the same period. Unless the three primary killers of the aged—cancer, strokes, and heart disease—are successfully attacked by modern medicine, we can expect little change in the death rates for developed societies.[15]

In the developing world the life expectancy for males and females in 1950 was 41.7 and 43.5 years, respectively. Life expectancy is projected to continue to increase until the turn of this century when it is expected to reach the United Nations-projected values of 61.7 and 64.5 years for males and females, respectively. The reason, of course, is due to the spread of better nutrition and of modern medicine in the form of supplemental feeding programs for pregnant women and mothers of newborn, and vaccinations against infectious diseases. The young have been the major beneficiaries of these processes. By the turn of the century we can expect a major slowdown in increases in life expectancy because the dramatic impacts of the initial transfers of modern medicine will already have been felt for several decades.

Migration

Migration is affected by such nonpopulation processes as war, famine, political persecution, and the seeking of a better way of life. All of these pressures may become more acute as the developing world struggles with providing the long-term basic human needs for their "baby boom" of the 1960s. The "boat people" episodes in recent years may be an early warning system of what the developed world might expect on a far larger scale as we move into the twenty-first century. In fact, forced or encouraged migration may be the strategy used by governments to address their population problems in the future. The West, and particularly the United States, must be prepared to deal with the *cause* of this potential migration—by helping to create the proper circumstances in the developing world that would deter migration—or else it will have eventually to deal with the *symptoms*: hundreds of thousands of people arriving at America's shore with pleading hands.

5 The Environment Issue

"Save the Whales!" "Ban the Bomb!" "Help Prevent Forest Fires!"
"Smoking is Hazardous to Your Health!" "Smog Alert!" "Caution
—Hazardous Materials!" "No Dumping!" "Unsafe for Human
Consumption!" "Please Do Not Litter!" "Make Love, Not War!"
"Red Tide Alert!" "Please Remove Tar Before Leaving Beach Area!"
"Conserve Energy!"

What do these admonitions have in common? At first glance,
they appear to represent a wide cross section of causes to which
segments of the general population attach themselves. Upon
reflection, however, one can observe a common thread among them
all. That is, they relate to some specific problem now viewed by
many citizens of this planet as part of the environment issue.[1]

Once thought of simply as the "outdoors," that part of one's
surroundings to be used in the pursuit of fulfillment and enjoyment,
the environment is increasingly viewed by laymen in much the
same light as by scientists. The environment, according to those
who work in this field, is a complex web of relationships and
interdependencies. It is the mutual interdependence that all plants
and animals in their habitats share in order to survive. Most but
not all problems labeled as "environmental issues" usually arise as
a consequence of the activities of human beings on the earth. Thus
emphasis is typically placed on the impact of human behavior on
nature, or the nonhuman environment.

Throughout history, human use of this planet has often resulted
in the nonhuman aspects of the planet being less well-off. This
scenario was given little attention in the past, however, for a number of reasons. First, because of the limitations of science and
technology, man had little ability to wreak havoc on his environment. Consequently, adverse effects were not observed. Second,
because their numbers were few and geographically dispersed, peo-

ple could generate only a marginal impact. Third, when problems were noticed, man either lived with them or, quite often, moved on to another geographic area. Fourth, the concept of delayed negative impacts on the environment was not part of human consciousness. Research had not yet uncovered the notion that time lag, sometimes for decades, had to be considered in projecting environmental damage.

Human concern about the effect of mankind's behavior on the planet began to emerge when these reasons began to lose their validity. Modern technology, embodied initially in the Industrial Revolution, began to project vivid pictures of large-scale abuse. Population growth rates increased dramatically, and with them came an escalation in the number of incidents of environmental degradation. With the coming of the last frontier (at least until outer space and the deep sea were conquered), the ability of the human race to migrate easily began to diminish. We were left to live among the visually apparent consequences of our past behavior. Modern medical and other scientific research uncovered the role of time lag in cause-and-effect relationships. Equally important, the human species began to understand the concept of an ecosystem—the idea that everything is related to everything else in an intricate complex of subsystems, that there exists worldwide a comprehensive integrative system with finite limits.

Gradually individuals, then groups, then governments came to see the problems firsthand and to perceive the global consequences of such problems. Early attempts to manage inland waters and protect forests, governments' initial response to perceived environment issues, culminated in the bringing together of the entire global community at Stockholm in 1972 to the *United Nations Conference on the Human Environment*. The conference, in the words of observers, was "the successor to the great voyages of discovery and exploration that made people aware of the shape of the world and the diversity of its lands and waters, rocks, vegetation, faunas and cultures."[2] The Stockholm conference was the culmination of a number of major developments in the post–World War II era addressing the environment issue. First, the scientific community was joined by environmentalists active in the ecological movement in their respective countries. Second, concern for the environment spread beyond the developed Western industrialized nations to both the socialist and developing worlds. Finally, the approach changed to embrace a much broader conception of the term environment. All aspects of the natural environment became matters of concern

—land, water, minerals, all living organisms and life processes, the atmosphere, climate, icecaps, the deep sea, the human condition, and all relationships therein. Perhaps the most important manifestation of this commitment to the environment is the official body created for implementing the precepts of the Stockholm conference, the United Nations Environment Programme (UNEP). This mechanism represented the synthesis of ideas for action that emerged at Stockholm. It became, in short, a coordinating body operating under the fundamental premise that responsibility for addressing environmental issues rests not with a specialized body but with every actor. As UNEP developed, it became not only a coordinator but also a creative body, an idea generator, and an evaluator. This development demonstrates further the global dimensions of environmental issues.

Historical Roots

Although modern technology has allowed environmental impacts to transcend national and even regional boundaries, limited versions of the same problems have existed since humans began to use the resources of this planet.[3] For example, rising sea levels in Holland caused by glacial retreat at the end of the Pleistocene Age must have represented a severe ecological crisis to the Upper Paleolithic reindeer hunters in Holland. Scholars of prehistory suggest that episodes such as these either were disastrous, sometimes wiping out whole populations, or creative, where society learned to adapt by creating new mechanisms. Examples of both scenarios abound. One controversial interpretation of why large mammals of North America became extinct points to early migrants from Siberia. These hunters easily killed the large animals and consequently the hunters thrived and their numbers grew rapidly, further reducing the large mammal population. Others argue, however, that the reduction of the animals' habitat caused their demise.

A second example is the plight of the early Vikings in Greenland. They lived in a marginal area where slight temperature or moisture fluctuations could be disastrous. Arriving during a warm climatic period (800–1000), they found their climate deteriorating after 1200. By 1500 they were extinct.

Another illustration occurred in the American Southwest. A recently developed thesis suggests that population grew as a consequence of increased agricultural productivity and sedentism (remaining in one place). Increased numbers meant that marginal land, land that could be made productive only with great effort, was needed for new habitation. Coupled with a change in the pattern of rainfall from spring to late summer, the new conditions created havoc with the ecosystem. Most of the northern part of the Southwest was eventually abandoned as a consequence, because neither new technological breakthroughs nor new levels of sociocultural complexity occurred.

These examples show that in preindustrial times it was not an infrequent occurrence for ecological stress to "win out" over human attempts at adaptation. In the industrial era, however, humans came to believe that they were masters of their surroundings. They had unbounded belief in science and technology as cure-alls for current and future problems. Environmental mastery was reinforced when this faith was joined by the rationalism and materialism of the late Middle Ages. Already believing that they were separate from nature, even above it, and could use it for pursuing noble ends, humans also came to believe that they could control it.

Linked by huge railway lines and busy waterways, large cities emerged. Attacks on the ecosystem were viewed as normal by-products of industrial progress, perhaps to be corrected at some later date when the problem appeared to be getting out of hand. Although science and technology, or more exactly, human inability to use science and technology correctly, were partly to blame, they were not the only reasons for environmental degradation. One scholar has suggested that a review of the literature about the antecedents of ecological problems reveals five possible explanations: population, affluence, technology, capitalism, and growth.[4] With the exception of the risk of nuclear war—and one might even make a sound argument in that case—dramatic increases in population size have served as a necessary condition for virtually every current environmental problem. Increased population has placed demands on energy, food, and other resources, while at the same time contributing to increased pollution. Most scholars who address environmental issues allude to the rapid growth of population as a major factor, particularly the dramatic increases (and rates of increase) in developing societies. Typical of this view is a recent statement by Lester Brown, informed observer of the world's resource base: "Until the rate of population growth slows markedly, improving the human condition will be difficult."[5]

Not all scholars, however, hold that population is a culprit, even in the rapidly growing areas of the developing world. One such author is Julian Simon, in the forefront of the minority who question the contention that population growth is at fault. Says Simon: "Population growth has positive economic effects in the long run. . . . . (It) is a moral and material triumph."[6] Although it is clear that the population theory of environmental damage has merit, one must look more closely at the causal links before being completely satisfied with the theory's plausibility.[7]

Those who argue that affluence has resulted in a wide range of negative environmental effects point to the correlation between major increases in the gross national product per capita in developed Western countries on the one hand, and high levels of pollution, resource depletion, and the destruction of virgin land on the other. The debate over the role played by affluence is much more pronounced than that for population. Although it is true that the correlation between gross national product per capita and environmental degradation is strong, the causal aspects of the link are much less certain. Barry Commoner, a noted commentator on environmental issues, argues that the significant increases in pollution cannot be explained simply by increased consumption. Commoner asserts that production processes are to blame. The producers of commodities rather than consumers must bear the major burden of responsibility.

Thus Commoner and others point to technology as the major cause of negative environmental impact. For them, new technological innovations have made the difference: "detergents, aluminum, plastic and inorganic fertilizers in place of soap powder, wood, steel and manure,"[8] disposable packaging in place of returnable bottles, more lead in gasoline, and increased chlorine production leading to increases in mercury consumption. Others disagree with this view, arguing that the environmental benefits of technology outweigh any costs. Robin Attfield finds a common ground between the two positions, suggesting that, although there have been undeniable benefits, ecological damage since 1945 owes much of its origin to technology.[9] Presumably, therefore, one may address immediate problems with greater technological clarity (although not necessarily with greater ease) than the less discernible long-term impacts that may come from the efforts of technology to solve those problems.

Capitalism has always been pointed to by Marxists as the major culprit for all of society's ills. In this case they are joined by many other thoughtful individuals who add the economic form of society to the technical dimension just discussed. The new technology was introduced because it yielded more profits. Consequently, by-products, no matter how unintended or controversial, have been tolerated, particularly when governments have refused to intervene or have been slow to act. Moreover, the link between capitalism and pressure for growth leads to institutional structures that are incompatible with the strategies of steady-state economies and local self-reliance ("small is beautiful"). In response to these criticisms, supporters of capitalism ask why, if capitalism alone is to blame, do severe environmental problems also exist in the planned economies of socialist and communist countries.

The final argument, a composite of the others, suggests that growth is at the heart of the matter, particularly growth applied to five areas—population, food production, industrialization, pollution, and consumption of nonrenewable resources. In this view, the linkages among these five contribute to the severity of the problem. The overarching theory forms the basis for the thesis advanced in the *Limits to Growth* reports. Although that thesis is at first compelling, these reports have come under a great deal of criticism, and much research remains to be done before the comprehensive, yet somewhat simplistic, growth theory can be embraced.

Difficulties of Analysis

We are left then with an absence of certainty with respect to the causes of global environmental problems. Those individuals who early recognized that the ecosystem was being adversely affected were handicapped in trying to pinpoint the causes, subsequent effects, and solutions. One observer suggests three principal reasons why those who issued early warnings were unable to convince many people that trouble lay ahead: (1) a lack of basic information (or gaps in the information) about critical aspects of ecological processes; (2) significant time lag before the full impact of some action or process is felt; and (3) the failure of those viewing a problem to acquire a comprehensive picture rather than a more narrow one based only on their own field of work.[10]

Inadequate information

Whatever the environmental issue, one is confronted with two kinds of problems relating to information about it. First, current knowledge about land, water, forest, grassland, and the atmosphere is rarely complete. This is particularly true with respect to knowledge about developing societies. Second, little historical data exist, particularly from the world outside Europe and the United States. In the study just cited, two basic examples are used to make the point: soil erosion and climate. We know little about soil erosion in a global sense: how much there is, what is causing it, and what are its effects. In the case of climate, despite the existence of the World Meteorological Organization for over a hundred years, little historical data exist for areas outside Europe and the United States. Satellite observation now yields information on both the developing regions and the oceans, but it only complements, not replaces, on-ground observation. Since the various systems mentioned above interact with one another—remember, everything is related to everything else—gaps in our knowledge about even one of the systems dramatically affect our understanding of the entire system.

Time lag

One fact that has become increasingly apparent during the last half of the twentieth century is that many of the effects of man's interaction with his environment do not occur immediately. Years and even decades may pass before the main impact is observed or felt. Even where suspicions exist about a potential cause, often the link cannot be positively determined because the appropriate research has not or cannot be completed. Cigarette smoking and the use of asbestos in the workplace are two examples of situations whose impact was felt only much later. In these two instances the evidence is clear and irrefutable, despite the pleas of the industries involved. The evidence is almost as clear for those who were exposed to fallout from nuclear testing programs. In each of these cases, however, it took years to discover the link and still more years for research to demonstrate the validity of the connection.

In other areas suspicions exist but scientific inquiry has not yet demonstrated the link. One such example is the relationship between diet sweeteners and cancer. Perhaps no other food additives have been subjected to more scientific investigation than low-calorie sweeteners. Some have clearly been shown to be linked to cancers in rats. For others, such as cyclamates, the evidence is less clear. In that case, the agent was banned in 1970 but the government has recently reevaluated the evidence with a view to partially rehabilitating it. Controversy remains, however, over cyclamates and other sweeteners and is likely to continue for some time. The example of sugar substitutes illustrates a major point. That is, the linkage between cause and effect may not be a direct and immediate one, and thus scientific research may not be able to document causality. As a result the average citizen is left to ponder the risk.

Specialized approaches

The third difficulty in analyzing the environment involves the contrasts between the concept of ecosystem and all its interrelated parts with the institutions and strategies designed to do battle with ecological stresses. One analogy that has been used is that of three blind men trying to describe an elephant. One holds the tail and concludes that the elephant is a snake; the next likens the leg to a tree; while the last holds the ear and describes a sail. The point is that it is just not a case of everyone's working on a piece of the puzzle and then fitting it together. Rather there are different research problems being suggested, and different research agendas being proposed, with findings, however relevant, slow to circulate throughout the network of researchers.

Environmental Problems

There are many ways to group those problems included in the phrase "the environmental issue." Some use the four basic elements understood by the Greeks—air, water, earth, and fire—and describe natural and man-made problems associated with each. Others use a much larger set of categories, including such topics as human settlements and terrestrial biota, that is, the natural living resources of the continents. Some focus solely on the type of activity causing the problem. Still others simply distinguish between natural and man-made problems irrespective of what part of the ecosystem is affected. Here we approach the problem of categorizing environmental issues by combining what we hope are the most useful elements of all of the above. In some instances the origin of the problem is the key; in others it is the current manifestation of the problem, and in other cases it is the process underlying the problem that is critical.

When the general population thinks of the environment issue the term *pollution* comes to mind—pollution of the atmosphere, waterways (including the ocean), and land. *Climatic change*, whatever the causes, is another common concept (some climatic change is caused by pollution, for example). The visible loss of natural resources represents an additional problem that has received wide publicity. This refers to the exhaustion of *nonrenewable resources* such as oil, gas, and other minerals. With respect to those objects found in nature as well as living things that can be reproduced, another common environmental problem is the tendency *to exceed* the *carrying capacity* of a resource. The carrying capacity is the maximum level to which a resource can be exploited indefinitely without going beyond its ability to replace itself. Carrying capacity is relevant for our fourth category, the *loss of cropland, rangeland, and forests*, as well as plants, fauna, and other inorganic objects that reside therein. The extinction of *animals and other living things* represents a fifth category, and another example of the carrying capacity being exceeded. Finally, environmental damage arising from the preparation for and the conduct of *war* concludes the list of environmental issues of general public concern. Let us now turn our attention to a further discussion of these six categories: (1) pollution; (2) climatic change; (3) depletion of nonrenewable resources; (4) loss of cropland, rangeland, and forests; (5) animal, insect, and fish species extinction; and (6) war.

Pollution

Pollution affects the air we breathe, the land we walk on, and the water we drink and use. Most but not all pollutants make their way to the oceans, either by runoff from land or inland waterways or by falling from the sky. Some pollution, such as oil spills, comes directly from the original source. Let us talk first about problems of pollution that affect the atmosphere.

Acid Rain   For some time an accumulation of evidence has existed to suggest that pollutants from the combustion of fossil fuels and the smelting of metallic ores create havoc with forests. A more recent problem is acid rain, that is, sulfur and nitrogen oxides that are changed by a chemical process in the atmosphere, then travel great distances and fall as sulfuric and nitric acids in rain, snow, fog, or even dry particles. In fact, acid rain falling on Sweden was one of the reasons why the Swedish government pushed for the United Nations Stockholm conference. Both air pollutants and acids are dropping on forests in far greater amounts than ever before, particularly on those in the wind paths of the industrial regions of Europe, eastern North America, and East Asia. Five to twenty times more sulfur than that provided by nature is added to the atmosphere in these regions.[11] Large amounts of the oxides cross international boundaries to fall as acid rain in another country. Much of Sweden and Norway's acid rain originates in Great Britain, Western

Europe, East Germany, and Poland. About half of that which falls on eastern Canada was generated in the United States.

A curious fact about the problem is that it might have unwittingly been created by the solution to an earlier problem. In order to combat local pollution caused by nearby emissions, tall smokestacks were added to power stations. This had the effect of diminishing the local effect but instead transferred the pollution across great distances. According to one source, the effects of acid rain have been dramatic:[12]

In the Katowice area of Poland trains are limited to forty kilometers an hour due to corrosion of the rails by acid rain.

In Sweden 20,000 of a total of 90,000–100,000 lakes are ecologically virtually dead or dying because of acid water; $4.5 million a year is being spent on pumping lime into the lakes to reduce acidity, and Swedish authorities have recommended that $40 million be spent yearly.

All the lakes in a 13,000-square-kilometer area of southern Norway are devoid of fish.

Two hundred lakes in the Adirondack Mountains in the United States are fishless.

In Canada 140 lakes are without fish, 1,000 more are damaged, and 48,000 more may be affected over the next decade.

A U.S. National Academy of Sciences committee has reported that even at the present level of emissions "the number of affected lakes in Europe and the United States can be expected to more than double by 1990."

The economic effect of acid rain on buildings, paintwork, and metalwork is probably high but has not been estimated.

Acid rain also dissolves heavy metals in the soil, possibly increasing the risks of metal pollution and poisoning.

Others have provided further documentation.[13] A 1984 survey revealed that half of the trees in West Germany apparently have some damage, a dramatic increase from only a few years earlier. In Czechoslovakia and Austria damage has occurred on an estimated half-million and four-hundred thousand hectares, respectively. Other countries throughout Europe also show significant forest damage. The problem promises to become greater, even as the international community attempts to deal with the issue.

Ozone Depletion   A decade ago there was a great outcry that the release of chlorofluorocarbons into the stratosphere was depleting the ozone layer. Public pressure was brought to bear to limit the use

Table 5.1   Sources of ocean pollution.

Water discharge or other process of activity potentially causing contamination	Baltic Sea	North Sea	Mediterranean Sea	Persian Gulf	West African Areas	South African Areas	Indian Ocean Region	Southeast Asian Areas	Japanese Coastal Waters	North American Areas	Caribbean Sea	Southwest Atlantic Region	Southeast Pacific Region	Australian Areas	New Zealand Coastal Waters
Sewage	x	x	x	x	x	x	x	x	x	x	x	x	x	x	x
Petroleum hydrocarbon (maritime transport)	x	x	x	x	x	x	x	x	x	x	x	x			
Petroleum hydrocarbon (exploration and exploitation)		x		x	x			x		x	x	x	x		
Petrochemical industry		x	x	x					x	x	x				
Mining			x					x		x			x	x	
Radioactive wastes	x	x	x				x		x	x		x			
Food and beverage processing	x	x	x			x				x	x	x	x	x	x
Metal industries		x	x		x				x	x		x			x
Chemical industries	x	x	x						x	x					
Pulp and paper manufacture	x				x					x			x	x	x
Agriculture runoff (pesticides and fertilizer)			x		x	x	x			x					x
Siltation from agriculture and coastal development						x	x	x			x				
Sea-salt extraction							x				x				
Thermal effluents						x	x		x	x	x	x			
Dumping of sewage sludge and dredge spoils		x							x	x					

Source: GESAMP (Group of Experts on the Scientific Aspects of Marine Pollution), "The Health of the Oceans," UNEP publication, cited in Martin W. Holdgate, Mohammed Kassas, and Gilbert F. White, eds., *The World Environment 1972–1982: A Report by the United Nations Environment Programme* (Dublin: Tycooly International, 1982), p. 80.

of fluorocarbons, or freon, in aerosol sprays and cooling systems. It is also understood, however, that gases emitted from high-altitude aircraft and nitrogen fertilizers contribute to ozone depletion.

The reason for the concern is that ozone absorbs ultraviolet and cosmic radiation. When the ozone is depleted, these dangerous forms of radiation reach the earth's surface in higher numbers, resulting in a great incidence of skin cancer in humans as well as damage to other species.

Water Pollution   The ocean and other waterways also suffer dramatically, whether directly or indirectly, as a consequence of pollution. Fifteen different sources of ocean pollution have been identified by researchers. These are listed in table 5.1 with the ocean regions that are affected by each. Pollutants reach the ocean through rivers, direct coastal outfalls, drainage from human habitats and farmland, deposits from the atmosphere, ships, and offshore structures such as oil rigs. Rivers are particularly potent avenues for pollutants, as most pollutants originate on land but are carried by the rivers to sea.

Worldwide attention typically focuses on such spectacular events as large oil spills that kill birds and fish and ruin recreational areas, or high metal concentrations such as the mercury in fish from Japanese waters that resulted in forty-one deaths in Minamata Bay in the 1950s and created widespread fear. Extensive mercury poisoning has occurred in Iraq in the last thirty years, while Sweden banned the sale of fish from forty lakes and rivers in 1967 because of high concentrations of mercury. With respect to oil spills, the Mediterranean area has only 1 percent of the world's ocean surface but 50 percent of all floating oil and tar.[14] But as the *Global 2000 Report* points out, the greater set of problems grows out of "largely unnoticed, and undetected, chronic low-level pollution."[15] That is why the oceans have always been viewed as mankind's ultimate dumping ground and have continued to receive waste at an ever-increasing rate.

We must also distinguish between the open ocean and coastal waters, for the coastal waters contain most of the ocean's productive capacity but form only a small percentage of its total area. The coastal ecosystems are likely to be more fragile while at the same time being bombarded by coastal development as well as by a larger and more diverse set of pollutants.

Another kind of water pollution is thermal discharge from factories and power plants. The increased temperature of the discharge reduces the dissolved oxygen in the water, speeding metabolic rates while depleting oxygen supplies. Thermal discharge has other impacts as well:[16]

Destruction of small organisms such as fish larvae and plankton entrained in the cooling water intake and poisoned by antifouling biocides

Reduction of fish abundance, biomass, and species diversity in downstream thermal "plumes"

Synergistic worsening of the stresses caused to most organisms by other factors such as increased salinity, biological oxygen demand, and toxic substances

Shifting of the balance among algae species to favor blue-green algae, which create taste and odor problems in municipal water supplies

Sudden changes of temperature during startups and shutdowns, causing deaths of many sensitive species

Take another case. In developing societies one likely future power source is hydropower, but plans that combine flood control, power production and irrigation have a tremendous impact on the environment. Such impact has included the following:[17]

The inundation of farmland, settlements, roads, railroads, forests, historical and archeological sites, and mineral deposits

The creation of artificial lakes, which often become habitats for disease vectors (carriers) such as the mosquitoes that transmit malaria and the snails that transmit schistosomiasis

The alteration of river regimes downstream by dams, ending the biologically significant annual flood cycle, increasing water temperature, and sometimes triggering riverbank erosion as a result of the increased sediment-carrying capacity of the water

The interruption of upstream spawning migrations of fish

Water-quality deterioration

Irrigation systems are another source of environmental problems. Humans have the capacity to "move mountains," but that process has an inevitable impact on the surroundings. The High Aswan Dam in Egypt is a good case of a substantial impact—for good or ill—on the immediate ecosystem caused by an irrigation project.[18] To begin with, one-hundred thousand people were relocated from the reservoir site. Ancient temples were flooded. Sediments that formerly enriched the floodplain as well as the Mediterranean Sea are now trapped by the dam. One casualty is the Egyptian sardine industry that once provided 50 percent of the country's fish. Waves and tides now erode the delta, resulting in an agricultural cutback. The year-round irrigation in the delta has elevated the water table and caused salinization. The disease schistosomiasis is spreading rapidly throughout the rural sectors as a consequence of the carrier inhabitation of the irrigation canals. Finally the water hyacinth, a floating plant, has now spread uncontrollably throughout the canal systems, interfering with water flow.

Climatic changes

Changes in the earth's temperature—up or down—represent another environmental problem. The atmosphere, and thus the climate, can be affected in three ways: (1) by changing the concentration of substances such as water; (2) by releasing heat into the atmosphere; and (3) by making changes in the physical and biological properties of the earth's surface.[19]

One concern is that the burning of fossil fuels causes build-up of carbon dioxide in the atmosphere that, in turn, leads to higher temperatures. In the past 125 years, 140 billion tons of carbon have been released into the atmosphere as a consequence of the burning of fossil fuels, and half of it remains there.[20] As the consumption of fossil fuels continues to increase yearly, so does the amount of carbon released into the atmosphere. Another way in which this phenomenon occurs is through massive deforestation and desertification, since more carbon is released in these processes as a consequence of its not being used by the displaced vegetation.

Carbon dioxide (CO_2) produces a "greenhouse effect" when sunlight reaching the earth's surface cannot dissipate back (reradiate) into space due to the CO_2 layer in the atmosphere. This trapped heat creates a warming effect. Scientists predict an increase of 1.5 to 3 degrees centigrade if the CO_2 concentration is doubled. Since fossil fuel consumption has been increasing by 4 percent per year, it will be only a short time (less than ten years) before we will approach this level.

Others argue, however, that the warmer climate scenario from increased CO_2 in the atmosphere may be misleading. They suggest that more clouds will be created, as will more particles in the atmosphere, thus stabilizing or even lowering the temperature. But we should not yet be willing to put down our guard. As one author has suggested, carbon dioxide "is the quintessential global environmental issue."[21]

Increased temperatures would lead to a gradual melting of the

About 40,000 pounds of new mineral materials
are required annually for each U.S. citizen

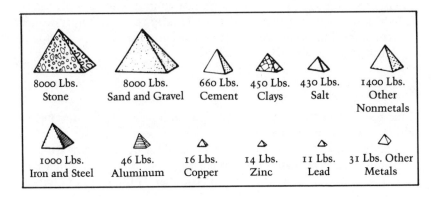

8000 Lbs.
Stone

8000 Lbs.
Sand and Gravel

660 Lbs.
Cement

450 Lbs.
Clays

430 Lbs.
Salt

1400 Lbs.
Other
Nonmetals

1000 Lbs.
Iron and Steel

46 Lbs.
Aluminum

16 Lbs.
Copper

14 Lbs.
Zinc

11 Lbs.
Lead

31 Lbs. Other
Metals

plus

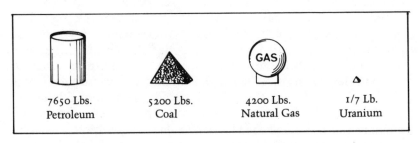

7650 Lbs.
Petroleum

5200 Lbs.
Coal

4200 Lbs.
Natural Gas

1/7 Lb.
Uranium

to generate: energy equivalent to 300 persons working around the clock
for each U.S. citizen

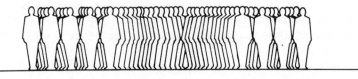

U.S. total use of new mineral supplies
in 1975 was about 4 billion tons.

Figure 5.1   Annual mineral requirements of U.S. citizens. Source: U.S.
Bureau of Mines, *Status of the Mineral Industries 1976.*

polar ice caps with a rise in the level of the ocean. Low-lying areas would become inundated. Agricultural conditions would also deteriorate in the equatorial regions (although they might improve in the temperate zones). A drop in temperature would have the opposite effect, hurting the breadbaskets of the temperate zones and requiring substantially higher levels of energy for heating.

We should not leave the environmental impact of climatic change without mentioning how nuclear war might affect climate. Later in this chapter we will detail the effects of war. One study by a team of scientists has concluded that even a comparatively small nuclear war would cause severe and long-term low temperatures (at least four months) a "nuclear winter," followed by an extended period of increased ultraviolet light.[22] While there are challenges from some circles about these findings and more research needs to be conducted, suffice it to say that a significant percentage of the relevant scientific community, including the Defense Department is enough concerned about this issue to make it part of their research agenda.

Loss of nonrenewable resources

Most of the earth's mineral resources are nonrenewable and are found in the earth's crust, called the lithosphere. Perhaps no picture better illustrates man's use of minerals than figure 5.1, a 1975 graphic depiction of the annual mineral requirements of each American citizen. As a consequence of this and similar analyses, projections of future mineral availability tend to be dire. Consider, for example, the life expectancies of 1976 world reserves of selected minerals at two different projections, static usage and projected growth, as predicted by the *Global 2000 Report* (table 5.2). These pessimistic predictions are typical and show cause for concern. But as the United Nations agency responsible for environmental concerns, UNEP, has suggested, many factors may push up these outward usage limits.[23] New deposits are still being discovered. Deposits known but formerly unexploitable because of cost can now be extracted economically through new processes of extraction and transformation. Recycling and/or substitution could lower future usage. Little is known of mining deposits at lower levels in the lithosphere (while new techniques for mining at deeper levels are being developed). Moreover, the bottom of the deep seabed where significant mineral deposits are found has not yet been tapped. Examples also abound of firm predictions made in earlier times that usually were proven false because of modern technology.

Table 5.2 Life expectancies of world mineral reserves.

	1976 reserves	1976 primary demand	Projected demand growth rate	Life expectancy in years[a] Static at 1976 level	Growing at projected rates
			percent		
Fluorine (million short tons)	37	2.1	4.58	18	13
Silver (million troy ounces)	6,100	305	2.33	20	17
Zinc (million short tons)	166	6.4	3.05	26	19
Mercury (thousand flasks)	5,210	239	0.50	22	21
Sulfur (million long tons)	1,700	50	3.16	34	23
Lead (million short tons)	136	3.7	3.14	37	25
Tungsten (million pounds)	4,200	81	3.26	52	31
Tin (thousand metric tons)	10,000	241	2.05	41	31
Copper (million short tons)	503	8.0	2.94	63	36
Nickel (million short tons)	60	0.7	2.94	86	43
Platinum (million troy ounces)	297	2.7	3.75	110	44
Phosphate rock (million metric tons)	25,732	107	5.17	240	51
Manganese (million short tons)	1,800	11.0	3.36	164	56
Iron in ore (billion short tons)	103	0.6	2.95	172	62
Aluminum in bauxite (million short tons)	5,610	18	4.29	312	63
Chromium (million short tons)	829	2.2	3.27	377	80
Potash (million short tons)	12,230	26	3.27	470	86

Note: Corresponding data for helium and industrial diamonds not available.
[a]Assumes no increase to 1976 reserves.
Source: U.S. Council on Environmental Quality and the Department of State, *The Global 2000 Report to the President* (Washington, D.C.: Government Printing Office, 1980), vol. 1, p. 29.

Accidental oil spills at sea have increased since earlier well-publicized episodes such as the spillage of 555,000 barrels from the tanker Torrey Canyon off Great Britain in 1966 and 77,000 barrels from offshore drilling rigs near Santa Barbara, California in 1969.[24] A shipwreck off the French coast in 1978 spilled 1.5 million barrels and destroyed 30 percent of local fauna and 5 percent of flora. Two million barrels spilled in the Caribbean in 1979 as a consequence of a collision. Off Mexico, 3.1 million barrels were discharged into the ocean from a blowout. In sum, during the period 1970–78 there were forty-six major oil spills totaling more than 8 million barrels. Larger oil tankers and more tanker traffic are likely to increase the number of oil spills. In addition to species damage, the cost of cleaning is estimated at $1,000 per barrel. Despite the environmental tragedy from oil spills, an even greater problem occurs daily where even a higher level of damage occurs as a consequence of tankers' normal dumping of excess fuel or the washing out of their tanks.

Loss of cropland, rangeland, forests

Each of these categories represents a separate kind of loss. Forests may (or may not) be transformed into cropland. Rangeland usually becomes deserts (the process called desertification), and cropland becomes unusable. Let us consider deforestation first. A major issue at the 1972 Stockholm conference, it continues to be widely debated. Some countries vigorously defend their right to cut down forests while others understand the broader implications.

What are the adverse consequences? First, the disruption of water systems is a clear consequence. In one study where twenty-four developing countries were found to have heavy forest losses, a critical water shortage appeared in sixteen of them and increased flooding occurred in ten.[25] Soil erosion is another dramatic result of deforestation.

Changes in climate represent a third major type of consequence, as suggested earlier, since deforestation increases the amount of carbon dioxide in the atmosphere. There are biological changes as well, as we will discuss later. Loss of habitat for flora and fauna invariably follows deforestation.

Desertification is another major problem. About twenty million hectares stop being productive annually as a consequence of becoming deserts, costing $26 billion a year.[26] This effect is caused not by climatic change but by humans—overcultivation, overgrazing, and salinization resulting from irrigation without adequate drainage.

The misuse of land sometimes has a relatively immediate impact on people in the surrounding area. Two cases in point are Ethiopia and Bangladesh. Recent drought in Ethiopia and severe flooding in Bangladesh were exacerbated by decades of land misuse. The cutting of trees for firewood led to deforestation, which in turn caused rainwater to run off in Ethiopia before it could soak in, thus removing productive soils in the process. Such creeping desertification is a major problem throughout the Sahel region of Africa. In Bangladesh, deforestation on the flanks of the Himalayan mountains has resulted in much worse flooding than previously occurred. One estimate is that 80 percent of the flooding during the annual monsoon season is now simply runoff that previously served to keep the upper regions green. Although erosion is a natural process, poor management makes the problem much worse. The standard loss is only six inches of topsoil. Without soil conservation, a leader in the field has suggested, "Management wears out the soil as surely as though you run a factory at full production without investing in repairs or maintenance. The factory will soon wear out; the land is no different."[27]

Species extinction

When the carrying capacity of a resource—living or inanimate—is exceeded, the resource cannot replenish itself. Consequently, each year's yield is lower than the year before until, in the extreme case, the resource disappears entirely. Extinction also occurs when humans overuse the habitats of other species. In fact, the destruction of habitat may be a more important reason for the loss of species than overexploitation. Farmers grow crops on the land, villagers gather firewood, lumber companies clear forests, engineers build dams, and construction companies erect developments. Thus the extinction of species is an unfortunate by-product of the use of land. Plants are also threatened by collectors who remove them wholesale, often pinpointing specific species. While it is difficult to determine precisely the magnitude of the problem, the best estimates suggest that of the three and ten million species of plants and animals believed to exist, 10 percent of flowering plants and over a thousand vertebrates (animals with backbones), are threatened.[28] For smaller species it is more difficult to acquire a true picture but it is likely to be just as grim.

World trade in wildlife and its products represents another problem. Not only are some of these species threatened with extinction as a consequence, but the introduction of exotic species into a new environment threatens the native species.[29] In 1979, $30 million worth of trade occurred in smuggled Australian wildlife. Some 350,000 birds are illegally imported each year into the United States, according to authorities. Six of the seven sea turtle species are threatened with extinction because of desires for their leather and shells and for turtle soup. The examples could continue page after page.

Why should the human race worry so much about these losses? There are many reasons suggested.[30] Economic benefits diminish because of lower yields caused by exceeding the carrying capacity. Plant availability is critical in the pharmaceutical industry, as about 25 percent of all prescription drugs are derived from plants while an additional 15 percent are of microbial origin. This percentage is likely to increase in the future. Finally, the loss of species is akin to an early warning system, much like the use of canaries to detect dangerous gases in the mines of yesteryear. Just as the canaries would die much sooner than the much more complex human bodies, the loss of simpler species demonstrates the potential for larger trouble in our fragile ecosystem.

War

According to the UNEP review of the last decade, both conventional and nuclear wars represent potential environmental problems.[31] These fall into three categories: (1) environmental consequences of current and past wars, including hazards from unexploded weapons, physical and biological effects of damage to soil and landscape, and human suffering; (2) environmental consequences of preparations for war such as diversion of resources from environmental development, impact of the armaments industry, weapons testing, military operations, and proliferation of nuclear technology; and (3) environmental hazards of future war, including conventional, nuclear, chemical, and biological warfare.

With regard to the first category—environmental consequences of current and past wars—unexploded munitions still remain a major problem. Some 150,000 to 300,000 remain in Vietnam, and one government report states that it continues to clear 300,000 to 400,000 bombs per year left from World War II. Concrete roadblocks, gun emplacements, abandoned airfields, and other installations constitute a problem as well. In Vietnam, chemical herbicides were responsible for the destruction of some 1,500 square kilometers of mangrove forest and damage to an area of similar size. One study suggests that there is no guarantee that original ecosystems will ever be restored.[32] The massive disruption of vegetation followed by widespread soil erosion, along with severe changes to the water support system and to the pattern of returning plants, suggest that restoration will be difficult if not impossible. But even more tragic is the disruption of societies caused by war. Close to 30 million civilians were killed in World War II, for example, while the

Kampuchean insurrections of 1975–77 resulted in over a million civilian deaths.

Preparation for war can also affect environmental issues, although less directly than war itself. In real terms, the rate of increase in global military expenditures was less during the 1970s than during the previous decade. However, the fact remains that the annual level of global military expenditures now totals more than $800 billion. Using this indicator to represent the problem of preparation for war, the scope has expanded in two ways. Vertically, there have been increases in total expenditures. Moreover, many more countries are now engaged in high levels of spending. Within the developed world, there have been continual increases in military spending. Developing countries have also increased their spending, largely in the form of arms purchases from the developed world. Unfortunately, those developing countries that can least afford to do so are diverting funds away from social programs to purchase arms. The developing world spent approximately 23 percent of the world military budget in 1983, twice the percentage of twenty years ago.[33] This increase has meant a dramatic growth in the international movement of armaments, and one consequence is the increased militarization of the oceans, stratosphere, and space.

The industrial process of weapons production contributes to environmental pollution. If one considers that military expenditures constitute between 5 and 10 percent of the world's gross national product, then the same proportion of pollution caused by all industry can be attributed to arms production. The problem is that all other factors are not equal, because the defense industry handles particularly hazardous materials. Between 1970 and 1980, 469 nuclear explosions were recorded, mostly weapons tests. Forty-one were atmospheric tests conducted by countries that have not signed the Limited Test Ban Treaty of 1963. The fact that most of the countries with nuclear weapons have abided by this treaty has improved the situation in atmospheric pollution as measured, for example, by the level of radionuclides in rain and in milk (caused by the ingestion of grass by cattle that have absorbed rainborne fallout). Other kinds of advanced weapons testing continue, although much less is known about their environmental impacts.

With regard to the hazards of future war, the possibility of nuclear conflict is not the only problem feared by environmentalists. The destructive level of conventional weapons grew steadily throughout the 1970s; aircraft carrying high-explosive cluster bombs or grenade clusters could deal a blow comparable to a tactical guided

Table 5.3   Hostile environmental modification techniques feasible in 1980.*

Basic natural systems	Type of effect	Military significance	Remarks
Atmosphere	Dispersion of cloud cover or fog	Ensures visibility in combat areas, airfields, and naval bases	Effective in limited areas as a tactical device
	Artificial creation of fog or clouds	Impedes surveillance by the enemy, and protects against light radiation from nuclear explosions	Effective in limited areas, under certain weather conditions as a tactical device
	Artificial creation of hail, snow, or rain	Damage to communications equipment and certain types of military equipment	Effective at certain altitudes in limited areas as a tactical device
Inland Waters	Changes in local water balance (destruction of dikes and irrigation works)	Impedes combat operations and logistical support	Effective on a tactical scale
	Action to affect the physical properties of water resources (pollution, infection)	Impedes combat and supply operations, disrupts operations in logistic areas	
Continental Ecosystems	Action to affect permafrost areas	Destroys road works and airfields, damages water systems	Possible for certain areas
	Stimulation of avalanches and landslides	Destroys road networks and impedes military operations	Possible only in limited areas as a tactical device
	Destruction of vegetation or soil cover	Impedes activities of enemy forces, disrupts agricultural activities	Effective as a tactical device

*Often under limited conditions only.
Source: Holdgate et al., *World Environment*, p. 609.

Table 5.4   The environmental impact of a one-megaton nuclear explosion.

Distance (km)	Effect
2.4	Reinforced concrete multistory buildings destroyed. Most people killed instantly.
4.6	Concrete buildings destroyed. Spontaneous ignition of clothing. Third-degree flash burns to exposed skin.
6.7	Brick and wood frame houses destroyed. Spontaneous ignition of clothing. Third-degree flash burns to exposed skin.
7.8	Spontaneous ignition of clothing and other combustion materials. Third-degree flash burns to exposed skin.
9.9	Third-degree flash burns to exposed skin.
13.6	Moderate damage to brick and wood-frame houses.

Source: *The Effects of Nuclear War* (Washington, D.C.: U.S. Arms Control and Disarmament Agency, 1979), quoted in Holdgate et al., *World Environment*, p. 607.

missile with a one-kiloton nuclear warhead. Chemical and biological warfare deliberately pollute the environment by the release of toxic chemicals or harmful microorganisms. At the end of the decade chemical weapons, which had once been banned, were again part of military planning. Although prohibited by international agreements, research and development on chemical weapons continue. In addition, there is mounting evidence that such weapons may have been used in several regional conflicts in the 1980s. Military planners have also considered environmental modification techniques; these involve a direct assault on the environment as a method of disrupting the enemy. Table 5.3 reveals the feasible techniques for altering the environment available at the close of the 1970s. Nuclear war, however, remains the greatest environmental hazard. The effects of even a single nuclear explosion are well documented. Table 5.4 shows the immediate impact of a one-megaton explosion, and table 5.5 reveals the twenty-four-hour effects of a ground burst (not the most lethal sort) of two larger bombs.

We have already talked about the "nuclear winter" study, revealing the likelihood of lowered temperatures in the event of a nuclear war. The study shows other likely atmospheric consequences as well: "obscuring smoke in the troposphere, obscuring dust in the stratosphere, the fallout of radioactive debris, and the partial destruction of the ozone layer."[34] Widespread fires and subsequent runoff of topsoil would also result, starvation would be rampant, and radiation sickness would be evident

Table 5.5   Some effects of ground-burst weapons within 24 hours of detonation.

Type of damage	Area over which damage may occur (hectares)	
	20-kiloton atomic bomb	10-megaton hydrogen bomb
Craterization by blast wave[a]	1	57
Vertebrates killed by blast wave[b]	24	1,540
All vegetation killed by nuclear radiation[c]	43	12,100
Trees killed by nuclear radiation[d]	148	63,800
Trees blown down by blast wave[e]	362	52,500
Vertebrates killed by nuclear radiation[f]	674	177,000
Dry vegetation ignited by thermal radiation[g]	749	117,000
Vertebrates killed by thermal radiation[h]	1,000	150,000

[a]Refers to dry soil. A subsurface burst could craterize four times as large an area as a surface burst. Nuclear warheads exploding above the surface would produce no craters at all if the burst were sufficiently high, but the nuclear and thermal radiation effects would then extend over larger areas.

[b]Refers to areas over which the transient over-pressure would be likely to exceed 345 kilopascal; this being the over-pressure for about 50 percent lethality among large mammals, including man. These figures are, in fact, augmented by reflected over-pressures that (depending upon height of burst, terrain, etc.) can more than double the total (so-called Mach front) over-pressures experienced at any distance.

[c]Refers to areas over which the early radiation dose would be likely to exceed 70 kilorad.

[d]Refers to areas over which the early radiation dose would be likely to exceed 10 kilorad.

[e]Refers to areas over which the transient wind velocity at the shock front, ignoring the Mach front, would be likely to exceed about 60 meters per second. Such a wind would be likely to blow down about 90 percent of the trees in an average coniferous forest or a deciduous forest in leaf.

[f]Refers to areas over which the early radiation dose would be likely to exceed 2 kilorad.

[g]Refers to areas over which the incident thermal radiation would be likely to exceed 500 kilojoules per square meter for the atom bomb or 1,000 kilojoules per square meter for the hydrogen bomb if the weapons were detonated on a clear day having a visibility of 80 km.

[h]Refers to areas over which, on a clear day of 80 km visibility, the incident thermal radiation would be likely to exceed that which would have a 50 percent lethality for exposed pigs (380 kilojoules per square metre for the atom bomb and 750 kilojoules per square meter for the hydrogen bomb.)

Source: J. P. Robinson, *The Effects of Weapons on Ecosystems*, United Nations Environment Programme Studies, vol. 1 (New York: Oxford University Press, 1979), quoted in Holdgate et al., *World Environment*, p. 608.

everywhere, not just in the areas of the bomb blasts themselves. The study concludes:

> Species extinction could be expected for most tropical plants and animals, and for most terrestrial vertebrates of north temperate regions, a large number of plants, and numerous freshwater and some marine organisms. . . . Whether any people would be able to persist for long in the face of highly modified biological communities; novel climates; high levels of radiation; shattered agricultural, social, and economic systems; extraordinary psychological stresses; and a host of other difficulties is open to question. It is clear that the ecosystem effects alone resulting from a large-scale thermonuclear war could be enough to destroy the current civilization in at least the Northern Hemisphere. Coupled with the direct casualties of perhaps two billion people, the combined intermediate and long-term effects of nuclear war suggest that eventually there might be no human survivors in the Northern Hemisphere.
>
> Furthermore, the scenario prescribed here is by no means the most severe that could be imagined with present world nuclear arsenals and those contemplated for the near future. In almost any realistic case involving nuclear exchanges between the superpowers, global environmental changes sufficient to cause an extinction event equal to or more severe than that at the close of the Cretaceous Period when the dinosaurs and many other species died out are likely. In that event, the possibility of the extinction of Homo sapiens cannot be excluded.[35]

While some thoughtful observers of the nuclear age are reexamining and even questioning these findings, all recognize the potential for environmental disaster.

In this chapter we have tried to show how this planet has been affected by the manner in which the human race has used its resources. This process of environmental degradation is not a new one but has been with us as long as the first human set foot on this earth. For much of history, however, people were not concerned about their impact, whether immediate or long-term.

The last two decades have changed our way of thinking about the environment. The evidence of decay has become overwhelming, in part because of man's ability to cause disruptions of such great magnitude. In this chapter we have pointed out the extent to which the human race has abused these four basic elements understood by the Greeks—air, water, earth, and fire—and we have also shown clearly that this planet is indeed a fragile ecosystem.

It is perhaps fitting that environment be the final issue whose problems we examine here. It can be argued that those individual problems identified as part of the population, food, and energy issues all contribute, in fact, to environmental decay. It should become clear as we move further ahead that there are linkages across the issues. At virtually every juncture these connections appear. These linkages are no more evident than when we examine the pluses and minuses of competing strategies for creating a preferred future environment.

Part III
Case Studies:
Applying the Conceptual Framework

In this third section of the text, we apply the conceptual framework outlined in chapter 1 to each of the issues. In chapter 6 we focus on the nature of the actors—their multiplicity and complexities—who are addressing global food problems. In chapter 7 we examine a number of competing values in the energy arena, focusing on alternative energy sources and the implications for traditional values were one energy source or another to be chosen. In the population area we talk about how governments have attempted to make policy affecting fertility and migration (chapter 8). Finally, in chapter 9 we describe six basic approaches to dealing with the environmental future and suggest that at this point in the history of the human race the international community has opted for what is termed an international regime approach.

6 Food: Competition Among Actors

In July 1985 millions of people in the developed world were made aware that hunger in Africa was a problem of enormous dimensions. The event, of course, was the heralded "Live Aid" concert of recording artists in the United Kingdom and the United States who performed for a worldwide audience on behalf of food relief for Africa. The Live Aid concert was certainly not typical of the kinds of efforts made to relieve the hunger problem, but it does provide insight into a problem that has been developing over the past two decades. The problem can be described quite simply. In the past twenty years, Africa has experienced two closely related trends: an extremely high rate of population growth, the highest of any continent in the world, and an extremely slow rate of increase in agricultural production. The problem does not extend over the entire continent of Africa. Neither the north, populated largely by Arab peoples, nor the extreme south has been drastically affected, although both regions have had to face difficulties with both population growth and food production. The real problem lies in the area known as sub-Saharan Africa, those countries that lie south of the steadily encroaching Sahara desert. This region is sometimes known as Equatorial Africa. The consequence of the two trends of high population growth and low agricultural productivity has been that sub-Saharan Africa has fallen steadily behind in its capacity to feed its own people. It is the only region in the world where per capita food production has declined in the past two decades.

The dimensions of the African food problem are enormous. In sub-Saharan Africa, according to the Food and Agricultural Organization (FAO) of the United Nations, twenty-four nations are suffering from serious food shortages.[1] According to the World Bank, per capita food production in the years 1979–81 was below that of the 1969–71 period in over two-thirds of the nations of Africa. The average for the whole region, using 100 as an index of per capita production in 1969–71, had fallen to 91 in the years 1979–81.[2] Quite simply, the average individual in the majority of African countries had less to eat at the beginning of the 1980s than at the beginning of the 1970s. Since these are all averages, of course, the picture for many individuals may be far more severe (and, for a few, less severe). Some estimates suggest that as many as one-third of all Africans suffer from malnutrition because of inadequate supplies of food. World Bank figures again indicate that the problem is widespread. Applying FAO standards of adequate diet (the value of 100 in this case equals 100 per cent of minimum caloric intake), only ten of thirty-four countries in the area meet the minimal requirement.[3] Some—Chad, Ethiopia, Guinea, and Mozambique —fall in the 70 percent range. Nine others are in the 80 percent range. The steady decline in these figures over the decade can be attributed in large part to the rapid increase in population during the same period. With the spread of medical technology and treatment in the postwar period, the mortality rate decreased dramatically and as a consequence population growth rose at an alarming rate. In 1983 Africa's population exceeded half a billion with a growth rate of over 3 percent per year. Much of this growth is concentrated in the sub-Saharan region, which contains 432 million of the continent's total of 538 million people.

Although population growth is an incontrovertible condition of the African food problem, it is by no means the entire problem. A number of other conditions have contributed to the growth of hunger. The most immediate of these has been a persistent drought, felt for some time, that has brought more famine to central Africa, especially across the Sahel region from Senegal to Chad. This drought-induced famine in 1984 finally brought the world's attention to the plight of the Ethiopians (and captured the talents of recording artists on a global scale to promote relief efforts), although this was the second time that such widespread famine induced by drought had struck that country. Still the drought itself has been the consequence of conditions caused by far more complex problems. Even when the rain returns, those problems will remain. Nor will the massive input of aid—from concerts, charities, governments, and international organizations—resolve the enormous problems that lie at the root of hunger in sub-Saharan Africa. In fact, the nations of Africa have been recipients of substantial amounts of aid for some time now. Without some mechanism to increase the level of agricultural production, aid will do little but provide temporary relief (and may even result in an unnecessary dependence on foreign assistance). The true nature of the problem of hunger in Africa arises then from a combination of factors, developed over a number of years, exacerbated by the rapid increase in population, and precipitated by the temporary onset of a series of droughts. Let us first examine some of those issues and then turn to the actors who are involved with the problems and the solutions.

One must first place the African food problem in the context of the overall international food system. As we have already seen in chapter 2, that system is predominantly based on the commodity characteristics of food. Like any other commodity, food moves from place to place through a system of trade. However, the purposes of that trade are not always the same. In the food-producing countries of the developed world, food is placed into trade for the purpose of securing income for the domestic agricultural sector. In the case of the United States, for example, nearly a third of all agricultural output goes into the international market. In the developing countries, food is traded internationally as an integral part of a development strategy. That strategy often concentrates on industrialization and largely disregards the agricultural sector. In those cases food is grown principally for export in order to gain foreign earnings to be used in domestic efforts to build an industrial base for development. We have already reviewed this picture in general terms. Often agriculture for domestic consumption is neglected in favor of the production of cash crops for export, the earnings from which may even be used to import food from abroad. This whole enterprise favors the large farmer and the urban areas, leaving the rural poor unattended. The small farmer is engaged in subsistence agriculture, taking care of his immediate needs, but not providing for domestic trade. The concentration remains on industrial development rather than on domestic agricultural production.

This general description of the developing countries' food situation in relation to the international market is directly applicable to the case of Africa. Here the situation was shaped initially in the division of the continent by the colonial powers during the nineteenth and early twentieth centuries. A number of characteristics of colonization contributed to the present framework of agricultural production in Africa. Africa was the most heavily colonized of the continents; only Ethiopia and Liberia have long histories of independence. Among the purposes of colonization, of course, was to bring increased income to the colonial power by importing goods from the colony or trading them overseas. Export-oriented crops were therefore a colonial strategy and helped shape agricultural usage in Africa. Some of that development was also intended to support European settlement of the colonial regions. The best agricultural lands were offered to these European immigrants as an incentive, denying fertile areas for use by native inhabitants. The latter tended instead to become employees working the land for landowners, with limited opportunity to gain monetarily from the experience. In a pattern typical of the colonial enterprise, Africans were discouraged and often institutionally denied access even to the knowledge necessary to develop modern agricultural methods. In fact, agricultural colleges and research centers are still rare in Africa. Those methods themselves, brought by the colonizers from Europe, were often not appropriate to the conditions of Africa. Although the absence of population pressures avoided the kinds of hunger problems faced today, the entire colonial experience thus left its mark on the structure of the agricultural sectors of the African nations in the postwar period.

As more and more African colonies became independent states, the structural foundation of agricultural production for export persisted. This seemed appropriate as a development strategy and after independence it became even more prominent. At the beginning of the development process the effort produced modest success, and the export of primary products including food increased through the 1960s. But by that time the situation had begun to change. While food production continued to increase, it had reached its peak by 1970 when measured in per capita terms. Thereafter, as noted, per capita food production began a steady decline of about 1 percent per year, because the effects of rapid population growth were beginning to be felt. The result was that the shortfall in food production had to be made up by importing food. Hence, export earnings were needed to pay for the unmet domestic food needs. As a result of this series of conditions, many African nations were now caught up in the vagaries of the international food trade. By that time the global food situation was not good. Because of a number of factors, not the least of which was the energy crisis of 1973, a period of food shortage developed on a global scale. Consequently the price of food (and the cost of food production) increased. Since a major problem is that the food-deficit countries of sub-Saharan Africa are among the poorest in the world, the market became tighter (the increased cost of food production reduced incentives to produce at the margin, the point where increased inputs yielded only slight increases in output), and the security of food imports for sub-Saharan Africa was further reduced. In such an environment, the low-income nations could not compete. Moreover, even the source of their income began to decline. Since the 1970s Africa has lost much of its role in the market. Between 1969 and 1971, Africa provided over 70 percent of the world's groundnuts (peanuts) but by 1984 that figure had dropped to 18 percent.[4] Similar reductions have occurred in other African food exports, reflecting price declines in some primary products (such as sugar, cocoa, coffee, tea, cotton, etc.) as opposed to the cereals (staple grains such as wheat) that Africa must import because its agricultural sector is not at present configured to produce them. In 1981, 27 percent of the earnings from food-related exports (including forest and fish products) of the nations of sub-Saharan Africa was spent to import cereals.[5] The sub-Saharan region found itself in a kind of spiral, unable to meet domestic food needs because of its burgeoning population, unable to compete in an international market of fluctuating prices, and unable to sustain the volume of food exports which had driven food policies.

Food Actors

We can now turn to explore in greater detail the treatment of these problems in terms of the actors involved. To do so we should first introduce the concept of food actors and place it in an appropriate context or framework. A food actor is any element—individual, institution, or agency—that has an impact on the global food system. Each of us is in fact a food actor insofar as we eat and therefore represent a part of both the consumption and demand components of the food system. Our individual impact on the overall system is of course quite minor, almost immeasurable in the larger picture. In the aggregate, however, individuals have a significant impact in the contribution of population growth to the problem of hunger in Africa. For our purposes, we are more concerned with those actors who have a major impact on the food problem and efforts to resolve it. These tend to be groups and institutions of some size that possess influence in the form of economic resources or political power and that can therefore affect the outcome of food issues. Often the actors involved have differing interests in those outcomes and consequently the food issue becomes a kind of arena in which the actors compete to attain their separate objectives. These actors whose interests are predominantly in the area of trade will seek to maximize their gains, working actively to select crops and buyers that will assure that future trading opportunities will continue to promote those gains. Other actors, such as the food-deficit nations, may wish instead to focus on security. They need to plan carefully for the right use of crops and reliable sources of supply at the most advantageous cost to their society. They are far less capable of tolerating the ups and downs of a market upon which the active traders pursue their own goals. Of course, the first priority for the consumer is an adequate supply of food. Cost is a major factor in the present global distribution system, so the ability to pay determines access to food. But regardless of the ability to pay, fulfillment of minimal nutritional requirements is a necessity for human existence. The actual competition among actors is more complex than such a brief illustration would suggest. But the outcome of the food problem is nonetheless determined by ongoing activity in this arena.

The rest of the chapter will make our framework clear by focusing on the competitive food actors in Africa. We divide the issue into three structural levels: international, national, and subnational. International actors are those whose actions and interests cross national boundaries in some way. This category includes several different kinds of actors. Some are intergovernmental. They are truly international actors in the sense that their activities are between (the Latin "inter") nations. These are generally formal organizations composed of the governments of nations interacting with each other to a greater or lesser extent. The World Food Conference held in Rome in 1974 must also be considered an intergovernmental actor. It was a one-time event but spawned a formal organization, the World Food Council. A second kind of international actor is transnational. Taken literally, this term means "across nations" and thus is meant to convey the status of nongovernmental actors whose activities cross national boundaries. Many such bodies, such as relief organizations (Oxfam and the International Red Cross, for example) and multinational corporations, operate in more than one country though generally headquartered in a particular state. A third kind of international actor is the supranational institution. "Supra" literally means above, so this term is meant to convey the sense that such actors are empowered to act over nations. There are in fact few organizations that can do so, and they have limited scope in which to act. The most prominent food actor fitting this description is the World Bank, which has become an active observer of and participant in developments affecting the global food system. The influence of the World Bank stems from its powerful financial position and the relative autonomy of its decision-making structures regarding the disposition of its funds. Since the 1970s the World Bank has become a major funder of food and agricultural development in the less-developed world.

The second category is composed of national food actors. National governments, most of which play a direct role in their own domestic agricultural policy, remain the most powerful actors in the global food arena. The flow of food between nations and in the broadest sense within nations is heavily influenced by the governments involved. Governments manage their food systems differently—they have different goals and strategies, often within their own structures—and those differences contribute to the outcome of the food issue.

Finally we need to include the category of subnational actors: groups—formal or informal—within nations, below the governmental level, that exert influence on food policy or food outcomes. In developed societies these actors tend to be quite formal, responding to the formal structures and processes of government. In the United States, for example, groups such as Bread for the World tend to adopt a broad political agenda. Still others are policy-oriented research agencies or information-dissemination groups. In less developed states, such as the newly emergent nations of sub-Saharan Africa, subnational actors tend to be much less structured. With these categories of actors in mind, we can begin to explore how they interact in the food problem in sub-Saharan Africa.

Food Issues in Sub-Saharan Africa

At this point we have looked at the basic shape of the food problem, especially in the context of the global food system. However, the impact of that system is contingent upon a number of other conditions within the sub-Saharan region. For a variety of reasons, including the colonial legacy and the dominance of the international food system, these African nations have been struggling to find a constructive set of agricultural policies. There has been little success, and sometimes little effort, in trying to address the social, economic, political, and international conditions that need to be overcome in order to implement constructive policies. It is useful, then, as we look at the role of actors in the food issue to examine those conditions in more detail. Although varied and complex, the conditions governing agricultural affairs in sub-Saharan Africa can be summarized in five areas: population dynamics, economic development, production capability, political-institutional constraints, and international influences. Many of the dimensions of these problem areas are closely linked. Resolution of the food problem as a whole will depend on recognizing and acting on those linkages.

Population dynamics

As already noted, one of the fundamental issues in the current African food crisis is the population growth that occurred in the 1960s. But, as we have also noted, the size of the population becomes a problem only when it encounters some other limitation, in this case the capacity to produce food. Population growth rates have therefore become a major component of the food problem. Sub-Saharan Africa is the only area of the world in which population growth rates have actually increased in the past two decades. In the 1950s the rate of population growth for all of Africa was 2.1 percent per year. By the 1970s it had reached 2.7 percent. By the 1990s the population growth rate is projected to be 3 percent. As a consequence, the size of the population is expected to double between 1981 and the year 2000. The bulk of this increase is due to the nature of population dynamics in the sub-Saharan region, where the population may quadruple by the turn of the century. Statistically, the rapid rise in population growth rates can be explained by the sharp decline in mortality in the region. That decline is attributable to the spread both of medical knowledge, allowing the eradication of many diseases, and of general improvements in the standard of living that affect infant mortality specifically as well as overall longevity. But a decline in mortality is not sufficient to explain such rapid population growth. The other factor was that birthrates continued at the same high rate. The demand for food expanded by a factor of one each time a child entered the population. Thus it became necessary to feed 15 million new persons each year as the population expanded. Consequently, population growth became a serious challenge to the capacity of the agricultural sector of Africa to provide enough food. We have seen that it could not do so. But the nature of the population change also made the problem worse. Among other consequences of this rapid expansion of the population is the fact that there is a young age structure. When famine and problems of hunger strike a population, the children and the pregnant or lactating mothers are most susceptible to its ravages. This rapid population growth, no matter what measures might be taken, will necessarily shape the food problem in Africa well into the twenty-first century.

What then can population actors do about such population problems? Ultimately, individuals or couples make basic decisions about having children. But these decisions are determined by a variety of influences that have contributed to the sustained high growth rates. Culturally, as we have seen, the memory of high infant mortality rates in the past impels people to have many children to ensure that there will be enough survivors to meet future family needs. Those needs include providing manpower for tending to the business of subsisting, and long-term provisions for the well-being of parents in their old age. Children in other words continue to be viewed as economic assets (even when the prevalence of malnutrition indicates otherwise). This attitude is ingrained for practical reasons; every new child is a potential source of income and social security. African women tend to choose to bear six children each. To turn the tide of population expansion, some form of control or planning is necessary. But little attention has been paid in Africa to such efforts.

After individuals, the most powerful actors in population policy are national governments. Here African governments traditionally have been reluctant to take on population control or planning. Indeed, in many places where governments have adopted any form of population policy at all it has been based on a posture of neglect or has been actively pronatalist (in Mauritania, for example)—that is, encouraging births as a means to expand the labor force in order to support economic development. Other nations have been constrained in taking a position on population control because of ethnic or religious influences. Thus for the most part African nations have been slow to recognize the impact of population on their capacity to survive. Only recently have some national governments begun to address population issues as an active part of policy. Kenya, with the world's highest rate of population growth, has recently adopted a population control policy.[6] In 1983 a report issued by the Economic Commission for Africa, an intergovernmental organization under United Nations auspices focusing on African economic problems, stated the true severity of the population problem for Africa. As a result an African Population Conference was convened in 1984. There forty-four African nations endorsed the need to focus on population planning. It is too early to tell whether these nations can repeat the dramatic success experienced in countries like China and India, but the trend seems at least now to be in the direction of change.

Economic development

The economies of the sub-Saharan nations are among the poorest in the world. In figures published by the United Nations Conference on Trade and Development (UNCTAD), twenty-five of the thirty-six nations identified as "least developed" are located in sub-Saharan Africa.[7] They suffer from a range of difficulties. In the first place, their economies are small and none of them has grown significantly in the past two decades. Several factors have contributed to this lack of growth (some of which we will address below in looking at political and institutional constraints), but our concern is with those actions that have an impact on food developments. Perhaps the most telling of these is the decision made by almost all the national governments of the newly emerging nations in the 1950s and 1960s to concentrate on industrialization. This decision complicated some of the already existing deficiencies of the agricultural sectors of the economies, especially the relative neglect that formed another part of the colonial legacy. As we have seen, in many respects the decision to industrialize was itself a response to the former colonial status of the new African nations. The economic systems of Africa had been structured to support the patterns of European colonial expansion. There was little if any concern for the indigenous economic foundation. Although formal political independence was achieved, these countries in fact continued to depend on the colonial pattern of exportation of a few primary products. More important, independence meant that this reliance was no longer supported by the structure of a larger colonialist economy. The economies of the newly emerging states were now national, yet because of the prevailing trading pattern they were still vulnerable to the shifts in the world economy dominated by the developed states, which continued to supply needed manufactured goods. In addition, the developed nations continued to provide the principal market for whatever products, primary or manufactured, that the new nations could produce. This lingering dependency, together with the small size of the newly independent economic units, formed the central challenge that the African nations were to face.

In the struggle for independence, therefore, economic development became an immediate focus for the governments of the newly formed African nations. There was competition among contending groups over what economic path—socialist or capitalist—would be followed. But all the nations placed a high priority on rapid

economic development in order to become self-sufficient and free
of dependence on the developed world. Moreover, development was
virtually universally translated as industrialization. In many cases
the national governments assumed responsibility for greater and
greater functions of society, such as education, public utilities, and
transportation. Much of the economic fabric of society then fell
under the control of a nationally directed economic plan whose
central feature was to build the industrial sector. This meant, among
other things, a concentration on urban development at the expense
of the rural agricultural sector. However, as we pointed out earlier,
such a concentration ignored the reality of the true economic base
of African society. The effort to build a labor force and move that
force to the city meant an increase in the number of consumers of
agricultural products and a decrease in producers. The bulk of the
food producers remained in the rural areas with little or no economic bonds to the growing urban industrial sector. As these developments moved forward into the 1960s and '70s, the comparatively
small urban populations began to exercise a disproportionately large
degree of economic influence in national policies. But the development plans never produced economic growth. After an initial surge
in the 1960s, the measures of growth, such as the gross domestic
product, were all declining in the 1970s and have become effectively level in the 1980s.

The economies of these African nations have proven to have limited flexibility. Thus, as food began to be recognized as a problem,
few feasible plans of action were available. Without economic growth
or increased earnings from exports (or outside financial assistance)
it was impossible to finance food production that was adequate to
meet the burgeoning need. During the 1960s food production,
although under conditions of economic neglect (as well as some
inherent constraints we will discuss next), had already reached its
peak. For a time, since this was a period of worldwide economic
growth, the impact of what was by now a declining rate of production per capita was not felt. But with the explosive increase of
energy costs, the fragility of most African national economies
became evident. The cost of energy reduced demand for the products that the African nations sold to gain export earnings to pay the
growing cost of food imports to make up the shortfalls in agricultural production. As the demand for exports slowed in response to
the global recession induced by the oil crisis, the cost of all imported
goods began to rise for the same reason. Inflation began to spread
throughout the African countries, as it did throughout the world.

But the less-developed countries with their limited flexibility were hit hardest. The African economies were now caught in the vise of their own development strategies. Refocusing economic resources toward the agricultural sector was extremely difficult. The decision to industrialize had been premature. By the time the fundamental shortcomings of the agricultural sector became evident, no economic base existed to finance food development. The financing of industrial development was itself intractable in the face of the lagging world economy. Whatever agricultural base existed for the national economy was devoted to the production of cash crops to gain export earnings to pay for the imports. But those earnings were already down. These factors increased the "opportunity costs" (that product which would need to be given up in order to gain something else) of redirecting economic resources into domestic agricultural production. The only exceptions to this constraining sequence were the few nations, like Nigeria, that had export earnings from petroleum and were therefore able to break the cycle. But even those countries could break the cycle only insofar as they could make up for their food deficits through imports (Nigeria spent over $1 billion on food imports in 1981, the highest level in Africa). The national governments of the sub-Saharan African region thus found themselves trapped in the premature economic decision to industrialize as a means of freeing themselves from the dependencies of the past. They ended up finding themselves victims of a new set of dependencies created by an international economic system in which they had little influence and almost no economic resilience. The most detrimental aspect of the weak condition of these economies with regard to the food situation has been the resulting poverty. As we have observed earlier, access to food is still a function of income. In the stagnant economies of sub-Saharan Africa, few have the opportunity to obtain the food that is available.

Production capability

The status of agricultural production capability is closely linked to the state of the national economies in the sub-Saharan region. In the decisions of the national leadership to seek economic development through industrialization, little attention was paid to domestic agricultural production. Indeed, as we have seen repeatedly, there has been a bias against such production. All of this process seems to belie the true character of the societies affected, since in fact the African societies are overwhelmingly rural and dominated by agrarian enterprise. This characteristic is illustrated in the fact that, on the average, three out of five individuals in sub-Saharan Africa still work in agriculture. This clearly reflects the difficulty of focusing on growth through industrialization. From 30 to 60 percent of the gross domestic product of these countries can be attributable to agricultural output. However, only 10 percent of investment goes back into the agricultural sector. That demonstrates how the stagnation of these weak economies is tied to the food problem. In essence then, what has happened in sub-Saharan Africa is that while demand has increased, production capability has deteriorated.

A number of factors are linked to this deterioration of agricultural production capacity. To begin with, the amount of land available for agricultural use in Africa is severely limited. Where land is available, often it cannot be continuously cultivated because of the fragile nature of the soils.[8] In order for the land to regenerate itself it must remain fallow for a number of years. Efforts to accelerate this process of regeneration, on the advice of outside specialists, have often proven damaging to the soil in spite of short-term positive effects on production. Much of the potentially arable land is also constrained by a wide variety of pests, which affect humans as well as plants and animals. The most damaging to humans is the tsetse fly, which produces the debilitating illness of sleeping sickness. Controlling it, like the many other pests, is a major undertaking requiring considerable inputs of pesticides that need to be imported and thus raise the cost of production.

The rainfall cycle in much of Africa is harmful to topsoils, coming in torrential periods that can wash away the already weak soil, so that erosion becomes a problem. Finally, the Sahara desert is advancing, its movement accelerated by efforts to overwork the land to obtain a short-term yield. Forty-seven percent of the land in Africa is simply too dry to bear any kind of cultivation. These inherent constraints on production would make it extremely difficult for the agricultural sector to respond to increasing demands of any sort, but it became virtually impossible to keep pace with the enormous population pressures that struck sub-Saharan Africa. The population literally exceeded the carrying capacity of the African landscape.

Production capability in this region is further constrained by the kind of farming that takes place. While overwhelmingly rural, the bulk of the agricultural sector is subsistence farming. African farming generally is quite simple and unsophisticated. Most farmers are small landholders, and their levels of productivity are generally low.

More important, from yet another perspective, these farmers are the very ones who have been neglected in development efforts. Where irrigation could be a significant help in increasing productivity, it is usually not available except to the large farms producing the export-oriented crops. Where investment has gone to the agricultural sector it has tended to go to the large, capital-intensive farms (plantations and ranches) devoted to the production of cash crops. These farmers have an inordinate amount of influence relative to the actual role they play in domestic food production. There is a technological gap manifested in the distance between the food demand and the attention paid to the small farmer capable of meeting that demand. A technological gap also exists in the relationship between the most prevalent means of production—by the small farmer—upon which domestic food production depends and the narrower but politically and economically more influential export-oriented production facilities. To expand production in the rural smallholdings requires attention that the national planners and the varied bureaucracies of these new nations have been unable or unwilling to give.

Political-institutional constraints

The role of the national leadership and the institutional support capabilities represent yet another problem for the production of food in sub-Saharan Africa. In the first place, the governments of these countries have been characterized by instability. Coups and revolutions, typical of the transformation of traditional societies, have been particularly prevalent in Africa since the beginning of the move toward political independence. Changes in the governments frequently have tended to be accompanied by shifts in development strategies, alterations of the institutional character of the regimes, and further confusion in the direction of development. Under the best of conditions the process of development is difficult and slow. Under prevailing conditions—with competing economic and political rivalries, often colored by tribal, religious, or ideological differences—the problem has been made even worse. Ethiopia, whose situation has focused so much of the world's attention on the African food problem, is a case in point. After seizing power in a military coup in 1974 the current leader, Colonel Mengistu Haile Mariam, instituted a sweeping program of agrarian reform. The planners of the program envisioned a complete change in the foundation of agricultural production in the country—land reform, peasant associations, government-controlled marketing, establishment of state and collective farms, and resettlement of agricultural areas.[9] In 1975 Mengistu nationalized all land and imposed an even more radical program of reform, with heavy and expensive emphasis on resettlement. The consequence was a clear resistance to change on the part of the peasant farmers, whose incentive to produce was subordinated to the government's exercise of control. Productivity declined and the overall production of food in Ethiopia was hampered (production increased at 1 percent while population increased at 2.5 percent).[10] Other controls restricted the movement of food internally by private traders, thus making it difficult to respond to the looming food crisis. In addition, the government suppressed warnings about the seriousness of the problem, delaying the capacity of others to respond. Finally, international efforts to provide assistance were shaped by the political posture of the Marxist regime of Colonel Mengistu. None of these factors was itself responsible for the subsequent famine, which was induced by widespread drought. But they made it worse.

In the development of the food issue in Africa the record of management in general has not been exemplary. One of the most disruptive elements has been government-directed pricing policies. Once again we witness the disregard for the role of domestic agricultural production in meeting the food needs of the populace. It is the familiar pattern based on the industrial priority of economic development. Following models of development drawn from outside of the African experience with the goal of rapid modernization, these governments have shortchanged rural society. One of the effects of government-controlled prices for agricultural products has been to keep them artificially low in order to provide an advantage to the new urban consumers. In many cases, however, these prices have been yielding returns below production costs, thus making it impossible for a farmer to market his produce at the break-even point, let alone turn a profit. Without a price enabling the farmer to meet his production costs it is hardly likely that there will be sufficient incentive to cause that farmer to increase production or to produce for market at all. In some cases farmers have smuggled their produce across borders in order to take advantage of better prices in neighboring countries.[11] Production for the domestic market has thereby been discouraged and the role of subsistence farming sustained by the policies promoted by national governments. For those governments, once committed to the development of the industrial sector, it has become a no-win situation. Once the scope and seriousness of the food problem were recognized, it was nonetheless politically infeasible to raise agricultural prices, for to do so would create discontent among the urban consumers who were not themselves economically well off to begin with. Efforts to shift prices have resulted in riots and civil disturbances in a number of countries.

The problems of such policy choices extend beyond pricing policies. In other areas, such as taxation or the valuing of currency within these countries, policies have seriously hampered agricultural production. Consistent with the emphasis on industrial development, national governments have used such policies (including pricing) to extract capital from the agricultural sector. Mismanagement has also included outright corruption in the administration of the economy as a whole that has carried over into the agricultural sector. At the same time two elements of the administrative picture in sub-Saharan Africa should be recognized. First, as we have seen, the problems facing the bureaucratic institutions of these countries are difficult and complex. Few of the individuals staffing the institutional structures given the responsibility for economic management, especially in the area of agriculture, have been adequately trained to deal with such complexity. The state grain boards established in many countries to oversee the production and distribution of grain, for example, typically have proved to be overstaffed and poorly managed, leading again to worsening rather than resolving the difficult issues relating to food. Second, because there are no simple solutions the food issues themselves have been further complicated by debates over which direction to take. In those debates competing Western models of development have been used with the advice and active participation of outside economic specialists. These models are drawn from an entirely different experiential, social, economic, institutional, and technical base that does not correspond to prevailing conditions in Africa. While superficially attractive, they too tend to worsen rather than improve conditions for agricultural development. Often this debate has been ideologically and politically colored as well, pitting market-based against socialist-based models of development. Little research regarding the applicability of either of these models to actual conditions has been conducted, and thus debates tend to focus on opinion rather than on fact.

International influences

As this last observation illustrates, the food issue in sub-Saharan Africa has been affected by the activities of a number of international actors. We have looked extensively at the impact of patterns of international food trade on the development of the food problem. For some time, regardless of the success or failure of measures taken to alleviate the inadequacy of domestic food production, it will be necessary to import food into this region. Few if any of the sub-Saharan countries are approaching a state of self-sufficiency. The cost of food remains relatively high, especially for low-income food deficit nations that have nowhere else to turn, and the price fluctuations of the market are likely to continue with only limited influence being exercised by these nations.

An important consequence of this inaction has been that international assistance will continue to play an important part in efforts to resolve the problem. The earlier efforts to provide assistance have proven to be flawed because they have frequently focused on the wrong kinds of aid. Many of the funded projects, such as those of the World Bank, were too extensive, tending to perpetuate the neglect of the small farmer who is at the foundation of African agricultural production. The World Food Council, established as a consequence of the UN-sponsored World Food Conference in Rome, was critical of such aid, urging instead a focus on solving the technological obstacles impeding production of small land holdings. Many other international actors have turned their attention to Africa. In 1980 Africa's own regional intergovernmental organization, the Organization for African Unity (OAU), issued the Lagos Plan of Action, which called for an increase in domestic resource inputs to food and agriculture. Unfortunately, efforts to reach the goals of the plan have repeatedly fallen short. In these and many other plans of action, small and large, that have emerged (including several initiated within the nations themselves such as Ghana's "Operation Feed Yourself" and Nigeria's "Operation Feed the Nation"), there have been a number of difficulties. Perhaps the greatest shortcoming has been the absence of coordination. The various international agencies and institutions have pursued their own objectives and schedules without reference to one another. As of 1982, forty institutions were offering financial and technical assistance for agricultural development in Africa through a wide variety of mechanisms.[12] These agencies now are making more of an effort to collaborate on approaches to the problem, but there is still a wide variety of ideas, many of which are generated outside of the African experience and thus may not be appropriate for the needs of Africans.

One of the most pressing needs that observers are emphasizing in sub-Saharan Africa is the development of an indigenous agricultural research capability. This effort has an international character. It is once again a carryover from the colonial pattern that provided no local support for learning and applying farming techniques to the African land.

In addition, there are also aspects of more recent origin. One of the shortcomings of African food development has been the limited application of the Green Revolution that contributed to advances in food production in Asia and elsewhere in the third world. There have been reservations concerning the Green Revolution stemming from its impact on indigenous species and other shortcomings. But in the case of Africa the revolution never got started. The varieties of seeds used elsewhere did not thrive in Africa's poor soils. Experts now recognize that in Africa there must be many varieties of plants rather than only a few in order to account for all the conditions of the region. Also much of the Green Revolution has been based on the infusion of large quantities of inputs—pesticides, fertilizers, and herbicides. These inputs are expensive and must be imported. In addition, given the inherent limitations of the African landscape, they are not always effective. Indigenous plant diseases have tended to be resistant to the efforts of control, the uneven African rainfall patterns make sustained application (without irrigation) difficult, and the perennial problem of poor soil places any effort on a weak foundation. Finally, much of the focus of the Green Revolution has been on plants that are not really staple foods in Africa.

The answer to these problems, according to many observers, is to build up an agricultural research base within Africa, where there are few university programs for such research and consequently few trained specialists to decrease reliance on outside assistance that may not have the capacity to understand the peculiar conditions of Africa. Much research needs to be done in such areas as irrigation, especially for small landowners, and on food crops and livestock adapted to the areas in which they are to be produced. Establishment of such a research base, however, is caught in the same constraints as the food problem as a whole. It is difficult to finance such programs in low-income nations with faltering economies. Private investors are discouraged by the lack of infrastructure and the problems of mismanagement noted above. Thus the bulk of aid will have to continue to come from public sources. International assistance agencies have begun now to shift their focus to such requirements and, once again, to coordinate their efforts.

Ironically, international assistance has never been in short supply in Africa. We can divide such assistance into two categories—emergency relief and financial assistance. In the case of the former, aid has been forthcoming. The Live Aid concert of 1985 was just one of many examples. As the plight of Africa has been more widely publicized, there has been an increase in private donations to a variety of organizations such as Save the Children, Oxfam, and the Catholic Relief Service. Even with such generosity, the relief has been unable to alleviate the tremendous suffering that has occurred. This has been due in part to the delay between warnings of the seriousness of the problem and the ability to respond to it and in part due to the same problems of mismanagement and limited infrastructure that contributed to the problem within the affected countries. Nevertheless relief efforts have been made.

Financial assistance, as the second category of international assistance, has also been present. The variety of donors seeking to assist food production in Africa are limited more by the difficulty in finding good constructive projects than by the lack of availability of funds. It is now generally recognized that assistance efforts in the past, bringing outside support, were ineffective. They tended to perpetuate the constraints in the food-deficit nations by relieving the pressure on the national governments to address and change their policies. Efforts now are intended to use assistance for the purpose of stimulating local response to the food problem.

Overlaying all of this troubled pattern of African food production is an odd paradox. As a continent, Africa has the potential to be self-sufficient in food production. Few specialists doubt the capacity of sub-Saharan Africa to develop a foundation to meet its food needs. The objectives are clear. Adequate food surpluses must be built up in order to absorb the vagaries of weather and market, and hunger must be alleviated. To accomplish these objectives, however, there are many obstacles to be overcome and the process is destined to be long and incremental. The instruments for change are additional carefully focused research,

patterned investment concentrated on domestic agricultural production, and development assistance effectively administered
both nationally and internationally. Ultimately, as is true of the
food problem everywhere, the conquest of hunger in sub-Saharan
Africa will depend on the elimination of poverty. That of course
is a much broader and even more pervasive challenge to global
development.

7 Energy: Value Trade-Offs for Alternative Sources

The global energy arena has undergone a series of remarkable fluctuations in a period of just over ten years. Yet remarkably little has changed. Virtually all of the conditions governing those fluctuations at the beginning of that period continue to exist. Nonetheless, the experience of the energy crisis contributed two new dimensions to the issue. First, there are many more actors who play a role and have a stake in the outcome of energy developments than at the onset of the crisis. Second, with the addition of new actors having differing stakes in the outcome, the value criteria applied to efforts to resolve the issue have expanded. In this altered setting we have seen that the sense of urgency that prevailed during the crisis of the 1970s has largely dissipated, but not the sense of imperative for change in the energy system. Something still must be done within a reasonably short period of time or the crisis and urgency will return with less time for adjustment and resolution. It is the imperative for resolution that brings the many energy actors into the picture. Whether they are producers, consumers, distributors, or members of some other group pursuing a nonenergy goal, energy actors take part in energy-related activities in order to achieve a preferred outcome from among all those anticipated. The choices to be made—in policy debates, in the commercial marketplace, in scientific research, or perhaps in humanitarian appeals—will be determined by the nature of prevailing values the actors hold.

The problems that arise in resolving the energy issue are a consequence of differences in value preferences that each actor or set of actors brings to the arena.[1] All actors obviously do not share the same values. The field of energy values can be divided into four broad categories. The first set of values are those pertaining to the economic characteristics of energy. As chapter 3 made clear, energy as a scarce resource is predominantly a commodity. Those with inadequate energy resources to meet their needs must obtain energy elsewhere through trade. Those who do have enough energy for their own needs have an incentive to trade that resource for some other valued good or service, and to do so at the greatest benefit to themselves. This interaction between consumer and producer —demand and supply in a commodity market—determines the price of energy.

A second set of values arises from the institutional framework of energy. The ability to participate in the determination of energy outcomes requires some form of institutional access. Nations, multinational corporations, interest groups within nations, even individuals, may compete to affect energy outcomes. Each acquires the ability to do so through the relative influence that can be brought to bear on the issue. Those possessing influence seek to preserve it; those without it seek to gain it, often by attempting to alter the prevailing institutional framework.

A third set of values arises from the impingement of energy on other societal issues. These values are based on recognition that energy exists in a broader social environment. For example, those who have the capacity neither to pay the price set in market competition nor to challenge the prevailing institutional framework are not able to lay claim to energy resources through either economic or institutional influence. They operate instead using criteria drawn from outside the energy arena itself, arguing that access to energy is a need directly related to human welfare and development. There are other areas, such as the impact of energy choices on the environment, where energy developments also affect broader social developments.

Finally, we must account for the effect on energy outcomes of nonenergy values. Actors with access and influence in the energy arena are also challenged by values that arise outside of that arena but that affect choices within it. Political commitments, especially those related to security objectives, tend to impose constraints on energy decision-making. Thus, in the face of a volatile and unsettled political situation in the Middle East, the United States nonetheless maintains a commitment to Israel that is manifested among other ways in efforts to maintain a military balance of power in the region. Those efforts in turn have meant taking positions contrary to those of powerful oil-producing nations.

A setting of scarce resources with multiple actors implies competition. The energy arena is just such a setting. The range of actions and values has so far turned largely on the continuing dominance of oil as a primary energy resource. But oil is a finite commodity. As we have already noted, within reasonable limits of accuracy the amount of available oil is known and is exhaustible. Thus the major issues that present themselves are these: How fast will petroleum resources be used? By whom will they be used? And, as oil becomes a scarcer and scarcer commodity, what resource will be chosen to replace it? Energy actors then compete in an effort to assure that the answers to those questions will be resolved in their favor. As a producing nation with the single largest proportion of known oil reserves outside of the communist world, Saudi Arabia may want to extend the economic life of oil for as long as possible. On the other hand, the major consumer nations of the developed world might be willing to accept some change in energy resources if it means a reliable supply at reduced cost, so as to sustain economic strength. Multinational corporations within those same nations may oppose such a pursuit because they value more highly their predominant role in the overall flow of energy under the oil regime that prevails. Still other groups will challenge that predominance by seeking alternative energy sources. Support for that position (or for some other position) may come from still other actors with values arising from self-professed humanitarian concern for equity or the future of the environment. With so much at stake in making choices in the energy arena and with the issue very much unresolved, values—or some combination of values—are critical to our understanding of possible energy outcomes. In this chapter we will explore some of the alternatives in the energy arena and the value trade-offs that apply.

Economic Values

Two energy values arise from economic considerations: assuring reliability of supply and achieving the most advantageous cost for energy. Reliability of supply entails the effort to ensure that there will be a sufficient supply of energy to meet the needs of society. When supply is unreliable it leads to fluctuations in the market such as those that characterized the energy crisis of the 1970s, when supply was interrupted by the politically and economically motivated Arab oil embargo. There are several effects from these fluctuations. First, in an unstable market a premium is placed on the ability to adjust to changing trends. The "oil shocks" of the energy crisis were felt most severely among the world's largest consumers, the major industrialized states of North America, Western Europe, and Japan. The reduced availability of energy imposed by the Arab embargo had an immediate effect on the economies of these states and induced a period of decreased growth and recession. But these were also the states most easily able to recover. While it took several years to make the adjustments necessary to reestablish a reliable base for supply, only the relative flexibility of these states allowed them to do so. In contrast, the lower-income, less-developed countries were already on the margin of economic flexibility. They too suffered immediate constraints on economic growth. However, because their economic foundation was much shallower than that of the developed states, any adjustments that they could make meant additional costs. As it turned out, the impact of the energy crisis led to impediments in planning, since economic development and energy are so closely linked. To compensate, the less-developed countries sought support from international lending agencies, both public and private. The process of lending to adjust for the changes induced by fluctuations in the energy market then contributed to the beginnings of another crisis, the debt crisis, in the third world. The energy crisis thus had a ripple effect throughout the system, the long-term consequences of which may not yet be fully felt.

The requirements of reliable energy supply can be met through either external or internal means, or by some assured combination of both. Externally, nations attempt to secure foreign sources for energy. In the contemporary oil-dependent energy environment, the large consuming nations have emphasized the short term in two ways. One has been to improve relations with existing suppliers. These efforts have necessarily focused on the Middle East and the major Arab producers. U.S. foreign policy underwent a significant change as a result of the energy crisis. The long-standing U.S. commitment to Israel was expanded in American diplomacy by efforts to resolve the underlying differences between Israel and the Arab states. In so doing it was recognized that a major political obstacle affecting the flow of energy to the United States and its allies could be alleviated. While not the only ingredient, certainly this element contributed to the vigorous pursuit by the United States of a peace treaty between Israel and Egypt, established in the Camp David Accords, and to the quest for a broader formula for peace in the Middle East (other nonenergy values, arising from U.S.-Soviet relations, also played a role).

Another change in direction for American policy was manifested in systematic efforts to improve relations in general between the United States and the Arab states by focusing increased attention on what are perceived to be the "moderate" Arab states. In particular, the United States has sought to improve its relations with Saudi Arabia. In 1981, though challenged by existing domestic support for Israel, the United States sold to the Saudis a sophisticated airborne warning system, the AWACS aircraft, together with fighter-interceptors and associated missiles. While once again additional considerations were involved in this sale, including U.S. efforts to keep the Soviet Union isolated from Middle Eastern politics, the predominant role of Saudi Arabia in OPEC and the vast Saudi petroleum production capacity were major considerations. Similar policy initiatives were taken by other consuming nations. In the face of the risk of interrupted supply through the Persian Gulf as a result of the Iran-Iraq War, Japan, one of the major consumers of oil transiting the Persian Gulf, has made a number of efforts—as yet unsuccessful—to intercede and provide a structure for diplomatic resolution of that conflict.

A second direction toward which consumer nations have turned in order to improve reliability of supply has been to seek out alternative suppliers. This effort has been aided by the effects of the energy crisis itself. The crisis was produced in part by sharp increases in the price of oil, which in turn provided an incentive for other suppliers—not bound by the cartel guidelines of OPEC—to enter the market. The decade following the crisis saw the emergence of many such producers. Consumer nations now improve their prospects for a reliable supply by drawing from more than one supplier, a condition that was not possible at the time of the energy crisis when supply was "inelastic," that is, when no practical alternative source was available outside of OPEC.

Internally, nations seek to provide supply reliability through self-sufficiency. The immediate response in the United States to the 1973 Arab oil embargo was President Nixon's declaration of Project Independence, indicating an intent to make the United States free from all imported oil by the year 1980 (a goal that was not achieved for a variety of reasons, despite conservation measures in both the United States and other industrialized energy-consuming nations and a number of shifts in the petroleum marketplace). This goal of energy self-sufficiency was adopted by virtually all the major consumers. At the same time serious consideration began to be given to the necessary trade-offs between short-term and long-term energy requirements. By applying a variety of measures, for example, the industrialized states were able to reduce the prevailing one-to-one relationship between economic growth and energy consumption, bringing the ratios down to about .7 percent of increased energy consumption for every 1 percent increase in economic growth. For many nations such efforts are not feasible. The less-developed countries, located at an earlier stage in the developmental process, once again have found it difficult to make adjustments in the ratio between energy usage and growth.

Such energy self-sufficiency may take two paths. One is to accelerate usage of domestic energy resources, so that a premium is placed on domestic exploration and the improvement of extraction and distribution systems for domestic supply. It should be noted that self-sufficiency in the current regime of reliance on nonrenewable energy resources is valid only as a short-term strategy. A nation may improve energy reliability for itself, but the underlying exhaustibility of resources in the overall system remains. Thus global supply is being reduced and eventually the problem of reliable supply will have to be faced unless other measures are taken. This problem may be illustrated by calling attention to those nations, such as Japan, for which self-sufficiency is not practicably within reach. Efforts to compensate for the unreliability of supply within the existing energy system therefore means seeking an alternative set of relationships, in which some other energy resource or a combination of resources plays a greater role. Japan has sought to build an energy system that relies on a variety of sources for energy, including natural gas, coal, and nuclear power (although oil remains the predominant resource), obtained from a variety of suppliers.

In addition to being sought through expanding use of domestic resources, self-sufficiency can be pursued through conservation measures. This approach is simply the other side of the production-consumption equation. Independence from external supply is enhanced by reducing demand. Thus major consuming nations have adopted conservation policies in response to the oil embargo. While such policies provided incentives, such as tax breaks, for individual consumers to conserve, the increased cost of energy proved to be most effective. Consumers sought greater fuel efficiency in order to lessen the impact of energy on their pocketbooks. Still such measures may not in themselves be sufficient to establish self-sufficiency. Conservation, like many of the other actions we have seen, concentrates on the existing set of energy resources.

It has been repeatedly the case that it is easier to focus on short-term responses than long-term trade-offs. Thus efforts to deal with the reliability of supply have tended to address the same economic conditions with which the problem was framed at the beginning, relying for the most part on the automaticity of the market to resolve differences in values. Despite its early emphasis on energy independence, the United States still possesses only ten weeks' worth of energy resources in its Strategic Petroleum Reserve should external sources be cut off altogether. Even with increased domestic development and decreased domestic demand, the *absolute* quantity of oil imported by the United States has not substantially changed; only the *proportion* of imported oil used in America has been reduced. That is, the United States is actually using more petroleum than at the beginning of the energy crisis. Regardless of efforts toward self-sufficiency, most consumer nations have continued to draw a stable proportion of their energy resources from external sources. To try to protect the reliability of those supplies they have favored the approaches of reinforcing relations with the existing suppliers and broadening the supply base by finding alternative suppliers.

A second economic value in the energy arena lies in seeking to obtain the most advantageous cost for energy. Here producers and consumers must interpret the value differently. The producer will benefit most from the highest price that the market will bear. During the 1970s the inelasticity of the market gave OPEC the capacity to control the conditions for the price of petroleum by coordinating both pricing and production. Thus the price of a barrel of oil increased in the market from just under $3 to nearly $35. From the producers' perspective that was certainly an advantageous cost. As the market began to fluctuate in the 1980s, however, this generalization became less certain. Greater emphasis has necessarily been placed on what the market will bear. New suppliers have entered the market and made it more competitive, and demand overall has dropped off relative to production. Under those conditions we have seen that the various producers have differing definitions of what constitutes an advantageous cost. Recall how the "low absorbers," reinvesting their profits ("petrodollars") in the industrialized states that have paid them for their oil, have sought to extend the market at high prices in order to take advantage of the long-term value of their product, expecting the rewards in future sales to balance out losses in the short term. But the "high absorbers," needing to invest their foreign profits toward their own development plans, have less capacity to wait for those rewards and therefore seek to sell more volume even at a reduced price because of their need to sustain the influx of foreign earnings to serve their development needs. These differing definitions of advantageous cost have added further to dissent within OPEC and to the growing fluctuations of the petroleum market.

Consumers of course have an entirely different interpretation of advantageous cost for energy. The consumer seeks the lowest possible cost for energy. Prior to the 1970s attainment of that objective was not a problem. Oil was plentiful and the interaction of demand and supply kept prices relatively low. An increase in demand due to economic growth and the entry of the United States into the international energy marketplace contributed to the series of events that precipitated the rapid increases in price of the 1970s. Attaining low-cost energy then became a more explicit and serious concern. Of course, oil is not the only energy source. But its domination of the energy system has meant that the cost increases and the more recent fluctuations have had major impact on consumers.

The effects of such fluctuations are often complex. For example, the non-oil-producing less-developed countries found that their reliance on exports of raw materials—in order to acquire foreign earnings to purchase needed imports—was constrained by petroleum price increases. The developed countries adjusted to the high cost of energy by cutting back their production (it became less profitable to increase output because the return on each unit of additional production was reduced by the increased cost of the required inputs of additional energy). In general, the cost of oil contributed to a deficit in the balance of trade, as more was being imported than exported, and to rising inflation in the industrialized countries. That phenomenon in turn spread throughout the international economic system. Third-world nations found themselves virtually priced out of the energy picture. The predominance of market mechanisms in determining energy flows meant that the major producers and consumers were setting the framework for global energy. The less-developed countries—neither major consumers nor, with a few notable exceptions, producers—lacked the industrial base, available export earnings, or domestic economic strength to compete. They either had to pay the going rate or seek intervention in order to reduce the cost to their society through separate funding or preferential treatment in the market. While some success was gained from international lending agencies and special reserves set aside by some of the major producers, the effort to obtain an advantageous cost was severely constrained in these nations.

Among the more damaging effects of the increased cost of energy was its impact on agricultural production. During the 1950s and 1960s the rate of growth of agricultural output worldwide was phenomenal, largely because of major inputs of energy. Farming became an energy-intensive enterprise. This was true not only because of the development of more extensive mechanization —internal combustion engines using petroleum-based fuels in farm implements—but also because of growing reliance on chemical fertilizers to compensate for nutrients taken from the soil. These fertilizers require large inputs of energy. Between 1950 and 1980 inputs of chemical fertilizers had grown by a factor of eight. Crop yields increased with each additional unit of fertilizer, but the same cost equation that applied in industry also applied in agriculture. As the cost of energy increased, the economic incentive to increase production was reduced and the rate of growth of agricultural production dropped off. The so-called Green Revolution, which increased crop yields through new seed varieties and heavy inputs of chemical fertilizers and pesticides (all energy-based), was also affected by increased energy costs. The impact of this Revolution was felt dramatically in Asia, but by the 1980s the cost of energy, combined with other constraints, began to show the limits of this dramatic effort to increase world food production (it should be emphasized that energy costs were not the only constrainig condition). Some of the neediest areas in the world, especially sub-Saharan Africa, were in part denied the potential of increased agricultural production because of disadvantageous energy costs.

Additional impacts of the quest for more advantageous energy costs among consumers have produced efforts to reduce the cost of energy by using it more efficiently, and have led to adoption of other energy sources into national energy systems. These efforts are linked to similar efforts with regard to improving the reliability of supply through conservation measures. Cheap and plentiful energy placed no premium on energy efficiency. High-performance automobile engines emphasizing speed and power exemplified the inattentiveness to questions of efficiency in the United States. There was neither an attempt to attract individual consumers to efficient products nor an effort to design such products through research and development. Now, throughout the developed world in particular, this trend has been reversed. There is a clear effort to provide energy-efficient products to the customer. The shift from inattentiveness to attentiveness with regard to efficiency is attributable to the value placed on the cost of energy largely because individual consumers felt the bite of the added costs of continuing at the same levels of usage. Similar approaches are evident beyond direct energy uses. For example, it is now common to find that garbage and other waste products that were once merely dumped are being converted to energy in small- and large-scale recycling plants. The cost of oil has also driven efforts to use other energy resources wherever possible. Many individual homeowners have installed woodburning stoves in order to reduce reliance on oil-fired heat. In the United States, easily convertible plants have switched from oil to coal because of the relative availability of coal. Solar energy, practical now for some small-scale uses, has also increased in prominence. There have been more ambitious attempts, not always with lasting success, to use nontraditional sources for energy—such as agricultural products ("gasohol"), geothermal energy, ocean gradients, and others. All of these efforts demonstrate that pursuit of advantageous cost, which moved oil into its place of prominence, is still at work among consumers, only now it is turning them away from oil to a variety of other resources.

Institutional Values

The institutional values that characterize the energy arena are regime maintenance and national and corporate autonomy. *Regime maintenance* derives from a social science concept referring to the prevailing structures that define a given system of institutional relationships. These structures determine access to decision-making and the exercise of influence. While the direction of change in the global energy system is unclear, one of the motivating forces in choosing a direction is the action of those in positions of dominant influence over the system to retain their control. We have noted in a number of different ways that the global energy regime is presently dominated by the actions of nation-states, acting as producers and consumers and to a somewhat lesser extent as distributors. Nations often operate both singly and in concert through intergovernmental organizations such as OPEC and the International Energy Agency. The second most influential participants in the prevailing energy regime are the multinational corporations. These nongovernmental international actors often pursue their corporate objectives without regard for the national policies that govern other actors (sometimes therefore they are referred to as transnational actors). We have also noted that the prevailing structures of today's energy regime, despite significant shifts in energy trends, remain focused on oil. Now, however, there are also a number of pressures on the oil-dominated energy regime.

These pressures come from three basic directions. First, there is the factor of the eventual exhaustibility of petroleum resources. In the foreseeable future some shift from petroleum will need to occur. When the energy crisis was at its height, the need to search for alternative sources of energy was pressing and it promised to have an impact on the energy regime. For regime maintenance, any such shift would probably mean realignment of relative influence. One short-term alternative to oil, for example, would be coal. Coal, like petroleum a nonrenewable fossil fuel, would extend the long-term choices for the global energy system by broadening the resource base for energy. But it would also remove from the major oil produc-ers their power over the system and place it in the hands of the major coal producers. This would mark a significant change, because the major coal reserves of the world reside for the most part in the industrialized sector of the North. The present role of the OPEC nations and other petroleum producers would certainly be dim-inished, and the current economic gains from oil would be lost.

The dominant coal countries are the United States, the Soviet Union, and the People's Republic of China. While there would be an evident economic realignment favoring the industrialized North, a move to coal would therefore also involve a political realignment as well. The Soviet Union and the United States are the principal rivals in the world today. China, while still underdeveloped, is mak-ing significant strides toward greater industrial development. Both China and the Soviet Union have domestic economic demands that would constrain their international roles as coal exporters. Both also would benefit from foreign-exchange earnings. If the major consumers in the developed states of North America and Western Europe are able to provide for their own needs, however, and the less-developed countries have little economic flexibility (less per-haps than they have now because of the diminished role of petroleum), then it is hard to envision how much of an interna-tional energy role coal might play. This scenario is of course oversimplified and speculative. Its purpose here is simply to illus-trate the point that any impending shift in energy sources, whether to coal or to some renewable energy source, will certainly alter the existing energy regime. Different actors will have different stakes in the outcome. Each will pursue the choice perceived as most advantageous.

A second set of pressures on the prevailing energy regime is related to the same kinds of choices just mentioned. Those pressures arise from the continuing tension between the developed North and the less-developed South. North-South tension has been manifested in two ways. First, the less-developed countries that currently possess petroleum reserves are understandably reluctant to relinquish the advantage which that resource provides. They have sought therefore to oppose any structural change in that system's reliance on oil. To maintain that regime, the oil-producing less-developed nations have favored efforts to improve the processes of recovering and processing oil, making it as durable a resource in market terms as possible. These efforts may operate in tandem with the role that the large oil corporations play, for they too stand to gain from extending the value of oil to the greatest extent possible. A second way in which the less-developed countries have challenged the developments in the prevailing energy regime has more profound implications. The nations of the South have tried to restructure the entire economic foundation that underlies the energy system (and other resource-based systems).

One restructuring effort is expressed in the demand for a New International Economic Order. This new order would attempt to compensate for the preference built into the market in which the major producers and consumers determine energy choice. It would substitute a system where all scarce resources would be considered global and therefore subject to distribution criteria drawn from human development needs, not economic influence. (This effort incorporates the value of equity and will be addressed in more detail below.) Another approach taken by third-world nations focuses on the claim that resources are global and not simply objects of economic competition open to the highest bidder. In other areas —exploitation of the seabed and food reserves—these countries have sought establishment of an autonomous international authority to allocate global resources. It should be noted that the developing nations, while they often form a voting bloc (known as the Group of 77, although there are over one hundred members now representing third-world views), are not always a coherent group. Particularly in the energy arena we have seen that the oil-producing nations are separated from non-oil-producing nations and that within the oil-producing nations there are important differences (for example, the difference between the "high absorbers" and the "low absorbers").

The final set of pressures is somewhat more difficult to define. These arise from the role of the multinational corporations that have been at the forefront of energy developments in the "oil age" in which we still find ourselves. The history of oil is closely linked to the evolution of these large, vertically integrated corporations that control much of the petroleum industry from the point at which crude oil is pumped out of the ground to the point at which it is pumped into a customer's gas tank. The multinationals thus have a considerable stake in the existing energy regime and take frequent action to sustain their role in it. This effort has focused principally on oil, challenged first by the increasing nationalization of petroleum by the governments of oil-producing states and more recently by the entry of these states into the full range of oil operations "from the wellhead to the pump" (the so-called "downstream operations"). The multinationals have continued to try to influence the national policies of various nations that can affect their continuing role. At the same time the multinationals clearly want to hedge their bets. This desire explains the expansion of investment and research by the oil corporations into alternative energy sources. When the energy crisis was at its height, these corporations expanded greatly in a number of areas related to petroleum—such as exploration for new fields, further exploitation of old fields, and development of additional distribution mechanisms. They also began to extend their investments in additional energy sources, including synthetic fuels and even nuclear power. Among their motivations in doing so was again a desire to maintain their own role in the larger energy system. The multinationals can be expected to continue to try to play as influential a part as possible in obtaining energy supplies and in pricing their products.

A second value, *autonomy*, is an institutional representation of interests similar to those that motivate self-sufficiency in pursuit of economic values. Autonomy is sought by both nations and corporations in order to preserve their capacity to influence others. National autonomy can be manifested in different ways. The non-oil-producing developing nations may achieve autonomy through the loose coalition of the Group of 77, which gives them some limited leverage to challenge the domination of the developed world with regard to resource questions in general. The developed nations, on the other hand, define autonomy in terms of their relative independence from the vulnerabilities of the pattern of distribution of energy resources that places control in the hands of a few suppliers. Thus they seek the capacity to make and enforce energy-related decisions independent of the influences of other countries. The oil producers of course seek just the opposite. That is why the trend toward nationalization of the oil fields and the more recent efforts to become involved in "downstream operations" have occurred in those countries. Oil producers outside of OPEC strive for autonomy from the control both of the developed world's consumers and of the OPEC structure. Oil producers also must look to their own energy requirements. Mexico, for example, which participates as an observer in OPEC meetings, limits its exports and production in order to have sufficient energy resources to meet its own development-planning objectives.

Corporations pursue strategies toward autonomy for reasons similar to those of nations—to be in a position to make decisions independent of other energy actors. However, the underlying bases for those reasons differ. Corporations are after profit and growth, and they seek to minimize risk and maintain stability. In pursuing autonomy, energy-related businesses will resist government energy or trade policies that are perceived to interfere in corporate decision-making. From either the national or the corporate perspective, autonomy is a means to stay as free as possible from influences outside the control of one's own decision-making institutions.

Societal Values

Two societal values operate prominently in the energy arena today —equity and protecting the environment. *Equity* presents a difficult problem in definition. While the concept seems clear in the abstract, it is hard to translate equity into operational terms. In the abstract, equity means a substantial degree of fairness in the allocation of resources. But by what criteria is fairness to be judged? Unlike the economic and institutional values, equity falls into a broader category of concerns. It raises issues of human welfare and challenges the characteristic patterns of economically and institutionally based exploitation that have governed distribution of most of the earth's resources. As resources become scarce, issues of distribution take on a more pressing form. Actors tend to be divided between those who have and those who do not.

With regard to equity, then, energy reflects broader divisions based on unequal allocation of wealth and resources worldwide. There is a growing gap between the developed nations of the North and the low-income nations of the South. Development efforts have sought to close that gap but have not achieved a notable degree of success. The developing nations still find themselves subject to the imbalances between trade in primary products and trade in manufactured goods, which leave them at a disadvantage in the world market (this imbalance is known as the "terms of trade" problem) because they cannot compete from their low developmental base. To solve the problem these nations must develop, but the current patterns impede that development and favor those already developed. Energy comes to bear on this picture in the way already mentioned. As the energy crisis emerged, the developing nations with growing energy needs were priced out of the market and were therefore able to gain access to energy resources only at the expense of other valued objectives (not all of which, it should be noted, are necessarily of broad social value, such as expenditures on arms). Internal corruption, mismanagement, and other problems are also a part of this picture.

The problem of equity has been particularly evident with regard to energy because of the heavy usage required at early stages of economic development, including the energy-intensive burden of agriculture noted earlier. The course of the decade following the energy crisis retarded third-world development plans. The standard for development, regardless of which of the available strategies is chosen to accomplish it, remains that of industrialization. Many resource issues, including meeting the food and employment needs of the population, are tied to that standard. Thus the less-developed countries have advanced a claim on resources based on equity—an equal right to the same foundation for development achieved by the industrialized countries of the North. Finding those resources not readily available, and even restricted in the case of energy because of increased cost, the nations of the developing world experienced the same slowdown in growth that the developed world experienced. But they were less able to absorb it. Hence they sought other means to compensate. First, international lending agencies tried to assist through low-cost development loans. Second, the OPEC countries established a two-tier pricing system, charging developing countries a lower price than the developed nations and thus providing a means to advance energy assistance to the developing countries. Both of these efforts presented their own inherent constraints. Funding through international lending—public and private—became part of a series of conditions that has led to a new "crisis" in the wake of the old—the "international debt crisis," in which economic growth in the borrowing countries has been insufficient to provide income to repay the loans. This has placed the borrowers in the precarious position of facing default with little option. On the other hand, the two-tiered pricing system is limited by the economic value of the resource itself. Only a limited amount of oil has flowed through this system. In short, despite claims of equity, energy cost increases have continued to promote the distance between the rich and the poor nations of the world.

Equity can also be a consideration for internal energy distribution. Here the domestic political system provides a more malleable setting than the international system in the allocation of scarce resources through income redistribution or through preferential programs favoring those judged by society to be disadvantaged. The argument turns on similar questions nonetheless. What are the standards for determining basic human requirements and for assessing who in the society are being denied? In many nations, such as the United States, this is a continuing controversy, with some actors seeking energy subsistence for all at a fixed minimal level and others arguing for another more flexible level of lower entitlement. Both governmental and nongovernmental programs exist to assist in these efforts. On the other side of the coin, these redistributive efforts are not always successful. In many countries there has been little diffusion through society of the gains made in the energy system. Major Arab oil producers, such as Kuwait or Saudi Arabia, while they have a high per capita gross national product, do not in fact spread the profits through the society. Energy assets are owned by a few who continue to control where these resources will be distributed. In developed societies, in the face of the energy crisis, the multinational corporations reaped enormous gains as a consequence of the increased price of energy worldwide. In the United States these gains were addressed in a "windfall profits" tax that sought to redirect some of the energy profit into research and development efforts and other methods of spreading the monetary advantages more equitably.

A second societally oriented value is concerned with the protection of the environment. This is a recent focus. Awareness of environmental degradation as a consequence of energy exploitation in the past, when it existed at all, was largely a local issue. There was insufficient evidence to cause concern about environmental risks. Now, however, a growing body of evidence demonstrates that the production, consumption, and distribution of energy present a variety of threats to the increasingly fragile environment in which we live.

Addressing these threats to the environment, however, involves considerable costs. Environmental protection is expensive, not only with regard to the cost of such things as antipollution devices on automobiles and scrubbers to remove pollutants from industrial exhaust stacks, but also in the lowered efficiency of energy usage when such devices are employed. Stack scrubbers, for example, operate on electricity that in turn adds to the energy burden of the industrial process. Moreover, assuming sufficient public support for the establishment of such controls, one must then question the capacity of the society to pay that cost. In the developing world, where again the economic margin is narrow, there is little to persuade newly industrializing societies to add environmental protection to the already high start-up costs of economic development. Many third-world countries simply disregard environmental protection as a value worth addressing, while wealthier, more highly developed countries are in a better position both financially and socially to support environmental programs.

.Virtually every form of currently feasible energy production, except passive solar collection, involves risk of environmental problems. The recovery of oil risks blowouts and fire. The shipment of oil on oceangoing tankers, as has been demonstrated many times already, risks collision and oil spills in coastal waters with serious and lasting damage to wildlife. The same risk exists for long-distance pipelines, such as the Alaskan pipeline.

With regard to coal, there are other equally problematic issues. Coal mining is a dangerous enterprise, with the constant risk of explosion and cave-in. More broadly, the strip-mining of coal has scarred the landscape, making it not only visually but ecologically unattractive. In only a few countries have there been efforts to require restoration of the land so scarred, and even those requirements are relatively recent.

Yet another area, nuclear power generation, presents additional risks. The safety hazards of nuclear power to society, though generally of low probability, have been brought dramatically to the fore by a number of accidents, most notably the Three Mile Island accident in Harrisburg, Pennsylvania, that threatened to spread dangerous radiation over a populated area. Beyond such risks, nuclear reactors often create thermal pollution from circulation of cooling water into surrounding rivers or the ocean. It is difficult to determine the cost of trade-offs in such instances of risk, but it is now recognized that there are societal factors to be considered in making energy production choices.

Similar environmental concerns are involved in energy consumption. Burning virtually any combustible fuel, whether it is oil, coal, or natural gas, produces various particulates, sometimes visible in the form of smoke and sometimes not. The pollution control devices now required on American cars are a legislated response to this environmental problem resulting from automobile emissions. The same problem exists at every level of fuel combustion. In this case, as we noted, the cost of controlling pollution is increased energy use. Combustion also produces carbon dioxide that is released into the atmosphere. We have seen how this gas, in itself harmless, has been shown to change the character of the atmosphere by increasing temperatures. Studies now exist that forecast global changes in climate and suggest a number of dire economic and political consequences.

Finally, there is the growing problem examined earlier of "acid rain," the consequence of particulates entering the atmosphere and being returned in the form of rain with greatly increased acidity. The results of acid rain have been felt in a number of countries where forests and lakes have been severely damaged by acid levels with accompanying damage to surrounding wildlife, sometimes to the point of extinction. The problem with environmental protection as a value is not evidence of its effects but incorporation of this value with the harder economic and institutional values that prevail. Few nations, corporations, or individuals are willing to sacrifice immediate energy needs to the longer-term state of the environment. Those advocating environmental concerns tend to be less influential than those promoting economic or institutional values.

Nonenergy Values

Often the energy arena is affected by actors who pursue values that do not arise directly from energy issues. The most prominent of these have to do with national security. In some respects, this nonenergy value may be related to the efforts to achieve self-sufficiency and autonomy. Concentration of oil production capacity in the Middle East, for example, has complicated U.S. energy policy because of security and foreign policy considerations peculiar to that region. The United States has maintained its long-standing commitment to a defensible Israel by providing both military and economic assistance. In part this assistance during the Yom Kippur War of 1973 precipitated the oil crisis. At the same time, the United States has also attempted to stabilize the volatility of the Middle Eastern political setting by keeping the military forces of the more moderate Arab states in the region in rough balance with those of Israel, in an effort to reduce the incentive for the use of force to resolve the profound differences that exist between the Arab states and Israel over the question of Palestine. The United States also has tried for much broader reasons to prevent or diminish the influence of the Soviet Union in the region.

These nonenergy objectives have not always proved to be compatible with immediate energy requirements. Diplomatic efforts by the United States to improve relations with oil producers in the area, such as Saudi Arabia, have been challenged continually by support for Israel (which has itself been tested by Israeli policies that are inconsistent with U.S. objectives). The trade-off between energy goals and foreign policy goals is difficult to assess in making policy decisions, because the two do not necessarily spring from the same set of interests.

National security has also been linked directly to energy because of concern for the military implications of interruption in oil supplies. The United States has always considered the flow of vital natural resources to be an imperative of its national welfare and has incorporated that objective into its overall strategy and force structure. When the energy crisis demonstrated the vulnerability of both the United States and its European allies, concern for such interruption was heightened. The secretary of state indicated that the United States would not allow itself to be "strangulated" and a study was conducted by the Congress to determine the feasibility of seizing the Middle Eastern oil fields (it determined that it would be infeasible to do so). The Soviet invasion of Afghanistan in 1979 elicited similar fears for the Persian Gulf region and President Carter enunciated the Carter Doctrine indicating that the United States would use military force if necessary to ensure the continued flow of oil through that region. A separate military command structure — the Rapid Deployment Joint Task Force (now the Central Command) — was established to deal with that eventuality. More recently the Iran-Iraq War caused concern among a number of nations dependent on that oil lifeline, again suggesting military responses to assure continued flow of oil resources. On a much broader scale continuing assessments are made of the energy status of the Soviet Union in terms of its overall military and economic balance with the United States. The Soviet natural gas pipeline to Europe was considered a potential threat to the security of U.S. allies, and for a period of time the Reagan administration sought to block its completion by imposing curbs on contractors from the West who were constructing it. Overall these kinds of concerns are sensitive to the potential vulnerability of American security interests that are affected by the global energy system.

As we have reviewed the range of values brought to bear in the energy arena, it is evident that the "harder" economic and institutional values tend to prevail. This prevalence reflects the predominance of economic and institutional factors in the shape and operation of the energy system as a whole. The functioning of the market and the regime that governs it are more determinative of energy outcomes than are the more general societal goals. Among all of the salient concerns, cost seems to predominate. At every level, from subnational to international, cost has driven various actors to try to enter the energy arena. Individual consumers have tried to reduce their own costs by making their homes and automobiles energy efficient. Oil-producing nations have sought to maintain a steady price for their commodity and consumer nations have sought to find alternative sources in order to make the pricing structure more flexible.

The period since the energy crisis has thus seen increasing fluctuations in the marketplace. Similar though less pronounced shifts have taken place in the energy regime. For a period of time, in the immediate atmosphere of the crisis, a number of efforts were made to change the prevailing institutions—alternative sources as well as alternative suppliers of energy were sought. At the same time those who controlled the energy system attempted to protect their roles. Now, with the price of oil once again declining, producers and consumers alike have found reduced incentives to make any changes in energy sources or the entire energy system. There is an irony here. For the future of the energy system as a whole, high-cost oil may be more beneficial than low-cost oil, for the higher cost spurs the search for alternatives. Those alternatives must come at some future date. The question of how fast and in what form they will come remains open.

8 Population: Government Policy-making

The foremost business of government is to make policies designed to affect the lives of its citizens. When policies are made to address problems in one area they frequently result in consequences, antici-pated or unanticipated, in other areas as well. In 1973 a law was passed in the United States to lower the speed limit to 55 miles per hour. This law was designed specifically to reduce the consumption of gasoline during the energy crisis of that year. It succeeded, but it also had some unintended results. Auto fatalities sharply declined as motorists slowed down. Thus the limit was retained even after the energy crisis subsided. As it turned out the 55 mile-per-hour speed limit, an energy policy, was also a population policy because, although unintentionally, the mortality rate was affected.

In this chapter we examine government's role in population matters. Specifically, we focus on historical and contemporary poli-cies designed to affect two of the three principal population processes —migration and fertility. As we learned earlier these two processes —together with the third, mortality—determine configurations of the size, distribution, and age composition of the population. Mor-tality policies are only briefly discussed because most of the legisla-tion affecting mortality focuses primarily on medical research funding, health laws, and the like.

Types of Policies

Government policies relate to population dynamics in one of five general ways: (1) the legislation is *not* directed toward population problems and has *no* effect on any of the three population pro-cesses at work; (2) policies are *not* directed toward population purposes but have an *indirect* effect; (3) they are *not* directed toward population purposes but have a visible, *direct* effect; (4) they *are*

Table 8.1   Relationship of governmental policy and population outcome

Type	For Population	Effect on Population
1	No	None
2	No	Indirect
3	No	Direct
4	Yes	None
5	Yes	Direct

directed toward population but, nonetheless, have little or *no* effect; and (5) they *are* directed toward population dynamics and have a *substantial* effect. These five scenarios are represented in table 8.1.

Many governmental policies, such as regulations on truth in advertising, have no relationship to population and thus fit into the first category. Most policies aimed at improving the quality of life fall into the second category, or even into the third, if the policy proves to have a direct effect. The case of the 55-miles-per-hour speed limit cited above, for example, brought reduced mortality and therefore clearly fits into the third category because it was not designed to affect population dynamics but, nonetheless, had a direct, visible effect. Other examples can be cited. In the nineteenth century, free public education legislation may have contributed to increased fertility rates by removing the burden of educating children from the shoulders of their parents. Opponents of current welfare programs argue that government assistance results in more children, although there is no scientific proof of a link. In another case, the development of four- and six-lane limited access highways radiating from major cities has led to the creation of large suburban ("bedroom") communities, where people work in the central city and live in the outlying areas. Originally these highways were developed to move people quickly through the city, but the inhabitants of the city itself, and thus the distribution of population, have been affected. The most recent transformation has been the movement of businesses from the center to the periphery so that goods and services can be better diffused around the country. Now workers need not drive to the central city area but can instead work closer to home. Cities, faced with declining vitality and a shrinking tax base, have responded with their own policies designed to lure people back to the center, both to work and to live. More such examples could be cited: compulsory vaccination programs, legislation to ensure safe water and food products, and so forth. All of these nonpopulation government actions have either indirect or direct population consequences.

There are of course many government policies that are clearly intended to affect one or more of the processes of fertility, mortality, and migration, and thus fall into either the fourth or fifth category, depending on their success. Government offers of free or cheap land to those willing to settle in frontier areas or depressed urban neighborhoods affect internal migration. Similar incentives were offered by colonial nations in the nineteenth and twentieth centuries and thus affected external migration. Tax funds for health programs are clearly designed to decrease mortality. Major advances in government-sponsored medical research have resulted in increased fertility as new discoveries allow couples who had been unable to have children to do so. Governments from time to time have not hesitated, unfortunately, to engage in policies and practices designed to *increase* mortality, especially in wartime. The strategic bombing of cities in Germany, England, and Japan during World War II was clearly designed to discourage further participation by these nations in the war through physical damage, injury, and even death to segments of the civilian population. Hitler's efforts to eradicate the Jewish race represent one of history's most despicable episodes of government manipulating with population variables.

Evolution of Population Policy-making

Throughout history governments typically focused on policies affecting mortality (in order to decrease it) or migration (allowing certain people to leave and others, principally workers or relatives of current citizens, to enter—known as optimal placement). Rarely did governments attempt to increase mortality (except in war) or decrease fertility. When fertility change was the target of policy action in previous eras, its emphasis was on enhancing births, not reducing them. The overriding question was always: is the human race able to survive? Life was hard. Disease, plagues, famine, and conflict were frequent. Death rates were high, and consequently birthrates had to be even higher if the human race was to survive and flourish. As a result, every authority—governmental and nongovernmental—encouraged high birthrates. The biblical exhortation to "go forth and multiply" has been a familiar refrain from religious and political leaders throughout history. All this encouragement through the centuries produced birthrates only slightly higher than death rates, meaning that the global population grew only slightly throughout most of the development of the human race. Governments thus resorted to a variety of economic, religious, and social incentives to encourage in-migration. In some locations throughout the globe, the United States being a good example, the impact of immigration on population dynamics was substantial.

In the developed world in the nineteenth century, the Industrial Revolution increased the need for workers and in-migration was encouraged. But soon the discoveries of modern medicine and their diffusion throughout the developed world reduced the death rate and, with continuing high birthrates, populations soared. This posed little or no problem during the nineteenth century because the population base was low and land was plentiful, particularly in North America for both American citizens and immigrants from Western Europe. Moreover, since this population pattern was closely associated with the Industrial Revolution, the advancement of technology had the direct effect of providing a better quality of life, including employment opportunities, for everyone. The death rate declined rather slowly, allowing society to make the necessary adjustments and thus minimizing problems. As a consequence, fertility reduction occurred at a pace deemed acceptable by government, and thus no direct action was taken to encourage a decline in births. By and large, growth rates within the developed world once again leveled off. Now, however, the problem of high births and deaths was replaced by one of low birth and low death rates. Where labor scarcities did occur, government policy sought to adjust by encouraging in-migration.

The situation was different in the developing sectors of the globe after World War II. The diffusion of modern medicine from the developed world dramatically reduced the mortality rate and, given high fertility levels, resulted in high growth rates. As governments in the third world became concerned with rapid population increases, they began to consider ways to slow this growth. Since population size is a function of each of the three population dynamics, governments had the option of influencing any or all of them. Indeed, some policies were implemented to encourage citizens to leave the country (out-migration), but their impact was minimal at the national level and even at the regional level. As we will learn later, migration policies were usually implemented for reasons other than their direct effect on population size. Only major movements of people from the developing to the developed world could have decreased third-world growth substantially in the 1960s and '70s, but the developed world would not adopt the necessary in-migration policies to accommodate such large influxes. A second option was the adoption of mortality policies encouraging deaths, a strategy that the world community would not tolerate. The only acceptable mortality policies are those that have just the opposite effect. They decrease mortality, adding to a country's net growth.

By process of elimination, therefore, the only way in which third-world governments could influence growth was by reducing births. Such efforts are called *fertility reduction programs*. Before 1950 there were rarely any attempts to limit population because governments did not believe that large population size and rapid growth rates were problems. This view has changed among most developing-world governments, but not without some difficulty. One problem is that even if the government wants to limit population, individuals may not desire smaller families. In some societies large families represent a symbol of status. Children also are wanted in order to take care of their parents when they reach old age. If parents believe that a high percentage of their babies will not live long—even though the government may have already introduced effective programs to combat high infant mortality rates—they will continue to produce more children than they may actually need until a few generations of child-rearing prove otherwise.

As the extent of the population problem became more apparent, national governments were still slow to make policy aimed at limiting fertility, because they did not yet understand the complexity of population dynamics. International governmental actors such as the United Nations were also slow to respond, not only because of limited understanding but also because of the fear of being accused of engaging in some form of ethnic, racial, or national genocide. It was left, therefore, to individuals and groups not affiliated with government (known as international nongovernmental organizations) to take the lead. In 1952 John D. Rockefeller, III, founded the Population Council and charged it with a worldwide agenda for population issues. The International Planned Parenthood Federation (IPPF), an independent agency focusing on family planning, also took an active role. Between 1952 and 1965 under the lead of the Population Council and the Ford and Rockefeller foundations, many research, training, and demonstration projects in population control and population planning were undertaken, primarily with private funds. The IPPF during this time concentrated on building affiliates in Asia, Africa, and Latin America while beginning to lobby national governments for appropriate action.

Table 8.2   Population policies around the world: a summary. Percentage of the population in each region or subregion broken down by government population policies (number of countries under each policy in parentheses)

	Government policy perception of nation's population growth rate		
	Too high	Satisfactory	Too low
World	60 (56)	29 (78)	12 (29)
More-developed countries	—	62 (25)	38 (8)
Less-developed countries	80 (56)	17 (53)	3 (21)
Less-developed countries (excluding China)	71 (55)	24 (53)	4 (21)
Africa	41 (19)	55 (26)	4 (16)
Northern Africa	80 (4)	17 (1)	3 (1)
Western Africa	14 (3)	77 (11)	9 (2)
Eastern Africa	33 (7)	67 (9)	—
Middle Africa	16 (1)	78 (5)	6 (3)
South Africa	100 (4)	—	—
Asia	90 (15)	9 (15)	1 (10)
Asia (excluding China)	84 (14)	14 (15)	2 (10)
Southwest Asia	45 (1)	36 (7)	19 (7)
Middle South Asia	98 (6)	2 (3)	—
Southeast Asia	87 (5)	11 (2)	3 (2)
East Asia	88 (3)	12 (3)	1 (1)
North America	—	100 (2)	—
Latin America	34 (19)	52 (11)	14 (5)
Middle America	94 (5)	6 (3)	—
Caribbean	67 (13)	33 (2)	—
Tropical South America	9 (1)	87 (6)	4 (2)
Temperate South America	—	—	100 (3)
Europe	—	67 (20)	33 (7)
Northern Europe	—	100 (7)	—
Western Europe	—	25 (4)	75 (3)
Eastern Europe	—	67 (3)	33 (3)
Southern Europe	—	93 (6)	7 (1)
USSR	—	—	100 (1)
Oceania	5 (3)	95 (4)	—

Source: Population Reference Bureau, *Intercom* 10 (November/December 1982): 6.

Beginning in the mid-1960s the United Nations began to address population directly, largely because of the prodding of the United States, which became a prime supporter of the UN Fund for Population Activities (UNFPA). These efforts followed the example of some

Western and Northern European governments that had already begun efforts to reduce fertility. Despite such initiatives the population of the developing world rose dramatically during this time, causing increased concern among third-world governments. These combined efforts led to agreement that world population ought to be put on the global agenda. Thus, under UN auspices, the World Population Conference was convened in Bucharest in 1974.

During the decade or so that has passed since the Bucharest conference, governments have exhibited a marked change in their attitudes toward certain population levels. Table 8.2 reveals the attitudes of governments throughout the world. As can be observed, within the developed sector a majority of nations (twenty-five) believe that their growth rate is satisfactory, although a minority (eight) feel that their rate is too low. That some developed countries hold the latter view is not surprising. Around 1973 fertility rates dropped below 2.1 births per woman in the developed world, which is the level needed to maintain population levels. In 1980 European nations added only 1.5 million to the world's population rolls. By 1984 three countries experienced an absolute decline (Hungary, Denmark, and West Germany), and three others were at zero population growth (Austria, Luxembourg, and Sweden). Six others were close to the zero level (0.5 percent annual increase in population or less). This is not surprising, as the average number of births per woman in these European countries at this time was 1.67 (1981 or 1982 data), and deaths began to outnumber births. Among the younger developed countries outside of Europe—the United States, Canada, Australia, and New Zealand—the drive toward lower rates was slower, primarily because of the impact of the post-World War II "baby boom" and immigration. But even the average number of births per woman in these countries was below the 2.1 replacement level (1.82 births).

As table 8.2 reveals, however, the developing world has a different view about growth rates. Of the 130 countries in this category, 56 believe their growth rates to be too high, 53 see them as satisfactory, and 21 see them as too low. However, only 20 percent of the third world's population resides in the 74 countries in the latter two categories, while 80 percent live in those 56 countries that believe their growth rates to be too high. It is primarily these 56 nations that have attempted to legislate fertility reduction.

World Population Conference of 1974

The year 1974 was declared the World Population Year by the United Nations, and the principal event, the global conference held in Bucharest, was attended by delegates of 136 countries as well as representatives of numerous nongovernmental agencies. Two opposing schools of thought were voiced at Bucharest. The industrialized world argued that population growth throughout the developing world was much too high, and that the only way to reverse the trend was to impose strong family population planning practices. The developing world, on the other hand, countered by arguing that the key to slowing population growth was economic development, and that the key to development was massive economic aid from the industrialized societies. "Development is the best contraceptive" was a phrase often used by the developing countries at Bucharest.

A World Population Plan of Action, representing a compromise between the two opposing viewpoints, was adopted. In essence, it affirmed that: (1) population and economic development are interrelated; (2) couples have freedom of choice but should have full access to both information and means for planning the number and spacing of children; (3) national governments have the right and the responsibility to formulate and implement population plans; and (4) international action and help, while not mandatory, is to be sought by national governments. Of particular note was the fact that for the first time in history governments were given the right by the global community to impose limitations on population size. But national sovereignty was not compromised, as international organizations such as the United Nations could not impose their will. They could offer help—aid and information—only if asked to do so. The global linkage for population was also affirmed, however, as the plan argued that "the growing interdependence among nations makes international action increasingly important."[1] Although migration received less attention than fertility at Bucharest, a particularly noteworthy principle of the formal Plan of Action argued against the use of race to control in-migration.

In the decade following the Bucharest conference significant strides have been made. Government assistance from the developed world has greatly increased. The network of relevant international governmental agencies has expanded as has their involvement. UNFPA has greatly expanded the nature and scope of its activities. A far larger number of countries have determined that the absolute level of their populations and/or their rates of growth were too high, and many of them have taken appropriate government action in establishing a national plan of action.

World Population Conference of 1984

Ten years after Bucharest, representatives of 149 countries and numerous other groups gathered at Mexico City in August 1984 to appraise the efforts made to implement the Bucharest plan of action. What a difference a decade had made! The developing world now clearly understood the urgency of slowing population growth. The earlier third-world argument that economic development would be the panacea for high growth rates was overshadowed by the recognition that the combination of extremely high growth rates with low levels of development suggested an outcome far different from the evolutionary demographic transition experienced by the developed world within the last century. Instead, despite a lowering of the growth rate in many societies, large food deficits have occurred, atmospheric and hydrologic systems have deteriorated, and economic and social standards at both the national and individual levels have been lowered. Moreover, as Lester Brown points out, the recent introduction of extreme legislation, such as China's policy of imposing tax and other penalties on couples having more than one child, and the completed World Fertility Survey also were effective by both dramatizing how deeply ingrained the high birth ethic is in the minds of third-world women and how far one country is willing to go to break this model of family practices. Of particular note, according to Brown, was the research finding that improved education and employment for women were more closely related to declines in fertility than any other economic and social indicators.[2] As a consequence, the final declaration passed at the Mexico City conference reaffirmed the Bucharest 1974 plan, while at the same time highlighting the experiences and findings of a decade of research and action.

These lessons are found in the first twenty-two points of the Mexico City Declaration, reproduced here because they capture the essence of the world community's beliefs on population.[3] The first five points set the stage for a discussion of population changes in the interim between the conferences.

1. The International Conference on Population met in Mexico City from 6 to 14 August 1984, to appraise the implementation of the World Population Plan of Action, adopted by consensus at

Bucharest, 10 years ago. The Conference reaffirmed the full validity of the principles and objectives of the World Population Plan
of Action and adopted a set of recommendations for the further
implementation of the Plan in the years ahead.

2. The world has undergone far-reaching changes in the past
decade. Significant progress in many fields important for human
welfare has been made through national and international efforts.
However, for a large number of countries it has been a period of
instability, increased unemployment, mounting external indebtedness, stagnation and even decline in economic growth. The
number of people living in absolute poverty has increased.

3. Economic difficulties and problems of resource mobilization have been particularly serious in the developing countries.
Growing international disparities have further exacerbated already
serious problems in social and economic terms. Firm and widespread hope was expressed that increasing international cooperation will lead to a growth in welfare and wealth, their just and
equitable distribution and minimal waste in use of resources,
thereby promoting development and peace for the benefit of the
world's population.

4. Population growth, high mortality and morbidity, and migration problems continue to be causes of great concern requiring
immediate action.

5. The Conference confirms that the principal aim of social,
economic and human development, of which population goals
and policies are integral parts, is to improve the standards of
living and quality of life of the people. This Declaration constitutes a solemn undertaking by the nations and international
organizations gathered in Mexico City to respect national sovereignty, to combat all forms of racial discrimination, including
apartheid, and to promote social and economic develpment,
human rights and individual freedom.

Principles 6 through 10 point to what has happened to population
variables in the interim. The evidence suggests that while growth
rates are declining, the contrast between the developed and developing worlds is striking, and the relationship between population and
development has become more evident.

6. Since Bucharest the global population growth rate has declined from 2.03 to 1.67 per cent per year. In the next decade
the growth rate will decline more slowly. Moreover, the annual
increase in numbers is expected to continue and may reach 90

million by the year 2000. Ninety percent of that increase will occur in developing countries and at that time 6.1 billion people are expected to inhabit the Earth.

7. Demographic differences between developed and developing countries remain striking. The average life expectancy at birth, which has increased almost everywhere, is 73 years in developed countries, while in developing countries it is only 57 years and families in developing countries tend to be much larger than elsewhere. This gives cause for concern since social and population pressures may contribute to the continuation of the wide disparity in welfare and the quality of life between developing and developed countries.

8. In the past decade, population issues have been increasingly recognized as a fundamental element in development planning. To be realistic, development policies, plans and programmes must reflect the inextricable links between population, resources, environment and development. Priority should be given to action programmes integrating all essential population and development factors, taking fully into account the need for rational utilization of natural resources and protection of the physical environment and preventing its further deterioration.

9. The experience with population policies in recent years is encouraging. Mortality and morbidity rates have been lowered, although not to the desired extent. Family planning programmes have been successful in reducing fertility at relatively low cost. Countries which consider that their population growth rate hinders their national development plans should adopt appropriate population policies and programmes. Timely action could avoid the accentuation of problems such as overpopulation, unemployment, food shortages, and environmental degradation.

10. Population and development policies reinforce each other when they are responsive to individual, family and community needs. Experience from the past decade demonstrates the necessity of the full participation by the entire community and grass-roots organizations in the design and implementation of policies and programmes. This will ensure that programmes are relevant to local needs and in keeping with personal and social values. It will also promote social awareness of demographic problems.

Changing the economic situation for women was recognized as one of the most important ways to bring about the desired changes in population. More research and dissemination of contraceptive technology represents the other important strategy for change.

11. Improving the status of women and enhancing their role is an important goal in itself and will also influence family life and size in a positive way. Community support is essential to bring about the full integration and participation of women into all phases and functions of the development process. Institutional, economic and cultural barriers must be removed and broad and swift action taken to assist women in attaining full equality with men in the social, political and economic life of their communities. To achieve this goal, it is necessary for men and women to share jointly responsibilities in areas such as family life, child-caring and family planning. Governments should formulate and implement concrete policies which would enhance the status and role of women.

12. Unwanted high fertility adversely affects the health and welfare of individuals and families, especially among the poor, and seriously impedes social and economic progress in many countries. Women and children are the main victims of unregulated fertility. Too many, too close, too early and too late pregnancies are a major cause of maternal, infant and childhood mortality and morbidity.

13. Although considerable progress has been made since Bucharest, millions of people still lack access to safe and effective family planning methods. By the year 2000 some 1.6 billion women will be of childbearing age, 1.3 billion of them in developing countries. Major efforts must be made now to ensure that all couples and individuals can exercise their basic human right to decide freely, responsibly and without coercion, the number and spacing of their children and to have the information, education and means to do so. In exercising this right, the best interests of their living and future children as well as the responsibility towards the community should be taken into account.

14. Although modern contraceptive technology has brought considerable progress into family planning programmes, increased funding is required in order to develop new methods and to improve the safety, efficacy and acceptability of existing methods. Expanded research should also be undertaken in human reproduction to solve problems of infertility and subfecundity.

15. As part of the overall goal to improve the health standards for all people, special attention should be given to maternal and

child health services within a primary health care system. Through breast-feeding, adequate nutrition, clean water, immunization programmes, oral rehydration therapy and birth spacing, a virtual revolution in child survival could be achieved. The impact would be dramatic in humanitarian and fertility terms.

No matter how successful the above strategies might be, the first effects of population dynamics of the last two decades still remain to be felt, and urbanization and migration will continue to be increasingly important. The next points summarize these effects.

16. The coming decades will see rapid changes in population structures with marked regional variations. The absolute numbers of children and youth in developing countries will continue to rise so rapidly that special programmes will be necessary to respond to their needs and aspirations, including productive employment. Aging of populations is a phenomenon which many countries will experience. This issue requires attention particularly in developed countries in view of its social implications and the active contribution the aged can make to the social, cultural and economic life in their countries.

17. Rapid urbanization will continue to be a salient feature. By the end of the century, 3 billion people, 48 percent of the world's population, might live in cities, frequently very large cities. Integrated urban and rural development strategies should therefore be an essential part of population policies. They should be based on a full evaluation of the costs and benefits to individuals, groups and regions involved, should respect basic human rights and use incentives rather than restrictive measures.

18. The volume and nature of international migratory movements continue to undergo rapid changes. Illegal or undocumented migration and refugee movements have gained particular importance; labour migration of considerable magnitude occurs in all regions. The outflow of skills remains a serious human resource problem in many developing countries. It is indispensable to safeguard the individual and social rights of the persons involved and to protect them from exploitation and treatment not in conformity with basic human rights; it is also necessary to guide these different migration streams. To achieve this, the cooperation of countries of origin and destination and the assistance of international organizations are required.

Principles 19–21 point to the increased commitment of all important classes of actors. Leaders of national governments—which retain ultimate sovereignty for population legislation—international governmental organizations, and international nongovernmental groups have all increased their awareness and their action on population matters.

19. As the years since 1974 have shown, the political commitment of Heads of State and other leaders and the willingness of Governments to take the lead in formulating population programmes and allocating the necessary resources are crucial for the further implementation of the World Population Plan of Action. Governments should attach high priority to the attainment of self-reliance in the management of such programmes, strengthen their administrative and managerial capabilities, and ensure co-ordination of international assistance at the national level.

20. The years since Bucharest have also shown that international cooperation in the field of population is essential for the implementation of recommendations agreed upon by the international community and can be notably successful. The need for increased resources for population activities is emphasized. Adequate and substantial international support and assistance will greatly facilitate the efforts of Governments. It should be provided wholeheartedly and in a spirit of universal solidarity and enlightened self-interest. The United Nations family should continue to perform its vital responsibilities.

21. Non-governmental organizations have a continuing important role in the implementation of the World Population Plan of Action and deserve encouragement and support from Governments and international organizations. Members of Parliament, community leaders, scientists, the media and others in influential positions are called upon to assist in all aspects of population and development work.

22. At Bucharest, the world was made aware of the gravity and magnitude of the population problems and their close interrelationship with economic and social development. The message of Mexico City is to forge ahead with effective implementation of the World Population Plan of Action aimed at improving standards of living and quality of life for all peoples of this planet in promotion of their common destiny in peace and security.

These principles are instructive because they accent the heightened awareness of the world's governments about the short- and long-term effects of present characteristics of population dynamics. While endorsing the Bucharest plan, world leaders realize that despite their best intentions forces have already been unleashed that continue to have substantial impact beyond purely population dynamics. The implications of the research finding that links education and employment for women on the one hand to decreased fertility on the other receive special emphasis in the Mexico City document. Delegates recognized that by the turn of the century the pool of fertile women will be the largest in history, and even more aggressive measures will be needed to curb the high number of potential births. A call was made for funding to improve contraceptive technology. Also noted was the change in social structures that will occur as a consequence of changes in the mix of the population processes. Increases in the percentage of children, along with urbanization and migration, will tax government's ability to respond to the special challenges of these phenomena. But the report ends on an optimistic note that at least consciousness is high and the commitment to action by virtually all segments of the international community is present.

National Fertility Reduction Programs

Since the emphasis at both Bucharest and Mexico City was on *national* solutions to population problems, we turn our attention now to how national governments have responded, first to combat high fertility rates and second to address migration concerns. There are two basic types of fertility reduction programs: *population planning* and *family planning*. Population planning programs are more extreme in nature as governments become very involved in trying, through a variety of incentives and disincentives, to convince couples to have fewer children. The latter include such policies as increasing taxes for more than a certain number of children, restricting housing, limiting educational opportunities, and establishing higher ages for marriage. Incentives include payments for voluntary sterilization and preferential treatment in housing, jobs, and education for one-child families. The major characteristic in population planning programs is that the governments intervene, providing rewards and penalties so that desirable family levels—determined by the government—will be met. In short, the limits to population are set and administered by governments.

Family planning programs represent a less extreme form of government intervention into the lives of families. In this type of strategy, governments do not set family limits but instead allow families the right to determine the number and spacing of children. If families wish to limit their size, governments will provide information, education, and the physical means to do so. But the key is that the family, not government, makes the decision. Once the decision is made to limit family size, the full weight of government is brought to bear to help the family carry out that decision.

The distinction between population planning and family planning is not as obvious as the above definitions suggest, however. Information about and the means for family planning quickly turn into incentives and disincentives. But some generalizations may be drawn. More extreme measures are typically used by Asian countries that have a longer history of high fertility rates. By contrast, the less extreme approaches tend to be favored by Latin American nations, whose problems are more recent and where Roman Catholic influences against fertility reduction programs are strongly felt, and by African nations that have been late to realize the adverse consequences of high growth rates.

For the reasons outlined in chapter 4, let us consider the African case, particularly sub-Saharan Africa.[4] Of the forty-two countries in sub-Saharan Africa, twenty-six provided some government planning services in 1984, but half of these were primarily concerned with the health of the mother and child rather than fertility reduction. About twenty countries also allowed private services by national family planning associations affiliated with the International Planned Parenthood Federation. But a recent study revealed that fertility reduction programs in Africa generally were weak.[5] Strong programs tend to be found only in the north and extreme south of Africa, not in the troubled sub-Saharan region.

Countries in Asia (excluding Southwest Asia), on the other hand, have been able to create more effective planning programs. Fourteen of the forty-three countries there had population planning policies in 1982, while many others had some government support. This is not surprising, given the much longer history of fertility reduction programs in the region.

Examples of Fertility-Related Policies

The above discussion summarized the extent to which the two basic fertility reduction strategies of family and population planning have been embraced throughout the world. Let us turn now to a brief description of specific policies and activities in a number of countries. Despite the heading of this section, not all of these programs are aimed at reducing population. Others are included to demonstrate that changing fertility levels upward is still a viable strategy for some countries.

Indonesia   At an earlier time the Indonesian approach was to encourage both births and migration, an unusual strategy for the world's fifth most populous country.[6] But by the early 1970s the government had launched a family planning program on an ambitious scale with strong support from foreign donors. It adopted flexible and innovative approaches through clinics, field-workers, incentives, targets, and "special drives." Apparently great success was achieved as the fertility rate in one major area (Bali) declined in five years from 5.8 to 3.8 children per woman (a reduction of about a third), and by a somewhat lesser number in Central Java, East Java, and Jakarta, the capital. These figures are astonishing when one considers that there are a variety of cultural forces mitigating against the acceptance of family planning programs. The government's goal is to cut its fertility rate in half by the year 2000.

Mexico   Officially, Mexico did not view its rapid population growth as a barrier to development until 1972.[7] Before then the government had a pro-birth (pronatalist) policy that had prevailed despite a growth in population of from 20 million to 54 million between 1940 and 1972. The reason is obvious. By 1960 the gap between births and deaths (the demographic transition model) was 33 per 1,000. By 1972 the growth rate was 3.5 percent, which means, if it continues, that the population will double every twenty years.

Some movements for change occurred in the 1960s as advocates of family planning became much more active. The government tolerated these activities—fifty-five planning clinics throughout the country by 1972—but did nothing to encourage them. One reason, of course, was the apparent influence of the Roman Catholic Church on government.

A national family planning program was announced in 1972 and the governmental turnaround occurred in a 1973 act of the Mexican Congress. This legislation focused on improving the quality of life for all people by carrying out an extensive program of family planning through the educational and public health services and the utilization of private services. By mid-1976 family planning services were available in 50 hospitals, 157 urban health centers, 500 semiurban centers, and 1,564 rural centers. Individuals in 6,000 rural communities not covered by the extensive services just mentioned were supplied with contraceptives. Family planning was added to many government agencies not normally in the public health area. The government embarked on ambitious programs of mass communication as well as population and sex education. The efforts yielded notable success as birthrates dropped and more ambitious goals were set by the government. Today, universal family planning is the government's highest priority and birth control is constitutionally guaranteed. Because of television, over 90 percent of all Mexican women know about family planning, and most want to use it.

China   Long a nation with substantial population size, China nonetheless has not always viewed these high numbers with alarm.[8] In 1911 Sun Yat-sen, founder of the Chinese republic, argued for increased population in order to preserve the Chinese race. But little change took place, and as a consequence the century prior to the 1949 communist revolution had been one of population stagnation. In the early postrevolutionary period most government action focused on reducing mortality. In this regard the Chinese government was successful. Couples were given some incentives for fertility—government workers received extra money for each new child—and population growth began to increase dramatically. The government reversed its attitude and began to discourage large families. Two family planning efforts were briefly attempted but had little effect. At this point the government launched a planning program in 1971 stressing late marriage, long birth intervals, and two-child families. The birthrate was virtually halved in just eight years (from 33.6 to 17.9 per 1,000). At that time planning efforts were intensified and focused on further reduction in family size with the one-child-per-couple movement. This latter policy was designed to counter the effects of China's "baby boomers" born in the 1960s entering their fertile period. Despite this new effort, however, the birthrate rose to 20.9 per 1,000. In early 1983 China further intensified its efforts by decreeing sterilization of couples with two or more children, although whether this policy is enforced or not has been a debatable point. These efforts suggest that the government was meeting resistance from the population, particularly in the rural areas, over its one-child policy. Within a year of this most recent campaign, some evidence surfaced that the government was softening its position in some cases, particularly if the first child was a girl.

Bangladesh   The country of Bangladesh is another Asian nation with vast problems due to population growth.[9] While its growth rate declined from 3.2 percent in 1962 to 2.3 percent in 1981, the latter rate is still unacceptable and forecasters predict a population of 125 million people by 1990. At the first press conference of the newly elected president in the early 1980s, population control was made the top priority. The resultant plan called for mass contraception and sterilization programs, upgrading of women's roles, and the deployment of an army of health and family planning personnel with information and supplies. It is still too early to judge whether or not Bangladesh will succeed with its fertility reduction programs.

India   This was the first country to initiate a nationwide government program of fertility reduction.[10] Begun modestly in 1952 with research and the establishment of some urban clinics for family planning, government population policy expanded in the 1960s with mass education and dissemination of birth control devices. By the mid-1970s, however, questions were raised about the likelihood of continued progress in the face of the lack of strong economic development. In 1975, therefore, Prime Minister Indira Gandhi introduced substantial incentives as part of population-planning efforts. State and local agencies adopted highly coercive measures, including sterilization of some two thousand women against their will.[11] Mrs. Gandhi's government was defeated in 1977, and voluntary compliance was reintroduced by her successors.

The sterilization of women after four or five children is the principal method of birth control in India today. Women in this category constitute the focus of 85 percent of all Indian contraception efforts. At present only about one-fourth of all adults between fifteen and forty-nine practice any contraception techniques at all. The Indian government has set out to raise those figures to 60 percent by the year 2000.

Eastern Europe   It is important to note that not all government fertility policies are designed to lower these rates. Some policies are pronatalist in nature, that is, they are designed to increase fertility. Most noncommunist countries of the developed world have become concerned about diminished growth rates, but have not really sought legislative measures, perhaps because subreplacement levels of fertility appeared only in the last decade.

In the early 1960s while the countries of Western Europe were in the midst of a baby boom communist Eastern Europe was experiencing a drop in the birthrate, primarily because of liberal abortion practices. The Soviet Union reinstated abortion in 1955, and was soon followed by all Eastern European nations except Albania

(East Germany waited until 1972). A dramatic turnaround in population growth occurred, causing government officials to become concerned about the future labor supply in an expanding economy, and even to worry about committing "national demographic suicide."[12] Restrictions on abortion soon appeared in four countries —Romania's were the most dramatic—and most of the nine Eastern European countries introduced cash incentives for successful fertility efforts. These incentives included "lump-sum birth grants, paid maternity leave, monthly family and child-care allowances, and even low interest loans for newlyweds which are progressively written off with the birth of each child."[13]

The impact of these pronatalist policies was short-lived, however, and birthrates declined in the early 1980s. The reason for this drop, according to some observers, is that the result of such policies was earlier births of two children rather than family sizes of three and four children. The typical attitude of East European families—that two children represented an optimal number—was not changed by government incentives. The reasons for such attitudes in Eastern Europe are many. Equality of men and women in the work force coupled with the women's continual traditional responsibilities in the home are important factors. Limited housing opportunities and the high cost of consumer goods also contribute to the desire for smaller families. At this time family attitudes rather than official government policy seem to dominate fertility patterns in Eastern Europe.

The Soviet Union   The population of the Soviet Union was estimated at 270 million in mid-1982 and is growing at the rate of 0.8 percent a year, down from 1.9 percent thirty years ago.[14] The decline is particularly acute among the Russian or Slavic ethnic groups within the Soviet Union. For example, the Russian Republic, far and away the largest of fifteen republics that make up the Soviet Union, is averaging only 1.9 births per woman, and the other two Slavic republics, the Ukraine and Belorussia, are averaging only 2.0 births. On the other hand, the Central Asian republics have births per woman rates of up to 5.8.

Thus the population problem as perceived by the Soviet government is that the established dominant nationality, the Russian, is not growing in numbers as fast as the rest of the country and will, in fact, constitute less than half the Soviet population by the end of the century. Unlike countries cited in the previous case studies, the Soviet Union is attempting to increase its growth rate, particularly among its Slavic population.

This Soviet effort began in earnest in 1981 when a set of measures was announced that were designed to improve life for "families with children, newlyweds, the growing generation, and ... women."[15] Nine million rubles ($12.2 billion) were to be spent in five years for state aid to families with children. The specific programs are rather comprehensive, including lump sum grants of 50 rubles ($67.50 at the official exchange rate in July 1982) for first births and 100 rubles ($135) for second and third births. Previously, progressive birth grants began only with 20 rubles ($27) on the third birth and 65 rubles ($88) for fourth births. Except for the allowances of single mothers, no plans were announced for increasing the present small monthly child allowance (4 rubles a month for third and "higher-order" children until age five; 12 rubles a month for all children until age eight in very-low-income families). For unmarried mothers, already receiving an extra 5 to 10 rubles a month per child up to the age of twelve, the plan called for an increase in the monthly child allowance. Maternity leave for working mothers, hitherto granted without pay for a year following a child's birth, is now partially paid for a year after birth. This began in November 1981 at 50 rubles a month for women in Siberia and the Far Eastern sectors of the low-fertility Russian Republic (where the subsidy amounts to 30 percent of the average monthly wage) and was extended by 1983 to 35 rubles a month to women in other regions (where the subsidy ranges from 21 percent to 25 percent of the average wage). Further extensions are planned.

Other fertility-stimulating measures have been authorized or proposed. More opportunities are provided for mothers to work part-time (part-time jobs accounted for only 2.5 percent of employment in 1974). Improved working conditions for women were instituted as they were barred from 460 occupations involving heavy or hazardous work—"the best-paying jobs for women with few skills".[16] These measures are also to include more and better day-care facilities for preschool children; improved housing conditions; increased leisure time for women-mothers (three extra annual leave days for mothers of two or more children under twelve); and "effective measures to ease housework." In any case, it remains to be seen how effective these Soviet pronatalist measures will be.

As these many examples show, in the last decade governments have not been reluctant to intervene in the fertility process. This lack of reluctance has been a function in part of the recognition that population dynamics do, in fact, have nonpopulation consequences. The global family of nations affirmed the right of governmental intervention during the 1974 World Population Conference, and individual nations have acted accordingly. But it remains to be seen what long-term effect such intervention will have on fertility.

National Migration Policies

We now turn our attention to national migration policies—both immigration (people entering a place) and emigration (people leaving a place). The 1984 Mexico City Declaration addresses migration in some detail, although the extent to which national governments are adhering and will adhere to such guidelines remains uncertain. With regard to internal migration, a number of principles are elaborated. First, government distribution policies should emphasize incentives rather than migration controls that are likely to infringe on human rights. Countries are urged to develop medium-sized towns and to reduce the inequities between cities and rural areas. Finally, a number of services to assist present and potential migrants are recommended.

With respect to international migration, the Mexico City document reaffirms the twelve recommendations found in the 1974 Plan of Action. Among the most important provisions are: voluntary international movement is to be facilitated without racial considerations; human rights considerations and other provisions of UN principles are to be operative; and treatment of migrant workers should be free of discrimination.

By the time of the Mexico City Declaration it became clear that certain types of migration need special attention. These include documented migrant workers, undocumented migrant workers, and refugees. The Mexico City recommendations affirm that documented workers should receive their full human rights, equality of opportunity and treatment for themselves and family, normalization of family life, and widespread information regarding these and other legal matters.

Undocumented workers present a particularly vexing problem because they are especially vulnerable to abuse. Again, the recommendations relating to them focus almost entirely on human rights concerns. The Mexico City conference also emphasized the vulnerability of refugees, alluded to international agreements that had been signed in 1951 and 1967, and urged governments to find durable solutions.

What is the record of national governments regarding refugees? A recent UN study addressing this question found that few countries

desire permanent immigration for demographic reasons.[17] Those
that encourage immigration do so because they equate size with
national security (as in Israel) or national identity (in the case of
Argentina), or because they want a different distribution of
population.

The United States is the only country that has adopted numerical limits to control immigration, doing so in 1921. At present,
270,000 migrants (excluding refugees who are treated separately)
may be admitted annually, with a limit of 20,000 from any single
country. Legislation during the last two decades has aimed at eliminating discrimination toward any particular group, although in practice old policies are hard to break. Family reunification is the cor-
nerstone of U.S. policy.

Unlike those of the United States, the immigration policies of
most other traditional receiving countries—Canada, New Zealand,
and Australia—tend to fluctuate more, as they are tied to economic conditions. Of course, certain classes of individuals are typically excluded: those with contagious diseases, criminals, the
insane, those likely to become public charges, and threats to national
security.

The picture is somewhat different among those countries that
are not the typical destinations for individuals seeking immigration.
There is little evidence that African governments—with the exception of South Africa—either seek or accept permanent immigrants.
Little government immigration policy can be found in Asia; most
action occurs for the sole purpose of creating a legal status in place
of a nonlegal one for long-standing residents. Israel desires increased
immigration and grants any person of Jewish faith the right of
immigration, but it no longer enjoys the success of earlier years. In
fact, there has been a rise in the emigration of Israeli nationals.
Most countries in Latin America desire certain kinds of immigration but are usually unable to attract such individuals, who would
rather migrate to a developed society. Argentina is perhaps the
best example of a country that has tied its destiny to successful
immigration policies.

Emigration policies differ in a number of ways. Countries tend to
encourage temporary rather than permanent emigration. However,
where there is significant emigration, it occurs because there are
either implicit policies or nonimplemented legal rules. Few African countries promote emigration, an exception being Rwanda
because of pressures on land usage. In Asia and the Middle East,
Pakistan, Korea, and Turkey have explicit policies to promote

emigration, while Jordan and Syria have encouraged it implicitly. In Latin America fourteen countries have significant levels of emigration, ten of which view it as being too high. El Salvador, on the other hand, encourages the emigration of its nationals. In Europe, both the Netherlands, for socioeconomic reasons, and Portugal, as a remedy for unemployment, have policies promoting emigration. In the former case the government provides financial assistance both enroute and after resettlement.

Within the communist bloc countries of Eastern Europe, there is much variation, from Hungary's flexible policies to East Germany's hard line. In East Germany, family reunification remains the principal motivation for those desiring emigration. The Soviet Union recently has allowed only three groups in large numbers to emigrate: Jews, Germans, and Armenians. A tightening of Soviet emigration policies and practices, however, suggests that the numbers are still not very large.

In sum, the four countries traditionally receiving immigrants —the United States, Canada, Australia, and New Zealand—have been accepting fewer than one million immigrants a year. Some Latin American countries, as well as Israel and South Africa, have selective policies for admitting permanent migrants, but the numbers have been less than desired. Israel and Argentina in fact have undesirably high levels of emigration in recent years. The two typical criteria for admission, family reunification or needed economic skills, result in the turning away of most who desire to emigrate. This in turn creates a situation where illegal immigration becomes a major problem, for the United States as well as for other countries. In recent years an increase in the number of refugees has meant added competition among emigrants for the limited number of spaces in the more desirable countries. In the United States, where refugees presumably do not compete for the 270,000 annual slots, the evidence suggests that when large numbers of refugees are admitted a corresponding drop occurs in slots reserved for nationals from the same region. We can expect that permanent immigration worldwide will be unlikely to increase, particularly to the traditional receiving countries.

Labor migration represents a different type of movement. With the decline in growth rates in Western Europe during this century, the labor shortage there was lessened by importing foreign workers. The policies of the European Economic Community since its creation in 1957 have resulted in a dramatic increase, particularly in the movement of workers from the poorer countries of the Mediter-

ranean basin. By 1973, fully one-seventh of the labor force in Western Europe consisted of labor migrants. However, the economic
recession of the last decade has resulted in a drop in the migration
of laborers.

Governments tend to adopt a low profile in policy-making in this
area, preferring to allow the private sector to determine foreign
labor needs. Among the Western European countries the French
government has taken a more active stance but without much
success. Governments of the developed world now typically focus
on managing the large pool of foreign manpower, particularly regarding how a major departure would affect the national economy. At
the same time, most governments have policies that encourage
workers to return home, thus easing the unemployment picture for
receiving nations. As the European economy brightens, however,
the cycle is likely to begin once again.

The movement of labor to the developing countries, particularly
to the oil-producing countries of the Middle East, has been a more
dramatic story during the last decade, although with a recent drop
in demand for oil from this region the flow of workers to the Middle
East has declined. A majority of labor migrants are from Asia, particularly India and Pakistan. More recently, dependents of workers
have been strongly discouraged from accompanying them. Government policies in the Middle East before the 1970s adopted a hands-
off policy, but the growing demand for workers led private firms to
adopt recruitment policies that still came under some government
control. Throughout the rest of the globe the typical government
policy has been bilateral, dealing with the exchange of laborers.
This model has been used repeatedly in western and southern Africa
and in Latin America.

Illegal migration represents still another type of international
movement. Obviously, because of restrictions on immigration, illegal movement occurs, but it is difficult to document the precise
numbers. The usual pattern is from the developing countries of
Asia, Africa, and Latin America to the developed world. But there is
also intraregional movement within the developing countries
themselves.

The United States has between four and six million illegal
migrants, by far the largest number in the world. The U.S. government has stepped up its efforts to stop the flow of illegal migrants,
while at the same time addressing the question of how to handle
those illegal aliens who have been in the country for a substantial
period of time. Progress appears to have been made on both fronts.

The pattern of periodically providing amnesty for long-residing immigrants has been a common response throughout the developed countries traditionally receiving migrants. Australia adopted such a policy on several occasions during the last decade, as did New Zealand and Canada. On the other hand, European countries have adopted a harsher attitude, perhaps because the numbers involved are lower.

Refugees present still another problem. The United Nations High Commissioner for Refugees (UNHCR) attempts to acquire voluntary repatriation. Usually this is achieved only when the refugee situation is a consequence of a natural rather than a man-made disaster. When repatriation is impossible, integration into the country of first asylum is the next step, particularly rural resettlement when possible. These principles seem sound, but refugees typically arrive en masse with their most basic human needs unmet. It is difficult for even the most developed of countries to engineer an adequate response. Witness how the United States handled the 130,000 Cuban asylum-seekers in 1980.

Clearly, the nature of the worldwide migration problem continues to grow as the global population increases and as individuals and groups become more strongly inclined to search far and wide for a sustainable quality of life. Indeed, as the developing world fights to provide adequately for its ballooning numbers, migration of any type as a solution for high numbers becomes increasingly attractive. Unless the world community deals with these issues, migration may well be *the* population problem of the twenty-first century.

9 Environment: Strategies for the Future

In chapter 5 we explored the many facets of the global environment issue, addressing six problem areas: pollution, climatic change, depletion of nonrenewable resources, loss of usable land (cropland, rangeland, forests), species extinction, and war. For each we described the nature of the current dilemma and how we arrived at such a state of affairs. We also examined a set of basic antecedents of these environmental problems. While there is generally less consensus about most of the effects of these factors, much agreement exists about what caused them. With or without certainty, however, we can still look to the future. In this chapter, we focus on a set of possible strategies and describe contemporary efforts to employ one of them by nations of the globe.

Approaches to the Future

Despite the pessimism brought on by the overwhelming nature of the problems and the difficulties of finding appropriate solutions, visionaries have not been deterred from thinking about the future and prescribing alternative conditions and strategies for a favorable outcome. Proposals for averting a possible future global catastrophe have been summed up by Marvin Soroos in a companion volume in this series.[1] It describes six approaches to cope with the future: international regimes, steady-state economics, centralized political authority, local self-reliance, global equity, and high technology.

International regimes

This approach is characterized by a loosely coordinated network of international organizations, multilateral treaties, institutions, conferences, and other arrangements, with varying degrees of support from national governments. This broad cadre of interested participants focusing on one global issue is termed an international regime. Many times a United Nations organization, often newly created, takes the lead among the network of actors, creates an action plan, monitors developments, educates interested parties, and prods official legislative bodies to action.

In the environment area many regimes come to mind. The law of the sea represents one such regime where a host of international organizations, multinational corporations, agencies of national governments, and other groups constitute such a regime. Within this context, one can even discern narrower regimes focusing on a particular area of concern within the law of the sea issue. For example, seabed exploration (or exploitation) was a major topic at the conference on the law of the sea which was concluded in 1982. The number of regime members for this issue numbered over a hundred: various members of national governments' bureaucracies (in the case of the United States, the Departments of Interior, Commerce, State, Defense, and Transportation), seventeen American multinationals as members of a U.S. advisory group, parallel groups from other nations, seven specific UN agencies that constituted an official group of experts, and many other international organizations.

A less specific strategy for establishing international regimes has been to organize global conferences to develop a focus for the creation of international regimes. This has become common in the years following Stockholm. Conferences have been held on a variety of issues and have in turn been the impetus either to initiate a new regime or to strengthen an existing one: for example, population (Bucharest, 1974 and Mexico City, 1984), food (Rome, 1974), women (Mexico City, 1975), human settlements (Vancouver, 1976), water (Mar del Plata, 1977), desertification (Nairobi, 1977), science and technology for development (Vienna, 1979), new and renewable sources of energy (Nairobi, 1981), the UN Law of the Sea Conference, which met in several places between 1958 and 1983, and a special session of UNEP's governing council in 1982. We will return later to case studies of environmental regimes in action but first, let us describe the remaining five approaches.

Steady-state economics

According to Soroos, steady-state economics represents an alternative to the widely accepted theories of economics that advocate maximizing growth. He alludes to the images of economist Kenneth Boulding who urged a transition from a "cowboy" to a "spaceman" economy, that is, from a notion of unlimited resources across a seemingly endless frontier to a concern for conservation of resources not unlike the limited provisions required by the closed system of a spaceship.[2]

Over a century earlier, John Stuart Mill first argued for steady-state economics and economists have sustained that argument into the contemporary era (led by Merman Daly).[3] Steady-state economists presume that the day of ecological reckoning can be delayed by moving away from the emphasis on maximizing extraction, production, and consumption, toward attempting to maintain a certain standard of living. But as Soroos points out, steady-state economics flies in the face of the long-established patterns of the normal growth model where even those at the bottom of the economic ladder benefit if their actual share of the economic pie declines. Without growth, the "have-nots" probably suffer disproportionately as unemployment and other problems increase. Proponents of steady-state economics reply that only growth requiring scarce resources or having adverse environmental impacts would be limited.

Central political authority

Many analysts believe that problems of the environment now exist because the human race, left to its own devices, has been unable to exercise proper restraint. This failure to respond properly, in the eyes of Garrett Hardin, is due to the tragedy of the global commons. The concept of the "commons" refers to the areas open to all in early village communities. Anyone with an animal herd could avail himself of the commons area. The "tragedy" of the commons stems from the tendency of each individual herder to continue to add to his own flock even though the eventual effect of all herders adding to their flocks would lead to the overgrazing and eventual exhaustion of the pasture (commons). The result of this overgrazing, of course, eventually leads to the death of everyone's flock. Translated to the international level, the global commons has been similarly abused as oceans have been overfished, resources have been extracted at an excessive rate by the privileged few, rivers and lakes have been polluted, and the oceans have served as the ultimate dumping ground.

What is needed to counteract the tragedy of the global commons is a strong, centralized world authority that will promote the common interests of the majority so that all benefit from the common heritage of mankind. Unlike limited government and maximum individual freedoms, a centralized political authority would curb the excesses of individuals who insist on excessive use of the planet's resources.

Robert Heilbroner, a cautious proponent of this strategy, argues that solutions to the problem may "be possible only under governments capable of rallying obedience more effectively than would be possible in a democratic society."[4] In short, he suggests that the political answer to the environment may lie in authoritarian rule: when taken to the highest level of organization, the answer lies in a powerful world government rather than a system of independent sovereign countries that cannot effect change beyond their own borders except by persuasion or force.

Local self-reliance

Instead of a centralized political authority, a move away from "big is better" might have the same desired result. Taking a cue from E. F. Schumacher's *Small is Beautiful*,[5] Soroos describes the movement to scale down large-scale modern industrial enterprises, replacing them with smaller, self-sustaining units that function "in tune with their environment." It may well be true that a strong central authority is needed to address the problems created by large complex societies. But it is not so with the "small is beautiful" approach with its focus on alternative and appropriate technologies that use rather than use up resources.

Global equity

Another strategy, although not a full-blown approach to solutions for the global environmental problem, argues that the inequities in the distribution of wealth between the developed and developing worlds have led to uneven development in which the "have" nations use resources at a disproportionately higher rate.

As Soroos suggests, in order to catch up the third world must find shortcuts to development. These include the burning of cheap, high-sulphur coal, the widespread use of pesticides harmful to the environment, massive land-clearing projects, and indiscriminate dumping of wastes. If both sides could agree to work together—the developed world helping its less fortunate neighbors and they in turn agreeing to pay the environmental price of development—then the global ecosystem might survive. More extreme proponents of global equity go further, arguing that only a total redistribution of wealth is the answer.

High technology

Other observers take a different position. They argue that science and technology have always provided answers for human problems, and that today's environmental crisis is no different. The key phrase is not "devising plans for living within what are currently perceived to be the natural limits of our environment, but rather transcending them by unleashing scientists and engineers to achieve technological breakthroughs that will make continuing growth possible indefinitely in the future."[6] Genetic engineering and space colonization are two examples of extreme proposals made by those advocating a high technology approach.

Dealing with the Future

Taken together, these six strategies are not mutually exclusive but rather have certain common elements. Upon further analysis, it is possible to combine the six into three distinct categories: high technology and global equity are similar in one sense: both really see no great change in patterns of absolute resource consumption. Technological solutions will allow continued growth, while global equity will spread the increased wealth much more evenly.

A second group of strategies is based on the concept of more stringent limits. Steady-state advocates adopt an economic approach to the setting of limits. Proponents of centralized authority argue that limits can be set only by a strong central political structure, perhaps even a world government. The strategy of local self-reliance represents what is essentially a social approach to setting limits.

Finally, unlike the other five, the international regimes approach represents a distinct category for a number of reasons. First, it is an incremental strategy that does not require major changes in the political, economic, and social structures despite its emphasis on the creation of networks. Countries give up bits and pieces of their sovereignty as the networks or regimes prove themselves to be workable mechanisms for resolving issues. When both representatives of national governments and private groups together recognize a problem and the need for solution, then the creation of appropriate processes and structures will follow. Success breeds success, both in the same issue area and in other areas. As we approach the end of the twentieth century, then, the concept of international regimes or networks represents the most likely course of action for future problem-solving.

Among these six strategies to cope with the future, global actors have tended to favor the international regimes approach. This approach best accommodates existing institutional structures while creating new frameworks to deal with pressing global issues such as the environment. In the case of the environment, an illustration of a highly specific international regime approach is provided by the United Nations Environmental Programme (UNEP), created at the 1972 Stockholm conference. UNEP was envisaged as a small unit of the UN Secretariat under the following guidelines:[7]

1. Environment is not another sector, but an interdisciplinary problem that must be considered in all sectoral activities.

2. No new institutions should be created with the sole responsibility for implementing environmental projects. Each UN agency should be responsible for the environmental aspects of its activities within its own field of competence.

3. A small entity (UNEP) should be created that would: (a) perform a "think-tank" function by producing innovative approaches and inspiring, motivating, and persuading already existing bodies to integrate the environmental perspective into their activities; (b) be a focal point for coordination of environmental activities in the UN system; (c) concentrate its professional competence in multisectoral areas that transcend the fields of competence of the sectoral organizations, such as monitoring oceans, human settlements, and deserts; (d) be nonoperational or, in other words, not carry out projects itself but delegate or encourage governments, member organizations of the UN, and nongovernmental organizations to do so.

4. In order to carry out its coordination role this new entity would have to "meddle" in the affairs of others, but should not divide responsibilities; rather it should promote interaction within the UN system and between the UN, other IGOs, governments, and NGOs, with the purpose of reaching joint definitions of goals and programs.

As you can observe, the strategy was to create a small group that "could motivate and stimulate the interaction of all the actors in such a way as to produce" policy.[8]

We have just seen how the international regimes approach represents the primary way in which the international community is addressing the wide array of environmental issues today. We now turn briefly to a discussion of the regime approach as it relates to the major environmental problems mentioned earlier.

Pollution

The first problem area is pollution: of the air, the land, and water. While the regime approach for ocean pollution is well established, the community of nations has been slower to respond to atmospheric pollution despite the growing evidence of the magnitude and scope of pollution of the air. The reasons are twofold. First is experience. Throughout the last thirty years we have witnessed a growing number of spectacular accidents involving oil spillage at sea. However, no comparable experience exists involving atmospheric pollution. Second is the extent of data available. Documentation of disastrous effects on the air has been produced more slowly, and international activity has focused on the preliminary steps of information gathering, global monitoring, and tests to demonstrate the link between atmospheric conditions and adverse environmental conditions, rather than on institutional responses to pollution itself. The international community has in fact done little to discourage transnational air pollution. There is a small body of international law which argues that nations shall be held liable for damage caused to the natural environments of other countries, and this responsibility was upheld at the Stockholm conference in 1972. Indeed, as noted earlier, the primary reason why the 1972 conference was called was because of concern about acid rain. There is little in international treaty law that directly addresses the question of transnational air pollution. The Limited Nuclear Test Ban Treaty of 1963 is the one exception. It is commonly viewed as an arms control treaty, but in reality it serves more as an environmental antipollution measure. In this treaty nations are prohibited from the testing of nuclear weapons in the atmosphere and in the ocean, and even underground if emissions from the blast are carried to another country.

Today acid rain continues to be considered the major atmospheric problem. Most international attention is focused on acquiring the necessary knowledge about its effects, through the efforts of UNEP's Global Environmental Monitoring System and the World Meteorological Organization's World Climate Program. In 1977 these organizations began to measure levels of sulfur, nitrogen, and specifically acid rain through a cooperative program in Europe. Fifty monitoring stations in eighteen countries are now operating.[9] Thirty-three countries in the UN Economic Commission for Europe—which includes Western Europe, Eastern Europe, Canada, and the United States—agreed in 1979 that long-range transport of acid rain should be limited, and eventually should be stopped. However, this action carries no legal sanctions.[10]

The binding actions that exist at present have been taken at the national level, the source of the acid rain.[11] The United States, West Germany, and the Netherlands have taken concrete steps. Today new power plants in those countries must employ scrubbers to reduce sulfur dioxide, and West Germany has tightened controls at existing plants that emit sulfur dioxide. Nitrogen oxide is more difficult to control, but Japan has attempted major steps to combat this problem.

Bilateral and multilateral agreements also have begun to characterize the regime approach to acid rain.[12] In March 1984 the "30 percent club" was created by nine European countries and Canada. So named because of their commitment to reduce sulfur dioxide emissions by at least 30 percent during the next decade, the 30 percent club had been joined by seven other nations by late 1984, and pressure is being applied on other polluting nations to join. Some members of the club have set goals higher than 30 percent; France, West Germany, Canada, and Norway adopted a figure of 50 percent. Once researchers acquire the necessary knowledge about the effects of acid rain, enough evidence might exist to prod the global community to take more substantial action in combating its adverse consequences.

The issue of ozone layer depletion received much more attention than acid rain did a decade ago, but the evidence of this problem is not yet convincing. As a consequence, action has been slow in coming.[13] At the urgency of the United States a group of experts prepared a world plan of action in 1977. Under it a coordinating committee was established by UNEP that subsequently has produced a yearly assessment of ozone layer depletion and its impact. Although the principal actions to control ozone layer emissions have been undertaken by national governments, particularly those belonging to the European Economic Community, the work of the committee has nonetheless been useful in raising public awareness. Sweden has called for an international convention to reduce the release of fluorocarbons into the atmosphere, an idea that UNEP has endorsed. However, until binding legislation is passed, governments are not required to take note of the concerns expressed in the scientific community.

Why has the international regime approach not resulted in more pronounced advances in dealing with transnational atmospheric pollution? Soroos documents a number of reasons in his study of environment policy-making.[14] The primary reason is that the relationship between polluting states and those countries downwind who receive the pollutants is often not reciprocal. Consequently, polluting countries have little incentive for absorbing the economic cost of controlling emission when those downwind are the only beneficiaries. Another reason is that given both the variability of wind currents and the intermingling of pollutants, it has been difficult to prove that environmental damage in one country is a consequence of pollution from another. A good case in point is the disagreement between the United States and Canada about who is to blame for the acid rain that is damaging both countries.

Among the more impressive success stories has been the national and international response to what was a major polluter of the land just two decades ago, the pesticide known as DDT. With the impetus of the publication of Rachel Carson's *Silent Spring* in the 1960s, the public became aware of the dangers of DDT. DDT was discussed at length at the Stockholm conference, although it was mentioned only by implication among the conference's set of recommendations.

Since that conference, the international regime approach has netted some results. National data about DDT are collected and published under UNEP's International Registry of Potentially Toxic Chemicals. The World Health Organization's International Program on Chemical Safety is studying the effects of different doses of DDT on humans. Twenty-one countries are participating in UNEP's monitoring of 343 food items for 34 pollutants, among them DDT.

At the national level, many countries in the developed world have banned DDT, while many more have reduced the number of permissible uses for it. The issue of DDT has subsided in the years since the Stockholm conference largely as a consequence of these actions but also because insects have developed a resistance to it. By the end of the 1970s there were 800 million cases of malaria worldwide but primarily in the developing countries caused by DDT-resistant strains of malaria-carrying mosquitoes.[15]

In contrast to the level of progress in dealing with atmospheric pollution, the international community has made great strides in addressing the problem of ocean pollution. The obvious reason, of course, is that laws relating to the ocean have a longer history than those relating to the atmosphere. Moreover, it is far easier to pinpoint the sources of ocean pollution. In other words, the international ocean regime is much more established. Since the time when man first began to use the ocean, nations have attempted to monitor and control the uses to which the oceans are put. Regulation of ocean pollution, however, is of a much more recent origin. International law provided few rules. This was primarily due to the widespread belief that using the oceans as the ultimate dumping ground presented no harmful consequences. As evidence mounted that shipping, dumping, and seabed and land activities all led to marine pollution, the international community adjusted its position.

The primary vehicle for addressing ocean pollution has been the vast network of treaties adopted since 1954. These include bilateral, regional, and general multilateral treaties as well as those embodied in the Law of the Sea Convention.[16] Some half-dozen focus on pollution from ships while one addresses dumping. No general multilateral treaties deal with pollution from either land-based sources or seabed activities. Those treaties relating to pollution from ships have been made under the leadership of the International Maritime Organization (IMO).

At the regional level, treaties have been adopted for the Baltic, Mediterranean, west Africa, Arabian/Persian Gulf and the Gulf of Oman, and the Red Sea and Gulf of Aden. With the exception of the Baltic Convention, UNEP's Regional Seas Programme has been instrumental in laying the groundwork and providing a common treaty framework. The Caribbean, southeast Pacific, and South Asia areas are expected soon to follow. A number of ad hoc agreements characterize the northeast Atlantic and the North Sea areas. The four Nordic countries—Denmark, Norway, Sweden, and Finland—have made two agreements on pollution, while France, Italy, and Monaco have adopted an agreement to protect their adjacent waters. In addition to general treaties, there are also many agreements dealing with more specialized problems of the marine environment. These efforts culminated in 1973 in MARPOL 73, an international convention for the prevention of pollution from ships. This new treaty designates special areas considered to be particularly vulnerable to pollution, where all oil discharges would be prohibited. These include the Mediterranean, Baltic, Red, and Black seas, the Persian Gulf, and the Gulf of Oman. Limits would be placed outside these areas on the amount of oil allowed to be discharged. Regulations also address procedures and equipment for reducing oil pollution.

Other treaties regulating the movement of ships require ship-owner insurance or other guarantees, place strict liability for pollution damage on the ship's owner, establish a fund to compensate pollution victims, prescribe a comprehensive set of design measures for safety, and address the dangers of explosions.[17]

Since the dangers of pollution were recognized, the international regime for ocean pollution has been rapidly developing, although some international efforts remain to be pursued.[18] Some treaties have not come into force and thus made a part of international law because enough countries have not yet ratified them. Better observance and enforcement of existing treaties must also occur. Nonetheless, the international regime in this area may serve as a model for addressing other problems.

In addition to a concentration on the oceans, international activity has also addressed problems with freshwater pollution. In fact, the United Nations has designated the 1980s the "Drinking Water and Sanitation Decade." The issue was also an important one at the Stockholm conference, which included seven recommendations in water management. This was followed by the UN Water Conference in 1977, which placed water squarely on the global agenda.

About a hundred countries contribute to UNESCO's International Hydrological Program, and 150 to the World Meteorological Organization's Operational Hydrological Program.[19] A joint monitoring system operated by WHO, UNEP, and UNESCO is now in operation, with data supplied by a substantial number of countries. Although the regime network is young, much hope exists for the future.

Climatic change

Efforts to address the problem of climatic change, particularly regarding the carbon dioxide level, have focused primarily on acquiring information about the processes involved. The World Meteorological Organization initiated the World Climate Program in 1979 with the aim of determining to what extent climatic change can be predicted and how the human race influences climate. As a consequence, 109 regional monitoring stations in seventy-one countries are now checking carbon dioxide levels.[20] Seventy more stations in sixteen countries are expected to be brought into service within the next decade. Several international conferences on climate and carbon dioxide were held in the decade since Stockholm. The most important of these, the World Climate Conference in 1979, concluded that carbon dioxide was the most urgent problem facing the nations of the globe today. The World Climate Programme represents a start, but the regime must be dramatically extended if the problem is to be adequately addressed.

Loss of nonrenewable resources

In contrast to many other environmental areas, the record in reducing the consumption level of nonrenewable fossil fuels has shown significant improvement. As a consequence of the energy crises of 1973 and 1977, there was an overall reduction in demand among the major oil consumers in the West. This reduction reflected a number of factors: slowing economic growth, increases in domestic inventories, less reliance on imported oil, and conservation. The decline in consumption, spurred largely by rising energy costs, provided an incentive for conservation and a search for alternative energy sources. It is now clear that there is a major turn away from oil as the principal energy resource. Unfortunately, this move is likely to take some time, and market forces will continue to rule the outcome. The transition from oil may differ from the earlier transition of coal to oil because it is being pushed by relative scarcity rather than being pulled by a more attractive resource. Nonetheless, a different but equally important factor may exist that is still a function of the resource. That factor is the relative cost of the alternatives. Countries that are major resource-users have made far fewer strides in cutting back on the pattern of usage for other nonrenewable resources. This is even true for resources for which the technology of extraction currently exists.

The UN held a Conference on New and Renewable Sources of Energy in Nairobi in 1981. A number of recommendations emerged, most of them counter to the interests of national governments. National governments tend to focus on reliability of supply, primarily for national security considerations, while the global community looks to an equitable distribution of what many believe to be the common heritage of mankind.

Where the technology does not exist, as in the case of the minerals on the bottom of the deep seabed, the international community is attempting to develop a more rational pattern of resource usage. This is particularly evident in the international ocean regime's attempt during the last two decades to counteract national encroachment, which began in earnest in 1945. Then U.S. President Harry Truman proclaimed national sovereignty for that nation's continental shelf, including the seabed resources. This "right" was subsequently embraced by most other coastal states. These countries were simply acting in the true spirit of the common heritage of the ocean, but they interpreted it to mean that the ocean bed was exploitable by those having the capability and inclination to do so.

For this and other reasons the UN held a series of law-of-the-sea conferences—known as United Nations Conference on the Law of the Sea (UNCLOS) I, II, and III—from 1958 until 1982. UNCLOS I produced an agreement on a coastal state's right of sovereignty for the resources on the continental shelf, that became effective in 1964. No progress was made on the deep sea resources issue in either UNCLOS I or II, however.

In 1969 the UN General Assembly took the first significant step in dealing with the deep sea resources by passing a resolution that:[21]

1 . . . acknowledged developing technology [that] was making the seabed accessible for economic exploration and exploitation.

2 . . . affirmed that the seabed is to be used only for peaceful purposes and its resources used for the benefit of all mankind (concept of common heritage of mankind).

3 . . . requested the secretary general to prepare a study on establishing an international regime to regulate the exploration and exploitation of the seabed. It also declared that all states should refrain from all activities of exploiting the seabed beyond the limits of national jurisdiction and that no claims to the seabed and its resources will be recognized.

Another General Assembly resolution in 1970 directed the secretary-general to study the issues relating to seabed mining, particularly as it affected the economic condition of developing and landlocked countries. The resolution also reaffirmed the common heritage principle.

UNCLOS III (1973–82) was a different story, however. It created an International Seabed Authority (ISA) patterned after the UN structure; a mining company called the Enterprise; a set of licensing, production, and price controls; and the mandatory transfer of technology. The ISA would operate on the one-state, one-vote principle, and would have control of who mined how much of which resource when and under what arrangements. The United States, as the country possessing most of the requisite technology, nonetheless was not guaranteed a seat on the ISA's council. For this and other reasons, the principal one being opposition to the ISA itself, the United States joined three other countries (Turkey, Venezuela, and Israel) in opposing the final treaty. But 130 countries signed the measure with 17 abstentions.[22]

Figure 9.1   Seabed regime network map. Source: Adapted with
modifications from Chadwick F. Alger, "Strategies for Increasing
Participation in Global Networks," paper prepared for the International
Studies Association Midwest convention in Columbus, Ohio,
November 6, 1981.

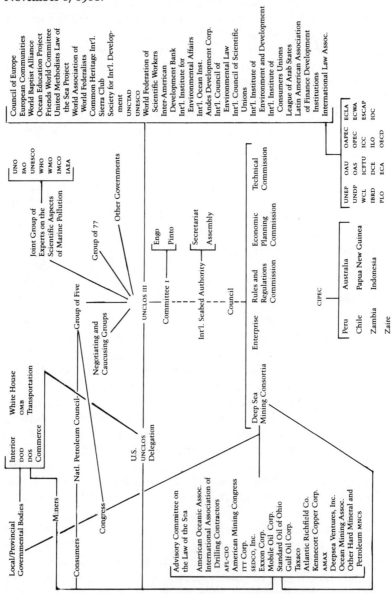

The complex nature of the deep sea mining regime can be seen by an analysis of both the formal negotiations of UNCLOS III and the informal discussions during the conference. In addition to representatives of national governments and international governmental organizations (IGOS), participants include many nongovernmental actors such as multinational corporations. Seminars were hosted by these groups, in one instance attended by 100 delegates and experts.[23] The regime also includes a wide range of actors from within various national governments, each representing a different domestic constituency.[24] One scholar has presented a schema of many (but not all) members of this regime in attendance at the conference. This diagram (figure 9.1) shows only part of the overall picture, but it gives a vivid portrayal of how the regime approach is being utilized to address global problems.

Loss of cropland, rangeland, and forest

In this area the response of the international community has been slow. Three tropical forests in West Africa are being monitored by UNEP, while that organization, UNESCO, and the Food and Agriculture Organization (FAO) have published a series of information reports. UNEP has held a series of meetings of experts to draft a plan of action but this has met political opposition from nations with extensive tropical forests that wish to protect their sovereignty over the forests.

The story is somewhat different with respect to desertification. As the Stockholm conference was being held, a major drought was also occurring in the Sahel region of Africa, in the path of the encroaching Sahara desert, and this brought the issue of desertification to the forefront. A UN conference on the subject was held in Nairobi in 1977, which drafted a plan of action. While consciousness was raised at Nairobi, however, neither the plan of action nor its promises have been carried out. A UN special account was formed to fight desertification but very little has been received. One group estimated that $2.4 billion would have to be spent annually over the next twenty years in order to carry out a plan of stopping desertification.

As one author has summarized: "A sorry tale. One of the world's major environmental issues was ignored at Stockholm, picked up five years later at Nairobi, and then allowed to drift back toward obscurity."[25] While this comment may be overly pessimistic, the fact remains that national governments do not give desertification programs high priority, cooperate with the UN system, or finance the effort in an adequate manner. The situation is no better with respect to cropland or forests.

Species extinction

Where once the international community accepted a nation's sovereignty over resources — living or inanimate — within its own boundaries, the prevalent view is that the common heritage of mankind prevails even if every member of a species is found within one country.[26] The government of that country thus has a unique responsibility to protect such endangered species, no matter how difficult. One author cites this example of the issues involved:[27]

> A Tanzanian delegate to a recent conference questioned whether it was right for the world to say to his country that it must guarantee the survival of these parks even if Tanzanians must do without adequate food, clothing, health, or education. He suggested, further, that if the international community is so strongly interested in preventing the extinction of the species of his country, then it should be willing to share in the economic cost of preservation.

Whether the international community was willing to share or not, this principle of national responsibility was adopted at the 1973 UNESCO Convention for the Protection of the World Cultural and Natural Heritage that established the World Heritage Trust to preserve those things of "universal value."

A major step was also taken in 1973 with the Convention on International Trade in Endangered Species of Wild Fauna and Flora (CITES). Having a current membership of close to seventy nations, CITES commits the signatories to refrain from all commercial trade in 449 species now designated as most endangered and to restrict trade in about 200 other species termed less endangered.[28] Obligations exist for both exporting and importing countries. Although fewer than half of the nations of the globe have signed the agreement, progress is being made. Consider this description of the implementation of the agreement:[29]

> A further mark of the convention's progress is that offenders are increasingly being arrested and fined (and even occasionally gaoled [jailed]). Fines, though, remain absurdly light in relation to profits, and on occasions prosecution still has to be brought by some

private body because the police consider the matter beneath their attention. In the USA, in November 1978, three companies were fined a total of $87,500 for shipping 2,500 alligator skins to tanneries in France. This may seem a large amount, but the shop value of that quantity of skins is $1,000,000, and one of the men involved had already received $140,000 from sales. In Hong Kong, in January 1979, a magistrate imposed the maximum fine of $1,000 (plus $400 costs) on the Hong Kong Fur Factory Ltd. for smuggling 319 cheetah skins from Ethiopia. The magistrate commented that the fine was quite inadequate in relation to the value of the cheetah skins, which were estimated by the fur factory to be worth $40,000 but more objectively valued at 25 times that figure.

Another strategy in dealing with this problem is to focus not on the species itself but on the habitat in which the species resides. During the 1970s a number of such multilateral agreements were signed by nations of the globe.

A good example of how cooperation among a group of nations culminated in a successful multilateral agreement is the story of the polar bear.[30] In 1965 scientists from the five circumpolar nations —the United States, Canada, Denmark (representing its then-province Greenland), Norway, and the Soviet Union—pooled their knowledge about polar bears. One alarming fact to emerge was that they were in danger of extinction in ten years. The countries contributed scientists to a Polar Bear Specialist Group, organized by the International Union for Conservation of Nature and Natural Resources.

Further research confirmed the earlier fears about extinction, and all Arctic nations were urged to protect the polar bear. In 1973 the five nations agreed to prohibit hunting of polar bears throughout the Arctic, with one minor exception of those few people who traditionally lived off polar bear hunting (and they were forced to use traditional weapons and techniques). Recent evidence suggests that the moratorium of the last decade has worked; the polar bear population apparently has doubled during that time.

Another excellent case is the story of whales.[31] The International Whaling Commission (iwc) was established in 1946 to regulate the catching of whales. It began to set quotas but these proved inadequate, and the whale population in most species continued to decline into the 1960s. Some argued that the iwc was dominated by commercial whaling interests. Whether or not that is true, there

Table 9.1   Principal international arms regulation or disarmament agreements currently in force.

Title of agreement	Signed	Entered into force	Number of states party[a]
Protocol for the Prohibition of the Use in War of Asphyxiating, Poisonous or Other Gases, and of Bacteriological Methods of Warfare	1925	1928	96
The Antarctic (de-militarization) Treaty	1959	1961	20
Treaty Banning Nuclear Weapon Tests in the Atmosphere, in Outer Space and Under Water	1963	1963	111
Treaty on Principles Governing the Activities of States in the Exploration and use of Outer Space, including the Moon and Other Celestial Bodies	1967	1967	80
Treaty for the Prohibition of Nuclear Weapons in Latin America	1967	1968	27
Treaty on the Non-Proliferation of Nuclear Weapons	1968	1970	111
Treaty on the Prohibition of the Emplacement of Nuclear Weapons and Other Weapons of Mass Destruction on the Sea Bed and the Ocean Floor and in the Subsoil Thereof	1971	1972	68
Convention on the Prohibition of the Development, Production and Stock-piling of Bacteriological (Biological) and Toxin Weapons and on Their Destruction	1972	1975	87
U.S.-Soviet Treaty on the Limitation of Anti-Ballistic Missile Systems	1972	1972	2
Convention on the Prohibition of Military or Any Other Hostile Use of Environmental Modification Techniques	1977	1978	27

[a]As of 31 December 1979.
Source: Martin W. Holdgate, Mohammed Kassas, and Gilbert F. White, eds., *The World Environment 1972–1982: A Report by the United Nations Environment Programme* (Dublin: Tycooly International, 1982), p. 614.

were two apparent problems. There were no separate quotas for each species nor was there any quota system among countries. The principle of the tragedy of the global commons seemed to apply as nations sought a variety of ways to acquire the largest catch as quickly as possible.

In 1970 the United States issued a ban on whaling and its products. At the same time the IWC began to introduce stricter regulations, including the lowering of allowable catch. The quota adopted in 1974 was based on the principle of the maximum sustainable yield for each species of whale.

The story has been a successful one although the actions of pirate whalers based in countries that have not joined the IWC did create some problems, as have the actions of Japan and the Soviet Union, which repeatedly violate IWC dictates.

War

The final environmental issue discussed earlier is war: consequences of current and past wars, consequences of preparations for war, and hazards of future war. Unlike the other environmental issues, war is one problem which has occupied the minds of world leaders for centuries. Much of the emphasis, however, has been on increasing the consequences of war for one's enemies. Thus larger armies and navies have been built, and research and development strategies have been adopted to create weapons with greater destructive capacity.

But even before the nuclear age, the international community sought to move away from the pursuit of mass destruction. Agreements were made to limit: (1) the numbers of weapons through institution of ceilings, freezes, or reductions; (2) the kinds of weapons during war, production, or testing; (3) the spread of weapons of certain kinds or to certain regions; (4) the conduct of war (the rules of war); (5) reducing tensions and building confidence by improving crisis communication and defusing areas of possible confrontation.[32]

Nuclear weapons, as demonstrated in Japan in the closing days of World War II, brought a new urgency to the effort. The postwar era has heard discussion about controlling weapons, although many observers are disappointed at the few successes. As the world entered the 1980s ten agreements were in force and are given in table 9.1. Others await ratification or are under negotiation at this time. Clearly an international regime for arms control has been created, involving virtually the entire world. The basic problem, of course, is that arms control, unlike some other environmental issues, goes immediately to the core of national security. Since the primary goal of a nation is its physical security, nations venture slowly, perhaps more slowly than in other areas, into making agreements. But with or without agreements, talking continues in both the multilateral and bilateral arenas.

The strategy of international regimes represents the preferred approach to the future environment, at least as evidenced by present behavior. Nations are willing to take incremental steps toward giving up pieces of their sovereignty to address an issue. Perhaps at this juncture of the human race, that is our best hope. It may be our only hope in the near future and it just might work. Should the consequences of environmental degradation continue to worsen, it remains to be seen whether or not the international community is willing to opt for a more radical strategy.

Part IV
Linkages and Future Prospects

In the concluding chapter, constituting Part IV, we look at how professional observers predict the future as it relates to the four global issues in this study. The emphasis is on a number of global models developed by these futurists.

10 The Future in an Interdependent World

> The interdependencies among peoples and nations, over time and space, are far greater than commonly imagined: actions taken at one time in one part of the world have far-reaching consequences that are often difficult to anticipate intuitively and are probably impossible to predict (totally, precisely, perhaps at all) even with computer models.[1]

This statement by the U.S. Office of Technology Assessment represents one of several common findings of five major global modeling studies conducted in the last fifteen years that we will discuss in this chapter.[2] As such, it has set the tone for this text. In this final chapter we will describe the nature of "the interdependencies among peoples and nations" and their effects on the new world agenda of global issues. In parts II and III of this text each chapter focused on a separate issue, but it was constantly evident, at least implicitly, that each issue was closely tied to an array of other factors drawn from outside its domain. Food, energy, population, and environment are all related and the linkages among them help to define the dimensions of each issue. Now we turn our attention to these linkages. Taking our cue from the five global models mentioned above and from other analyses of the future, we will summarize where the world may be heading, utilizing a series of alternative assumptions or differing scenarios.

Before examining each of our four global issues in some detail, we turn to the five global models' efforts to provide a comprehensive picture of the world of the future. A model is intended as a replica of reality. In this case, a *global* model, the replica is a computerized mathematical simulation of the world's physical, economic, and political systems. It represents a useful way of dealing with a large amount of information under a set of consistent assumptions.

Table 10.1 Five global models.

Model	Date	Historical base period	Projection time horizon	Geographical regions	Alternative scenarios[a]
World 3	1972	1900–70	2100	1 (global)	11
World Integrated Model (WIM)	1974	1950–75	2025	10 (later 14)	17
Latin American World Model (LAWM)	1976	1960–70	2060	4 (later 15)	7
United Nations Input-Output World Model (UNIOWM)	1977	1970[b]	2000	15 (3 blocs)	13
Global 2000	1980	Not consistent	2000	5 to 28 (not consistent)	12

[a]Number of computer runs, sensitivity tests, or policy scenarios examined by Office of Technology Assessment in the text of appendixes of this report.
[b]System structure and behavior in 1970 were verified through comparison with cross-sectional data dating back to 1955 or 1960.
Source: Office of Technology Assessment, *Global Models, World Futures and Public Policy*. (Washington, D.C.: Government Printing Office, 1982), p. 3.

As a tool of analysis, each model is used to study the interactions and future implications of past events and current trends. The past (and present) is often thought of as the best predictor of the future. We have seen, however, that governments make policy in an attempt to intervene and alter predicted outcomes perceived to be unfavorable. Without such policy intervention, the projected trends may yield results that are unacceptable to policy makers and average citizens alike. Thus a global model, having built into it the presumed linkages across the issues, evaluates the likely impact of various policy options. Table 10.1 provides basic information about the five models.

General Findings

Although these models differ greatly with respect to their purposes, techniques, findings, projections, and prescriptions, they have drawn surprisingly similar conclusions about the present and future of the world. Let us describe briefly some of these. The most fundamental conclusion of these models is that population and its use of the physical capital of the globe cannot grow indefinitely on a finite planet without eventually causing widespread hunger and resource scarcities.[3] However, despite some popular beliefs or views, the authors of these global models suggest that there is no physical or technical reason why the basic human needs of individuals throughout the world cannot be met today and into the foreseeable future. Thus they point to factors other than physical limits as the cause of global problems. Primarily, their conclusion deals with the unequal distribution of resources as well as the consumption of them. It is not the absolute amount of a resource but the manner in which that resource is distributed geographically, and how (and by whom) it is used, that in the latter part of the twentieth century affect the ability of the global community to provide basic human needs. The models caution, however, that the absence of absolute physical limits does not necessarily imply that there are easy or practical solutions to the problems brought about by their physical, political, or economic accessibility.

The studies conclude in fact that the continuation of current trends is likely to result in growing environmental, economic, and political problems. They suggest that "business as usual" is not a "palatable" future course. This assumption is made despite the fact that these global modelers assume technological progress; indeed, they argue that technological advances are essential. Most important, however, no set of purely technical advances tested was sufficient to bring about a satisfactory outcome. The obvious implication of the inability of technological progress by itself to bring about the desired results is that such change must be accompanied by social, economic, and political shifts as well. In short, policy intervention and changing life-styles are two additional requirements for the creation of a satisfactory future.

What is the nature of these shifts in policy and life-style? The modelers do not answer that question; they assert only that the world's socioeconomic system will be in a period of transition over the next several decades and that it is likely to look quite different from the present one as a consequence. These modelers do, however, argue for immediate action since effective measures will likely be less costly now than later. Moreover, they argue that cooperative long-term approaches are likely to be more beneficial for everyone than competitive short-term approaches. They further caution that many existing plans and agreements, particularly those related to long-range international development programs, are based on assumptions that are inconsistent, either with other assumptions or with physical reality. Finally they argue that if dire *global* consequences occur, they will likely center on the problems of pollution and resource availability. Other kinds of problems will tend to manifest themselves in a much more dramatic and immediate fashion at the *regional* level, as in current food problems found in sub-Saharan Africa.

In short, there is a consensus that indefinite growth cannot continue, at least without adapting our socioeconomic political environment to account for such growth. Policy intervention is thus essential, with or without such growth, if the human race is to continue to enjoy the quality of life that its most fortunate members now enjoy. Some observers disagree with these generalizations, however. The late Herman Kahn, formerly chairman of the Hudson Institute, and Julian Simon, a university professor, are two individuals who have written and campaigned against the consensus suggested above. Argues Kahn:[4]

> the basic message is this: Except for temporary fluctuations caused by bad luck or poor management, the world need not worry about energy shortages or costs in the future. An energy abundance is probably the world's best insurance that the entire human population (even 15–20 billion) can be well cared for, at least physically, during the many centuries to come. . . . except for the occasional regional fluctuations caused by natural disaster, inappropriate policies or the misapplication of resources, the long-term prospect is for adequate food supplies. By "adequate" we mean both an increase in amount of food per capita and improving nutritional balance in the countries of the world currently deficient in either of these respects. Indeed, within two hundred years we anticipate that—if desired—it will be possible to increase world food consumption to the level of the United States today.

Julian Simon in his book *The Ultimate Resource* makes similar arguments. Simon asserts that while it may be true that increased population causes more problems, "in the long run the most important effect of population size and growth is the contribution of additional people to our stock of useful knowledge."[5] Increased population, in short, is a "bonus." Simon argues, "the more people, the more minds there are to discover new deposits and increase productivity."[6] He concludes his analysis of current trends this way:[7]

Is a rosy future guaranteed? Of course not. There always will be temporary shortages and resource problems where there are strife, political blundering, and natural calamities—that is, where there are people. But the natural world allows, and the developed world promotes through the marketplace, responses to human needs and shortages in such manner that one backward step leads to 1.0001 steps forward, or thereabouts. That's enough to keep us headed in a life-sustaining direction. The main fuel to speed our progress is our stock of knowledge, and the break is our lack of imagination. The ultimate resource is people—skilled, spirited, and hopeful people who will exert their wills and imaginations for their own benefit and so, inevitably, for the benefit of us all.

On closer examination, certainly Simon and perhaps Kahn are closer to the findings of the global models than it first appears or than they themselves have believed. Simon sees our largest weapon as people, and people make policy. People react or respond to problems with imagination and foresight, and they adjust to dislocations in the systems, on some occasions more easily than others, sometimes sooner rather than later. But adjustments have always occurred. Those societies that did not adjust have disappeared from the face of the earth.[8]

Future Projections

It is clear that policy intervention is likely to affect future levels of resources as well as the nature of accompanying problems. The above discussion has dwelled only on generalization about the capacity of the earth itself and of the human race residing there to provide answers. Let us now turn to a discussion of future alternatives for each of the four global issues discussed in this text.

Food

In general, one finds several alternative scenarios being projected for future food supplies. The most optimistic projections assume rapid economic growth, technological progress, decreased population growth, and continued large reserves of easily developed agricultural land. While regional projections vary greatly, global projections tend to be relatively similar, at least among the five world models considered in this chapter. For example, four of the five models predict that the world will have difficulty supplying food to some of its population during the next twenty years. This is a function of the assumption that there will be diminishing marginal returns to agricultural inputs and increased cost for land development as a consequence of a decrease in the amount of undeveloped land. There are, in short, agricultural limits that lead to this short-term projection.

Price projections vary far more than projections of food supply, and for poverty-stricken individuals the amount one has to pay for food influences the supply available. The models differ, however, on the nature of technical progress. One model assumes that most of the increase in agricultural production will come from more land under cultivation; another assumes increases in yield per acre; and still a third assumes an increase in both the amount of land under cultivation and the yield per acre.

Let us consider in greater detail the forecast in the *Global 2000 Report*, first mentioned in chapter 1.[9] This report offered three sets of projections: Alternative 1, a median projection assuming the continuation of current growth rates; Alternative 2, an optimistic projection assuming good weather, lower population growth, and higher per capita food growth; and Alternative 3, a pessimistic projection using the opposite assumptions. Perhaps unfortunately, a significant climatic change was not part of any of these alternative scenarios. Each of the three projections offered several important conclusions. Among these were the following:[10]

"The world has the capacity, both physical and economic, to produce enough food to meet substantial increase in demand through 2000. . . ." Having the capacity, however, does not ensure that it would be fully employed.

Near-record growth in demand is predicted, driven equally by growth in population in the less-developed countries and growing affluence in the industrialized countries. "The world's food sector must grow at near record rates simply to maintain the bench mark per capita consumption levels reported in the late 1960s and early 1970s."

As a concomitant to the high growth in food production, there will be increases in the resources committed to such production, that is, land under cultivation and the increased use of capital-intensive technology such as fertilizers and pesticides. "Land-man ratios decline throughout the projection period, however, and the productivity gains needed to keep up growth in production come at increasing real cost, particularly if sharp increases in petroleum prices are incorporated into the analysis."

These general conclusions may in fact hide a darker side of the trends predicted under each of the three alternative scenarios. In Alternative 3, the chronic scarcity scenario, the supply of food is substantial but more or less permanently insufficient to meet existing demand; therefore severe malnutrition will become a fact of life, at even worsening levels. In Alternative 2, world abundance produces an optimistic scenario, but that simply means that the food supply will remain above or at least equal to demand; therefore hunger and malnutrition disappear as significant food problems. In Alternative 1, the median scenario, some projection of the present pattern will continue, implying that chronic malnutrition will also continue (and even worsen in so-called poverty pockets of the developing world) with food prices varying according to the cyclical nature of the world harvest and policies adopted by individual governments. One author, Wallerstein, characterizes these three projected futures as a doomsday scenario (Alternative 3), a radical-breakthrough scenario (Alternative 2), and a muddling-through scenario (Alternative 1).[11] But what would have to happen in order for a radical breakthrough in the availability of food to emerge? Wallerstein suggests that either important new technological innovations, such as advances in nuclear fission or genetic alterations, must occur, or that a fundamental restructuring of the social and political fabric of societies will have to take place in the capitalist developed world. Since he believes that there are likely, at best, to be only marginal technological achievements, then the critical factor is a change in the way in which the global food system is structured.

The *Global 2000 Report* concludes with the following pessimistic prediction:

Agriculture is now and will continue to be based largely on depletable resources; at present these depletable resources . . . are being consumed, extinguished and eroded at rates that cannot be sustained indefinitely . . . for the foreseeable future, there is no end in sight to increasing population levels and to escalating needs for agricultural production . . . unless the pressures of these resources are addressed and resolved, at least in part before the year 2000, it appears virtually certain that the world's per capita food production will slow, stagnate, or even decline during the first half of the 21st century.[12]

Energy

Energy projections take into account future availability and price—in other words, the factors of supply and demand. The models under analysis in this chapter tend to include a finite resource base. The resulting prediction is that depletion will raise prices, slow industrial production, and dampen future economic growth. That is, there will be energy problems because there are energy constraints. As a consequence, the models conclude that there will be a short-term transition away from a dependence on the conventional finite sources of petroleum and natural gas, and that major decisions must be made concerning priorities among three future energy choices: coal, nuclear energy, or solar power. The models further predict that well into the next century coal, energy conservation, and conventional nuclear power may not be enough to sustain continued economic growth throughout the world. As a consequence, some additional energy sources—breeder reactors, fusion, and large-scale solar power—may be needed. Again, however, these alternatives would require changes in socioeconomic and political structures.[13] As suggested above, solar energy, rather than being the only source of energy, is quite likely to be used in addition to other sources and would have to be accompanied by a decline in the demand for energy, probably through energy conservation. Solar energy would also require a decentralized political situation. Energy decisions could not be made at the international or even national level. Rather it would be left to local units to decide the amount and nature of any emphasis on solar energy.

Nuclear energy on the other hand requires complex central decision-making. The start-up costs, moreover, as we have learned repeatedly in the last decade, are tremendous and are typically accompanied by a larger and more complex set of problems heretofore unanticipated.

Coal remains an abundant resource, but like petroleum it is not distributed in an equitable fashion throughout the globe. As we have learned from the actions of OPEC, when supply inelasticity exists (a few actors control the supply), problems can arise. In the case of coal, the United States, China, the Soviet Union, and even Australia might play the role in the twenty-first century that OPEC has played in the contemporary era. Environmental problems with coal are also substantial, since we do not yet have adequate pollution-control technology that would allow us to rely on coal as our major energy source.

In the most recent past the sense of urgency about energy issues raised in the 1970s has been replaced in the 1980s by talk of an "oil glut," suggesting that the energy crisis is over and that we are now once again in an era of plenty. But this is only a short-term phenomenon. There has been an overall reduction in demand among the major oil consumers in the West that reflects a number of factors: slowing economic growth, increases in domestic inventories, less reliance on imported oil, and conservation. The decline in consumption was spurred largely by rising energy costs, providing an incentive for conservation and a search for alternative energy sources. One way of observing the impact of such incentives is to note the marked changes that have taken place in the United States in the nature and performance of automobiles. There is some evidence, however, that such adjustments, while extending the profile of demand, have not altered its fundamental inelasticity — the availability of alternative products to meet consumer needs. Despite their increased efficiency, automobiles still run on petroleum products.

As we discussed earlier, the development of energy policies over the past decade has largely reflected considerations of costs. The energy crisis of the early 1970s emerged from short-term factors, economic and political, and occasioned short-term adjustments, also largely economic and political. These adjustments, not the emergence of long-term energy policies, have brought about fluctuations in the petroleum market. Many of the policies selected and supported were designed to alter supply and demand, primarily of petroleum sources.

The fluctuations of the past decade from the energy crisis to the currently projected oil glut have not substantially changed future global energy prospects for the long term. Trends do suggest a turn away from oil as the principal energy resource, and long-term projections support this movement, although there are disagreements about timing and relative distribution among the above-mentioned alternative sources. We do know that the transition is likely to take some time. Events seem to indicate that the pattern of petroleum usage can be extended by the kinds of adjustments that have taken place, particularly those that have occurred in the consumption sector—fuel-efficient automobiles, decentralized home heating, and other conservation measures. It also seems probable that market forces will continue to rule the outcome. Therefore, the kinds of fluctuations that have taken place recently may become the norm rather than the exception, and energy futures will indeed be dictated by the kind of successful commercialization that one or another energy resource acquires. A new resource will replace oil as the dominant source of energy when it becomes commercially more feasible. Feasibility includes not only the actual cost of the resource itself but also the cost of the entire system associated with it. Furthermore, the resource must be tested in the commercial arena not only against the oil that it is replacing but also against other alternative resources. The prospects for a change thus seem to favor slow, incremental adjustments dictated by market forces. In terms of the resource characteristics, the transition from oil may differ from previous transitions because it is being "pushed" by relative scarcity rather than being "pulled" by a more attractive resource. In the end, however, neither the finiteness nor the uneven pattern of distribution of the world's petroleum reserves has been greatly altered by anything that has occurred in the past decade.

Population

In addition to the five global models, three other analyses project future population. Their results are summarized in table 10.2. There is wide agreement in the population projections for the year 2000, the range being from a low of 5.8 billion to a high of 6.5 billion. The reason for this consistency is that we have relatively clear information about the number of reproductive-aged females between now and the year 2000. Our major uncertainty relates to the number of children that each will bear. At the global level, of course, migration does not affect the total number of people on this planet. Only fertility and mortality levels influence the population of the world as a whole. With respect to mortality, we are likely to see little significant change in the developed world unless, as we have seen, three major causes of death among the elderly—heart disease, strokes, and cancer—are severely limited by new discoveries of medical science. In the developing world the biggest change has been a drop in the infant mortality rate. We can expect this steady decline to continue, particularly into the next century.

Fertility is another matter. As described in chapter 8, fertility reduction programs have expanded dramatically in the developing world. China's success is likely to serve as an inspiration for other countries, and we can expect to find fertility rates declining throughout the third world. Thus, although we know the number of women of child-bearing age throughout the developing world, we must reserve judgment about the number of births to expect per woman.

Table 10.2   Comparison of population projections.

Projection source	Projection	Population in year 2000 (billions)
World 3	Standard run	About 6
World Integrated Model	Standard run	6.4
Latin American World Model	Standard run	6.4
United Nations	High	6.5
	Medium	6.2
	Low	5.9
U.S. Bureau of the Census	High	6.5
	Medium	6.2
	Low	5.8
CFSC	High	6.0
	Medium	5.9
	Low	5.8
World Bank	Standard	6.0
Harvard	Standard	5.9

Source: Office of Technology Assessment, *Global Models*, p. 3.

reserve judgment about the number of births to expect per woman. Government intervention, particularly regarding fertility, has therefore become an important influence on whether the lower or higher estimates for the year 2000 will be realized. If additional countries adopt family planning or population programs, if they are accepted readily by the general population—and we have too little experience with countries in Africa, for example, to know how likely this will be—then we may find the lower limits of population size being realized by the turn of the century.

Let us consider the projections contained in the *Global 2000 Report* by the U.S. Council on Environmental Quality and the Department of State. Three scenarios are used in this report, which draws heavily from figures produced by the U.S. Census Bureau. Depending on the assumptions made, this study suggests three future levels of population—high, medium, and low. Table 10.3 describes changes from 1975 to 2000, based on the medium projections. As you can observe, the medium prediction is for a population of 6.35 billion by the end of the century. Given successful fertility programs now in place, it is quite likely that actual population will be short even of this mid-range projection.

Table 10.3   High, medium, and low population projections.

	Total population (millions)		Net growth 1975 to 2000		Average annual growth rate (percent)
	1975	*2000*	*Millions*	*Percent*	
Medium series	4,090	6,351	2,261	55	1.8
High series	4,134	6,798	2,664	64	2.0
Low series	4,043	5,922	1,879	46	1.5

Source: U.S. Council on Environmental Quality and the Department of State, *The Global 2000 Report to the President* (Washington, D.C.: Government Printing Office, 1980), p. 10.

Environment

As the world's population increases, the need for food rises, and our conventional energy supply diminishes, further environmental degradation becomes likely. But beyond this generalization the reports of the five global models that we have examined do not focus much on environmental impacts. An exception is the *Global 2000 Report*. In addition to one major section devoted to environmental projections, this report focuses on other areas related to the environment as well, such as climate, water, forests, fuel minerals, and nonfuel minerals. It places a major emphasis on the impact of future trends on agriculture: "Perhaps the most serious environmental development will be an accelerating deterioration and loss of the resources essential for agriculture."[14] These effects include:

> soil erosion; loss of nutrients and compaction of soil; increase in salinization of both irrigated land and in water used for irrigation; loss of high-quality crop land to urban development; crop damage due to increased air and water pollution; extinction of local and wild crop strains needed by plant breeders for improving cultivated varieties; and more frequent and more severe regional water shortages—especially where energy and industrial developments compete for water supplies, or where forest losses are heavy and the earth can no longer absorb, store, and regulate the discharge of water.[15]

This quotation succinctly describes likely environmental consequences as we move into the twenty-first century with the corresponding impact on agricultural production. But the future of the environment affects the quality of life beyond agricultural production. It remains to be seen whether the fundamental global response —the international regimes approach—will be able to stem the tide of environmental degradation.

While many advocates of alternative futures for all of the issues we have addressed here suggest a variety of extreme approaches to problem-solving in the global arena, much of the international community has instead opted for a more incremental strategy, and international regimes support such a strategy. This is not surprising, given the absence of a hierarchy of authority in the international system. Nation-states are reluctant to give up their sovereignty too quickly, and do so only when confronted with a problem that is both challenging and requires the cooperation of other nation-states. We have tried to demonstrate in this text that the global problems of food, energy, population, and environment have such characteristics. The most fundamental change in the last several decades is the emergence of a wide consensus that these problems exist, and even a wide agreement about the nature of the problems. The international community has begun to act. If the prevailing instrument, international regimes, does not work, then we can expect to find more extreme strategies being faced by the global community. Until then we must place our trust in that path selected by governments throughout the globe.

Appendixes

In chapter 1 we outlined briefly a conceptual foundation. The four articles that make up the appendixes have been written by specialists in each aspect of that foundation. They go beyond the basic information provided in chapter 1 and describe in much greater detail the nature of the four components of the conceptual framework: actors, values, policy, and the future. These articles are condensed versions of larger work commissioned by the Global Issues Project and carried out by the four authors—Chadwick F. Alger, Robert S. Jordan, Richard W. Mansbach, and Dennis Pirages.

A   The Role of Actors in Global Issues
Robert S. Jordan

The struggle for power and influence among groups of human beings, characterized herein as "actors," did not, of course, originate with the emergence of the modern territorial state. Nor is the phenomenon of nationalism, so applauded in the nineteenth century and deplored in the twentieth, the only means of describing the tendency of human beings, when gathered in collectivities, to distinguish between "friends" and "enemies."

But human beings in communities everywhere—whether recognized as nations or states—have always had to strike an effective balance between the two seemingly opposing principles of authority and liberty. On the one hand, authority is necessary to maintain law and order within the community. On the other, human beings want some liberty to decide how they will live a life that offers more than the struggle for physical survival, either from the natural elements or from coercion. The methods that have been used to balance authority and liberty, and the values that sanction these means, make up the subject of study of government. Although no form of world government has yet emerged, this discussion of the role of actors in global issues indicates the directions in which contemporary international society is going in attempting to create some order and coherence out of the disorder of competing national states struggling for power and influence, which characterizes the latter half of the twentieth century.

At the national state level, the condition whereby the citizen gives his loyalty to a variety of groups is known by the term "multiple loyalties." Although the state demands primary allegiance, every citizen also has loyalties to other groups within the state. These loyalties can embrace the family, the church or other form of divine worship, the tribe or ethnic group, the trade union or professional society, or the political party. One of the reasons why there is international disorder is that there are elites in some societies, such as those in the armed forces, the church, the party (in a single-party state), or the tribe, that claim a loyalty that challenges the primary loyalty demanded of citizenship by the state.

This is because groups of people who are completely different have often been brought together by accidents of geography, military conquest, and local and external political rivalries. The likelihood that these various otherwise unassimilated groups will form themselves into a coherent nation-state can be determined by the extent to which they cooperate in common enterprises such as self-defense against external enemies, the acceptance of similar concepts of political authority and legitimacy, the development of interdependent agricultural and commercial communities, and collective religious worship. Another measure is the extent of intermarriage. But most important of all, different groups must accept a common future that binds them to each other.

It is precisely because in today's world the attempt to reconcile nations (ethnic groups) with states (defined territorially) is meeting with widespread resistance that an examination of the various actors involved in either helping or in hindering this process is appropriate to this book.

The State as International Actor

In the last quarter of this century we are witnessing how the long current of ancient tribal or ethnic hostilities has persisted even in Europe as well as elsewhere, and has continued to influence the very structure of present-day international relations. In fact, can we continue to use the term "international" to describe these relations? The impact of modern technology on warfare, on political and other forms of communication, on the movements and migrations of peoples, and on values and ideas, have created conditions in which the state, although still the dominant or rather the primary actor, is not the *only* actor of consequence on the international political stage.

The term *actor* signifies much more than simply the modern version of the territorial state as the primary force in the world. An examination of the various roles performed by the state (whether on behalf of or in response to public or nonpublic demands), reveals how complex this actor is. Such an examination also reveals how constrained the state is as it attempts to monopolize political power within its territory in its own interests. Preserving its territorial integrity and the legitimacy of its system of government, in the face of increasingly restless and demanding domestic nationalities or interest-groups (as the case may be), has become itself a major source of domestic tension that spills over into international conflict. This is why simply defining actors as groupings of people derived from the evolution of the state would seriously miss the point in our attempt to understand the major global issues facing mankind.

Furthermore, when we examine the global issues confronting mankind, it seems increasingly clear that their resolution to the benefit of all—and this may consist only of devising forms of damage control—means reliance on the efforts of intergovernmental organizations. This is especially true for the global issue of *energy*. OPEC, whose counterpart among the oil-consuming industrial states is the International Energy Agency, (IEA), has played a pivotal even if declining role. In the case of *population*, individuals make the crucial decisions that collectively add up to a global issue. Governments, and intergovernmental organizations such as the United Nations Fund for Population Activities (UNFPA), can help influence such decisions, of course, but domestic or international nongovernmental organizations such as religious or social welfare organizations can help shape attitudes toward reproduction and family planning, perhaps just as effectively.

Governments and intergovernmental organizations, together with domestic and international nongovernmental organizations, share a concern for the global issues of *environment* and *food*. It is true that states, at the regional and subregional levels as well as within their own territories, play a crucial role in coping with environmental degradation. But nonstate actors such as multinational corporations also are involved, especially as regards industrial pollution, as are various natural resource interest-groups dedicated to the preservation of animal or plant life.

Thus there are many forms of domestic organizations and international nongovernmental organizations that respond to the same global issues of concern to intergovernmental organizations. While the former set of actors tends to be single-issue or special-interest in character, states identify their roles as actors in so many different ways that no categorical listing of states according to respective global issues would suffice. For example, there is always the potential that the cohesiveness of the third-world Group of 77 will be weakened by other loyalties.

The range and variety of intergovernmental organizational activity devoted to global issues are thus much too great to delineate here, and they are growing by leaps and bounds. For example, before the creation of OPEC, development bank activities were largely confined to a few regional banks along with the World Bank Group (IBRD and affiliates); today there is a proliferation of development banks based on cultural affinity, political cohesiveness, geographical propinquity, and shared trade or economic needs. Consequently, the emerging "global village" is marked by diversifying and decentralizing tendencies as much as by the opposite trends—global centralization leading to world government is so remote a possibility in these pluralistic times that it cannot be considered even as a potential ultimate actor. As has been illustrated, one important reason is that the state, even though it remains central to the international political system, is increasingly often found to share its centrality with various nonstate international actors, most but not all of which are nongovernmental organizations, as well as continually being exposed to internal challenges to authority.

The proliferation of transnational activities by government officials also can contribute to citizen awareness of global issues. As a headline in a story about an international meeting of mayors of thirty-three cities from around the world put it: "Conference in Boston underscores fact that woes are universal while solutions are not."[1] In some states agrarian reform is viewed as an essential factor in solving the problems of burgeoning cities; in other states creating or reinforcing neighborhoods is viewed as the essential factor. In Mexico City, as another example, geological conditions have created tremendous problems as the population growth has become unchecked. In all states, urbanization is affecting the global issues of concern to us, and subsequently to our children.

According to the U.S. government report, *Global 2000 Report*, the average citizen, wherever located, may well look back to 1980 as better times. By the year 2000, the report speculates, another 2.35 billion people will have arrived on the planet; food production, although estimated to increase by 90 percent (faster than the population) will bring fouler water because of pesticides and will bring polluted air because of the increased use of energy (primarily coal). However, the food will be maldistributed, so that there will continue to be widespread chronic hunger, with resulting political instability and violence in the poorest two-thirds of the world. If the state cannot cope with these conditions, what other recourse is there?

Nonstate International Actors

If the analysis of the state as an actor in global issues appears complex, the analysis of nonstate international actors is even more so. These would include, for example, domestic and international nongovernmental organizations and international scientific and professional associations.

Domestic and international nongovernmental organizations

Intergovernmental organizations interact with domestic and international nongovernmental organizations through formal affiliations, such as those provided by the United Nations Economic and Social Council (ECOSOC) and by the United Nations Educational, Scientific, and Cultural Organization (UNESCO). As already pointed out, many nongovernmental organizations can be useful sources of information as well as lobbying agencies. Many cooperate with intergovernmental organizations in carrying out development projects.

Often such nonstate international actors will interact at the local or national levels with appropriate agencies or ministries of governments. This has occurred most frequently in such activities as health, nutrition, family planning, disaster relief, refugee resettlement, or education. It is sometimes overlooked that, within a state international nongovernmental organizations can often work closely and harmoniously with governments; only when an element of domestic or international political conflict enters do tensions arise. Unfortunately, this tendency is growing rather than diminishing, partly because of domestic hostilities that spill over beyond the territorial boundary of a state into the global political arena. This has happened not only in Southeast Asia, where incessant warfare has resulted in mass starvation and forced involuntary migration, but also in Central America, the Horn of Africa and in the Persian Gulf.

Some international nongovernmental organizations have memberships based wholly at the national level, and some have memberships that operate wholly internationally. For some, the headquarters usually acts as a networking clearinghouse; for others, the headquarters tends to be more directly engaged in projects that are carried out either entirely by the organization or in cooperation with other voluntary or governmental agencies.

Many domestic or international nongovernmental organizations accept contributions from intergovernmental organizations or from governments, some rely wholly on voluntary or private donations, and some draw on other kinds of sources. How this affects an organization's "nonpolitical" character is not always easy to discern. For example, very effective humanitarian international nongovernmental organizations exist that rely largely on governmental support. This support could occur through the form of provisions of office space or other facilities, or through secondary (loaning) officials from governmental bureaucracies, as well as through direct funding.

In contrast, the United Nations Children Fund (UNICEF) raises money through voluntary national committees that solicit private contributions along with governmental contributions. The United Nations University and UNESCO also have effectively used this means to attract funds and general citizen support. Such national committees are not exactly private because often governments lend moral if not some financial help to their efforts at attracting funds.

A few international nongovernmental organizations have profit-making objectives. They may be nonprofit corporations created or sustained by profit-making multinational corporations such as ITT or Exxon, and are expected to raise revenue over and above operating expenses. Other such organizations may take the form of charitable foundations, such as the Ford or Rockefeller foundations, that carry on international research or operational activities funded at least indirectly from profits in the form of return on investments.

In fact, some of these nonstate actors command more resources than some states.

The largest charitable foundations are valued at many hundreds of millions of dollars, but more to the point is the fact that the largest multinational corporations are greater, in terms of capital and other resources, than most of the member-states of the United Nations. Unfortunately, this trend will probably continue, especially for the so-called "most seriously affected" states—the non-oil-producing developing states. Sometimes the "most seriously affected" category is identified as the fourth world, to distinguish it from the relatively wealthier or more favorably endowed members of the third world.

International scientific and professional associations

With memberships drawn from many states, international scientific and professional associations can serve both as information-transfer mechanisms and as lobbies for particular causes. This is especially the case, for example, with the global issue of *environment*. There is no general consensus as to what constitutes a universally acceptable definition of the environment issue; instead, there is a melange of contending groups—some governmental, some nongovernmental but profit-oriented, and others nongovernmental but voluntary in funding and staffing. Even though the United Nations Environment Program (UNEP) carries the major responsibility intergovernmentally for coping with environmental problems, it shares this responsibility with many international scientific and professional associations.

The development and use of *energy* is a global issue that arouses strong interest among international scientific and professional associations. Dependency on fossil fuel sources by the industrialized states has led to a search for energy alternatives, and since the scientific community must be relied upon to discover and seek access to such alternative sources, these nonstate international actors are an important part of the issue. Nuclear energy figures prominently as a controversial alternative, but it is not the only one.

In effect, scientific and professional associations can develop foreign policies of their own that are implemented in domestic politics by targeting other associations and various levels of government, and in international politics through intergovernmental organizations and networking nonstate actors. Besides being evident in trade unions, similar patterns of behavior can be discerned in the International Chamber of Commerce, the International Cooperative Alliance, the International Union for Conservation of Nature and Natural Resources, the International Council of Scientific Unions, and the International Union of Local Authorities, as further examples. Their memberships consist of professionals who collectively attempt to influence public policy-making and who are tied together internationally through an association (union, chamber, council, etc.) that seeks to influence policy-making through its membership and through its presence in various international intergovernmental and nongovernmental activities.

Subnational/transnational actors

Subnational/transnational actors are groups that do not necessarily fall under the control of a single governmental authority. These can include refugees, migrant workers, emigrating members of intellectual and scientific elites, international civil servants, etc. These actors sometimes challenge the authority of the state and sometimes reinforce it. They often have their own ethos or code of conduct, share welfare concerns among themselves, have established customary or legal definitions of membership, and are susceptible to widely variant national attitudes or control. Forms of international legislation concerned with human rights, basic human needs, or educational and employment conditions offer some protection from exploitation or persecution by the state to these groups.

The plight of refugees presents a particularly difficult and challenging dilemma. Their numbers are increasing as subnational hostilities are transformed into transnational conflicts that in turn encourage outside intervention. These conflicts are partly the result of the creation of new states whose boundaries divide rather than unite ethnic or tribal groups.

Around the world, there has been rising concern over what to do with migrant worker populations. Usually these "guest workers" are from states or regions where poverty is widespread. In the nineteenth century and earlier, distinctions on the basis of race were often made between the host population and its migrant workers, but especially since the Nazi period of domination in Europe this distinction has given way to distinctions based on nationality or cultural attributes based on such factors as language or religion.

The migrant worker problem between the United States and Mexico became diplomatically acute, for example, when the United States perceived that Mexico had the capacity to be a primary oil and gas source for the United States. As a consequence, Mexico became more insistent that Mexican migratory farm workers should not be harassed or discriminated against. Thus the migrant worker now is a significant nongovernmental actor in the interstate relations of the United States and Mexico. But even more important, in transnational terms, the migrant worker has become a fixed presence in the economic and social life of those states (provinces) of both Mexico and the United States that form the international boundary between them. The "foreign relations" of the respective adjacent states (provinces) are as important as those of their respective federal governments, on this issue.

Since many migrant workers make up the educated cadres that perform technical or professional services not otherwise available in a developing host state, they may be considered part of the so-called "brain drain elite" problem. The brain drain phenomenon is not new in history; the expansion of the European industrialized states into the non-European world (including North America) was partly to provide a social and economic escape route for surplus skilled populations. After decolonization, the colonial expatriate usually would return home (less often in French territories than in British), but his indigenous replacement would not remain happily in place. Even though the chance to remain within one's own ethnic or cultural group in a recognized high-status career was welcome, the lure to go abroad and to remain there often was greater.

Domestic political instability, including tribal or ethnic rivalries, was one consideration. Often the most Westernized of the new elite groups were singled out for discrimination politically. Also, having been educated abroad and exposed to the technological and social amenities that this provided, these professional elites often preferred to return to these surroundings rather than be deprived of them in their native land. Thus the fact that the public health service of Britain is made up of increasing numbers of Pakistani and Indian doctors is not accidental; the presence of persons of South Asian and Middle Eastern ancestry on the faculties of many American universities and in research institutes also is not accidental.

Many studies have been made of the brain drain phenomenon, most of which recommend improving conditions at home as the most effective inducement either to retain these persons or to encourage their return. Sometimes the developing country itself attempts efforts at recruitment within the host country: the Nigerian government has engaged in this activity in the United States for several years, with negligible results. One distortion of this practice is that, rather than simply job recruiting, the home government may have political motives in mind. An example occurred in 1980 when both the British and the United States governments expelled members of the Libyan diplomatic missions in London and Washington on grounds that they were harassing their expatriate nationals under instructions that might also have included political assassination.

An international elite that has come in for widespread criticism is the international civil service. This term is a bit misleading, for there is no single "international civil service"; rather there are many forms of international bureaucracies that have differing policies and functions.

Career international civil servants are better insulated from national political pressures than those who are on short-term contracts, or who are seconded (loaned) to the organization. It is an open question, however, whether an intergovernmental organization can fulfill its mission if it claims such political insularity for its employees. Especially since the end of colonialism, for example, the trend has been toward ensuring on the part of the majority of the member-states of the United Nations, its specialized agencies, and other bodies, that the needs of the poorer and newer states be given higher priority. This is the motivation behind the so-called North-South dialogue. One reflection of this trend has been pressure for increasing the number of nationals from the newer states in the secretariats of intergovernmental organizations.

The host of technical experts that roam the world, giving their services to intergovernmental and international nongovernmental organizations, national agencies, and private voluntary agencies alike, are themselves important subnational/transnational actors. Incrementally, they have altered the conditions of life and even mandated national programs in developing countries that, if imposed even by well-intentioned donor states, would not have been acceptable.

In a sense, this type of civil servant is more transnational rather than international. Their careers are among states rather than within only one state and are like the careers of many employees of transnational corporations. They provide channels of communication for new ideas and technologies that can help to focus national energies in socially and economically constructive rather than destructive ways, and hence can reduce the danger of conflict (whether subnational or transnational) that is self-defeating developmentally. Because impoverishment is becoming a source of human suffering that threatens to embroil mankind in more and more conflict, the international civil servant who is engaged in economic, social, and humanitarian activities may well perform a crucial even though limited role.

The Various Roles of Actors

Participation in decision-making

In order for a society to remain stable, there must be created among *all* the people in that society means whereby they can feel themselves to be a part of their society. These means can be symbolic as well as literal. A flag and the cross of Christianity or the Star of David have been as constructive symbolically as the ballot box. Literally, the New England town meeting served this purpose in America just as effectively as the linking of the trade unions with the Labour party did in Britain.

Increasingly, and especially in field-level operations of international organizations, whether intergovernmental or nongovernmental, there is an emphasis on the value of such participation in community decision-making. Also, there is increasing awareness that the "consciousness-raising" of all people—those being acted upon as well as those performing the actions—is in and of itself a part of the process of defending or restoring human dignity to mankind. Without this participation, the prospect of long-term success in dealing with global issues is cloudy.

Within many developing states the richer elites have gotten richer, and the rural and urban masses have gotten poorer. Even though the total wealth in a state may have increased, the distribution of the wealth has been sharply inequitable. How to overcome this process has preoccupied donor and recipient states alike, and formed an important part of the strategy formulated for the United Nations Third Development Decade of the 1980s. One way has been to give the least advantaged sectors of the population the opportunity to participate in the decisions that affect their economic and social futures. In other words, participation can be seen as a means to "end-run" the well-entrenched domestic elites who have not allowed the fruits of development to be shared widely. The challenge to intergovernmental and international nongovernmental organizations, as the primary actors in the development process, is to devise politically acceptable means to accomplish this participation without running afoul of the ruling elites who control the levers of political power. So far the attempt has met with only limited success.

Looked at another way, the principle of participation is an extension of the principle of one-state-one-vote in intergovernmental organizations. Many of the smallest and poorest states that are insistent on their right to speak for themselves in international forums are unwilling to give their own people the same right at home, or, alternatively, they speak in the name of the people even while acting in the interests of the few. Such behavior leads to social and political dissatisfaction and unrest. In any event multilateral diplomacy is becoming more a fact of international life, and therefore the principle of representation linked to participation will play a greater role in the resolution of global issues.

Priority-setting

International actors, and especially the nonstate kinds, can assist in rearranging the domestic priorities within and between developed and developing states, especially regarding human and physical resources, although to a lesser extent when the resources are committed to military purposes. Where national interests are involved, these actors can bridge differences, provide a figleaf of political acceptability, or act as humanitarian agents of governments to facilitate resource transfers that can affect the transformation of domestic priorities. Food relief and refugee resettlement activities are examples that have already been discussed.

However, if outside agencies, whether intergovernmental or international nongovernmental, move too insistently to establish their priorities for development, resentment and resistance can emerge from the recipient states. This was not the case in the early postcolonial period; today it is a fixed rule that no international project can be devised or carried out without the consent of the host government. The tribulations encountered by intergovernmental and international nongovernmental organizations alike in providing food relief to Ethiopia is a case in point. In another case, President Nyerere of Tanzania stressed self-reliance and rural development long before it became fashionable; the fact that his particular methods of achieving these goals have not been too successful should not detract from recognition of his sincerity of purpose or political awareness. Also, even where massive industry-based projects have proven disproportionate to the resources committed to them or to the benefits gained, eventually they may prove themselves worthwhile. Hydroelectric systems and road transportation networks fall in this category.

International nongovernmental organizations have played a role in priority-setting that is often not appreciated, as already pointed out. Perhaps, however, if even greater notice were taken, their role would be reduced even further. This would be unfortunate because even though they are heavily staffed by Westerners who work in primarily non-Western societies, these organizations are often able to reach to the village level more effectively than agents of national governments. In education, public health, nutrition, and housing, they have helped to create new attitudes and improved conditions. The process has not been dramatic or sudden; rather it has taken place incrementally, over years and even decades.

Even as nationalist pride and sensitivity can frustrate the best-laid national development plan, there are counter tendencies that should be noted. For example, the inauguration of the European Parliament within the structure of the European Communities brings into play interaction among national political parties that cannot help but influence both national priority-setting (whether legislative, executive, or mixed), and multinational priority-setting (whether carried out through bilateral or multilateral means). Other forms of multinational consultation and decision-making have sprung up: the Andean Pact, the Association of Southeast Asian Nations (ASEAN), the Council for Mutual Economic Assistance (CMEA), the Organization for Economic Cooperation and Development (OECD), and the project activities of the various forms of development banks.

Within the United Nations, accompanying the restructuring process of the economic and social sectors that has been going on for several years, emphasis has been given to greater coordination in planning and priority-setting. The structure of the Economic and Social Council, for example, has been revised to provide more coherence and focus to its activities. Whether this process can overcome the essential diversity and decentralized nature of the United Nations system as a whole remains to be seen.

Agents of change

It is a truism to say that the only constant in human affairs is change; but in today's world the rate and nature of change produce unforeseen consequences, and this is worrisome. Even to speak of "global issues" a decade or two ago, let alone define them precisely, would have been unusual. Today, contemplating "planet Earth" is a universal pastime.

One result is the popularity of so-called networking, whereby disparate groups scattered throughout the world and throughout the disciplines of knowledge self-consciously create systematic means of communicating with each other. The United Nations University sees networking as its primary method of operation, as do a number of domestic and international nongovernmental organizations. There is even an International Association of Institutes of Advanced Studies to help coordinate elite bodies. UNESCO, of course, has served as a clearinghouse for ideas, as have also during the last decade the various ad hoc global conferences sponsored by the United Nations devoted to such global issues as environment, food, population, human settlements, women, and (in the context of special General Assembly sessions) disarmament and development.

The need for a sense of continuity in life-style and personal values is now recognized as universal, even though this need may be expressed in many cultural ways. The implied superiority of one particular cultural or social tradition over all others is manifestly being rejected. The imposition of Western-created science and technology on non-Western cultures has not brought with it the unquestioned adoption of Western cultural or social traditions. Instead an inchoate melding process seems to be occurring throughout the world, which prizes diversity as much as if not more than uniformity.

Even in authoritarian political systems, cultural and social pluralism has proved difficult to stamp out. Nonindigenous populations have been evicted from many of the new developing states—for example, the Syrians from West Africa and the ethnic Chinese from Southeast Asia—in attempts to eliminate not only economic disparities but also social and cultural patterns that are perceived as threats to traditionalism. Assimilation of nonindigenous traditions, on the other hand, has been widespread, which illustrates the nonrational and contradictory character of the situation.

Legitimizing political forces in society

Actors, especially those affecting subnational/transnational relations, can validate or legitimize the political forces in society, whether regarded as constitutional or otherwise. They can also create new forms of domestic political organizations, or discredit old ones. Where the societies are ethnically fragmented, or where the political system is unsure of its constitutional footing, these actors can influence the conduct of affairs rather substantially.

The formal method through which political authority is transferred within a State used to be a prime measure of constitutional efficacy. Especially since decolonization, self-appointed groups claiming to speak for the "people" and promising elections, have played fast and loose with written constitutions. In other words, constitutional *practice* is becoming a more important and accurate gauge of political legitimacy than constitutional *authority* based on a written document or on custom. This trend becomes transposed into the international arena only partly through the participation of national governments in intergovernmental organizations, important as this is.

The right to speak on behalf of the population of a state is often not clearly established. For example, at the 1979 United Nations General Assembly, there was open disagreement as to the credentials of which government claiming to represent the Democratic State of Kampuchea (Cambodia) should be recognized. The ruling regime in Afghanistan has been accused by a large majority of the General Assembly of being nonrepresentative and subservient to an outside state.

International nongovernmental actors sometimes get caught up in these conflicts, usually because of attempts to ameliorate the human suffering and environmental destruction that occurs. Reports such as those issued by Amnesty International or by special agencies concerned with human rights can focus world attention on a particular situation, but if the hostility is deep-seated, the conflict can assume a life and momentum of its own, as we can witness in Lebanon.

Information-transfer function

Actors can perform an information transfer function by establishing networks of information. Some of this could be of the "disclosure" variety, such as the work of the International Commission of Jurists; some can be seen as being of the monitoring variety, such as the work of various peace research institutes, the International Labor Organization, and the United Nations Environment Program, and some can be seen as humanitarian/operational, such as food relief organizations like Save the Children. The uses to which information collected and disseminated by international nongovernmental organizations are put depend in part on the receptivity of governments, and governments often resent revelations by outsiders of such unpleasant matters as famine conditions, human rights violations, maltreatment of minority groups, or wasting of wildlife or other living resources.

Not to be underestimated is the information-gathering capability of the United Nations and various regional intergovernmental organizations committed to economic and social development. The Organization for Economic Cooperation and Development, the World Bank, and the United Nations Development Program all produce widely respected statistical and analytical reports that can form the basis for program and policy commitments by governments and other intergovernmental organizations. Domestic and international nongovernmental organizations also rely on such reports.

Finally, networks of scholars and academicians are constantly being created, and sometimes these networks are institutionalized through, for example, the United Nations University, and sometimes they are purposely self-liquidating. The ease of air travel has helped to make possible such groupings. The Goals, Processes and Indicators of Development Project of the United Nations University is one example; the Obstacles to the New International Economic Order Project, cosponsored by the Center for Economic and Social Studies in the Third World and the United Nations Institute for Training and Research, is another.

Interest-group politics

In a pluralist, multipolar, decentralized international political system, the question of method in resolving disputes has assumed an importance equal to and in some instances greater than the question of substance. Interest-group politics at various levels of national and international decision-making, involving others besides governmental actors, has imposed on the international system the necessity to search for new ways of bargaining to resolve differences. The sharp shifts in power relationships among the state-actors have further disrupted established forms of international political discourse. The dilemma of the TWA hostages seized in Lebanon in 1985 is but one instance.

Although bloc relationships and commitments still exist and play an important role as a form of interest-group international coalition politics, the nature of the coherence of these blocs has become more complex. The politics of resource scarcities and of comparative economic advantage can be added to the politics of territoriality and ideology as major motivating elements in foreign policy-making. But traditional (that is, precolonial) cultural and societal forces have also entered into national calculations of advantage and self-interest. The result has been a cluttering of the channels through which intergovernmental political discourse, so carefully cultivated in the nineteenth and twentieth centuries, takes place. The "cacaphony of the deaf"—many voices raised but none listening—threatens to short-circuit established diplomatic practice, with nongovernmental and even antigovernmental domestic and international actors dominating the ability of a state to develop and implement a coherent and rational foreign policy.

Not all nongovernmental political interest groups are committed to the notion that force and violence are required to achieve their ends, however. Depending on the nature of the governmental regime (or regimes) involved, other methods are often adopted. Where a multiparty political system exists, domestic and international interest groups find it easier to achieve their purposes by operating within the domestic and international system. Where a single party or other form of authoritarian political system exists, there has been a tendency for political interests to operate outside of or against the domestic and international system, an example of which is terrorism used both as a tool serving the interests of the state and as a tool used against the state.

Internationally, authoritarian single-party and multiparty systems alike have found it expedient to work with or through domestic and international interest groups. It is only partially correct to claim that authoritative "nongovernmental" interest groups operate as agents of their governments; they possess a degree of discretion and freedom of action to influence the people of their own state and the international audience that should not be overlooked, and even should be encouraged when possible. That is why the activities of such organizations as the World Federation of United Nations Associations, or the Conference of Nongovernment Organizations in Consultative Status with UNESCO, can be useful elements of the international political dialogue.

The ability of mankind to think globally is a recent phenomenon; with a few exceptions, it dates only from the age of celestial exploration. The "spaceship Earth" concept, as far as global issues are concerned, stresses the need to recognize the interdependence of all peoples in order to cope with the pressures that technology, population, resource scarcity and limits, and economic expectations impose.

Paradoxically, at the same time in history that globalism is emerging as a reference for domestic and international policymaking, there is also a resurgence of nationalistic particularism, that takes several forms. One is a reversion to traditional (precolonial or anti-Western) cultural and social patterns and values; another is the pervasiveness of ethnicity as a motivation for group behavior; a third is the failure of political ideology to provide a guide for the future and a measuring rod for the present; a fourth is the inability of advanced scientific and technological capacity to assure social and political stability; a fifth is the capability of the technology of communications to exacerbate as well as to ameliorate these conditions.

Therefore, to classify actors as either state or nonstate can itself be misleading: the state is not a monolithic entity, nor are nonstate actors entirely divorced from the state. There is an intermixing of one with another within both the domestic and global context.

B Values Orientation Toward Global Issues
Chadwick F. Alger

The twentieth century may come to be recognized as that period in history when representatives from all parts of the world, from a diversity of religious, philosophical and ideological persuasions, first attempted to draft standards for human relations intended to have universal validity. Such standards have been attempted in the past by specific groups yielding principles for human relations such as those found in Judaism, Christianity, Islam, socialism, communism, syndicalism, etc. Such principles were even further defined by great conventions of believers from many parts of the world. The difference between those attempts and the current ones is that now, largely under UN auspices, people from a *diversity* of traditions seek to find common ground by defining values for humankind that are accepted by all. Building on the UN Charter which expressly mentions human rights seven times the Universal Declaration of Human Rights (December 10, 1948) asserts that "a common understanding of these rights and freedoms is of the greatest importance," and that these rights include "life, liberty, and security of person."

The Declaration, like other great declarations, including the U.S. Declaration of Independence and the French Declaration of the Rights of Man, is not a binding legal instrument. But it has had an impact on the constitutions of many countries, particularly those of the newly emerging nations who have "accepted the Declaration either in whole or in part as their basic laws."[1] The declaration has also inspired numerous international conventions or structures now in force: elimination of racial discrimination, elimination of slavery, abolition of forced labor, opposition to discrimination in employment, opposition to discrimination in education, advocacy of the political rights of women and the consent to marriage, etc. But the most sweeping efforts to implement the declaration have been in two documents, the International Covenant on Economic, Social and Cultural Rights and the International Covenant on Civil and Political Rights, both adopted by the General Assembly on December 15, 1966, and now ratified by over fifty countries.[2]

Universal ratification of these conventions is likely many years away. Actual implementation in countries that have ratified them will be far into the future. But that reality should in no way detract from the Universal Declaration and its implementing conventions and covenants as significant landmarks in defining minimum global standards. They give people everywhere standards against which to judge their status and instruments that can be used in justifying efforts to improve human conditions. It is a mistake to look to a single institution, such as a world court, or even to judicial bodies alone as means through which evolving global values will be further defined and implemented. This will come through a diversity of means, in a variety of settings, international, national, and local. Not insignificantly, both the Covenant on Economic, Social and Cultural Rights and the Covenant on Civil and Political Rights assert that:

> the individual, having duties to other individuals and to the community to which he belongs, is under a responsibility to strive for the promotion and observance of the right recognized in the present Covenant.

These rights will also be further defined and implemented in the great global debates that are a hallmark of our age—debates characterized by special UN conferences on topics such as Human Environment (Stockholm, 1972), Population (Bucharest, 1974), Food (Rome, 1974), Women (Mexico City, 1975), Human Settlements (Vancouver, 1976), Water (Mar del Plata, 1977), Desertification (Nairobi, 1977), World Development (New York City, 1978), and numerous Law of the Sea conferences.

These great global debates have not been held out of a desire to clarify abstract principles. They signify efforts to cope with threats to values that have crystallized into global issues. For example, environment became an issue only when air, water, and land became polluted by nuclear fallout, oil spills, DDT, mercury, and phosphates, thereby posing a threat to human existence. Before this occurred, air, water, and land were valued but did not constitute an urgent issue because these resources had not been threatened. Environmental pollution is but one example of the way in which modern technology has created new issues. New technologies for transportation, communication, production, and distribution have rapidly increased the density of human settlements and contact among them, thereby increasing the agenda of issues within societies and between societies.

A Framework for Viewing Values in Global Issues

The purpose of this essay is to offer a simple framework for thinking about values in the context of an array of global issues. This framework reflects one person's effort to comprehend emerging values in global issues in this century. It should be obvious that people with different kinds of training, experiences, and personal values would have done this task quite differently. Nevertheless, it is believed that any road map over complex terrain is better than none at all. Values do not have a static meaning. Their meanings undergo a process of change and clarification when they are threatened. For example, the concept *peace* appears in many languages, reflecting a deep concern of most of humanity for thousands of years. But the exact meaning of peace to specific people changes, depending on the concrete nature of threats to peace and on human experience in devising solutions to these threats. Thus the first element in our framework emphasizes dynamic interaction among definitions of values, threats to values, and experience with solutions to meet these threats.

The growing list of global issues reflects the fact that new technologies for transportation, communication, production, and distribution have spilled across the entire globe—creating a vast array of linkages among the countries, societies, cities, and even villages of the world. These linkages have spawned global issues with respect to environment, energy, food, and population. For an issue to be global, it is not necessary that everybody or even most people in the world perceive it as a global issue. An issue is called global either because a network of people in widely scattered places around the world believe it to be an issue or because a substantial number of people in one part of the world assert that an issue is manifest on a global scale.

Another part of our framework exemplifies how in this century reactions to threats to values, in the context of global issues, have produced efforts to protect values that lead to value clarification and change. The values selected for this exposition are: international peace, national self-determination, national development, international economic equity, national autonomy and self-reliance, ecological balance, basic human needs, and participation. A major part of this essay portrays the way in which these values have been clarified and redefined and how this sometimes has led to new values. The selection of these eight values, and the order of their presentation, is admittedly arbitrary. Other people might include other values, or might change them. Nevertheless, these values are prominent enough to support the assertion that an important exchange of ideas about the human condition is taking place and that these ideas, on a global basis, are an indispensable element in efforts to cope with transcendent issues. This global exchange selects the values and specifies meanings that have relevance to global dialogue. This is not to say that values such as peace, self-reliance, and participation originate in response to global issues. The origins of the deep longing in the human spirit reflected by these values are extensively entwined in human history, philosophy, and religion. We are only saying that meaning relevant to global issues emerges out of global dialogue.

This dialogue provides a continuous dynamic to the evolution of global values. We assert that the eight value themes just listed seem to be evolving into other value themes, such as the value of life in the sense of staying alive. Finally, our framework asserts that underlying efforts to define standards for human relations on this planet seem to drive still more enduring quests. It is not suggested that these are wellsprings from which all values reflected in global issues flow. Rather, they seem to represent the aspirations toward which humanity is striving.

Eight Evolving Value Themes

International peace

The prominent place given to international peace throughout the twentieth century—in the Hague Conference, in the League of Nations Covenant, and in the United Nations Charter—underlines the importance of this value in a global context. Opposition to war had arisen earlier out of a variety of philosophical traditions. Mo Ti, a fifth-century Chinese philosopher, asserted that killing and conquest in war are crimes similar to murder and theft, though far greater in their consequences. He rejected war as a criminal act and as an economic waste. Based on his respect for human life, the Dutch scholar Desiderius Erasmus (1466–1536) deplored war as brutal, wicked, wasteful, and stupid, believing it unprofitable to both victors and vanquished. William Ellery Channing (1780–1842), a pioneer in the American peace movement, believed that war dehumanizes those who participate and always brings more evils than it removes. Just before World War I, an English publicist, Normal Angell, wrote a widely circulated book, *The Great Illusion*. He too considered war wasteful to both victors and vanquished and thought military preparedness to be wasteful and futile.[3]

Unfortunately, opposition to war is not easily converted into policies that will bring peace. In this century a number of approaches have been advocated and practiced. The concept of balance of power had its heyday in the eighteenth and nineteenth centuries, fell into great disrepute after World War I, but has since made a comeback. A nineteenth-century diplomat described balance of power as "the maintenance of a just equilibrium between the members of the family of nations [which] should prevent any one of them becoming sufficiently strong to impose its will upon the rest."[4] The means for acquiring a balance of power against a potential aggressor consist not only of national military forces but also of alliances. A problem with balance of power according to Nicholas J. Spykman is that "states are interested only in a balance which is in their favor. Not an equilibrium, but a generous margin is their objective. . . . The balance desired is the one which neutralizes other states, leaving the home state free to be the deciding force and the deciding voice."[5]

Thus declared efforts to prevent war through balance-of-power strategies have often produced counter-alliances and arms races that have increased tension. Many attribute World War I to this kind of process.

Three approaches were employed in the early twentieth century in an effort to overcome the shortcomings of balance of power as an approach to peace: peaceful settlement, collective security, and disarmament. All were incorporated into the League of Nations Covenant. Peaceful settlement can involve a variety of techniques, negotiations between the parties, mediation and arbitration by third parties, and judicial processes. The instruments of peaceful settlement are fundamentally different from collective security, which relies, like balance of power, on the deterrent effect of military power. In collective security, members of a system agree to come to the aid of any member who is a victim of aggression. In this case military power is still used as a deterrent, but in the form of a preponderant power of a community of nations, rather than as an instrument of individual nations or alliances.

Some see the possession of weapons of mass destruction themselves as a cause of war. This had led to the espousal of universal disarmament as a route to peace. As succinctly stated by Inis Claude: "Whereas pacific settlement proposes to leave states with nothing to fight about, and collective security proposes to confront aggressors with too much to fight against, disarmament proposes to deprive nations of anything to fight with."[6]

A great transformation in peace thinking took place with the advocacy of functionalism by David Mitrany. In *A Working Peace System*, an essay first published by the Royal Institute of International Affairs in London in 1943, Mitrany moved emphasis from military deterrence, procedures for dispute settlement and disarmament, to emphasis on eliminating the underlying causes of wars through organizing joint projects involving experts from different countries in activities devoted to solving common problems.[7] The practice of functionalism, accompanied by some degree of success, has had considerable influence on approaches to peace and on the definition of peace itself. Increasingly, international cooperation in trade, investment, agriculture, monetary policy, technological development and transfer, communication, education, and many other fields are considered to be policies in the pursuit of peace. The image of peace based on this positive approach to problem-solving has come to be called *positive peace*, in contrast to peace defined as absence of large-scale violence that is now called *negative peace*.

National self-determination

A second value that looms important in world affairs is national self-determination, usually rivaling peace in attracting the devotion of humanity. People in all parts of the world, in all eras of human history, have sacrificed their personal treasure and lives in the interest of avoiding domination by outside authorities. Many people will not buy peace if the price is subjugation.

While national self-determination is an end in its own right for many members of nationality groups, for others self-determination can be viewed as a means for acquiring peace. For example, outside support for the breakup of the Austro-Hungarian and Turkish empires in Europe after World War I included not only those who valued self-determination for its own sake but also those who believed that the subjugation of certain nationality groups caused instability inside these empires that continually threatened international peace.

While national self-determination is a widely accepted global value, the application of the value is still a matter of deep dispute. Has the breakup of the overseas colonial empires ended obstacles to self-determination? Are people still being deprived of self-determination within the borders of states created from colonial holdings in Africa, Asia, and America—for example, Somalians in Ethiopia, Palestinians in the Middle East, Kurds in Iran, Iraq, and Turkey, or American Indians in North and South America? Are people still being deprived of self-determination within the borders of Europe—Scots, Bretons, Basques, etc.? Much of the violence in the world today flows from demands by nationality groups within countries for greater autonomy. With a few exceptions, such as apartheid in South Africa, UN members have not made what could appropriately be called "internal colonialism" subject to the principles of the Universal Declaration. Existing nation-state borders deny self-determination to hundreds of nationality groups, many with distinctive languages, customs, and religion developed over a thousand years or more.

The problem of internal colonialism is a great unfinished task in global value clarification. Some believe that any kind of outside intervention—even enunciation of standards—could cause great instability and violence by creating disputes about many national boundaries. On the other hand, internal colonialism is already causing much bloodshed every day around the world. There seems to be little doubt that the transformation in the nation-state system that self-determination has already fomented has not yet run its course. What is in doubt is whether those who hold power will agree to the wider spread of self-determination through peaceful means or whether it will have to be pursued through violence.

National development

The arrival of the third world in the UN, and its emergence as a force in world politics in other settings, was to give higher priority and new meaning to another global value: national development. This was signified by the United Nations' calling the 1960s the First Development Decade and the 1970s the Second Development Decade. Development emerged as a global value in response to the disparity between wealth possessed by people in the industrialized countries of Europe and North America, and the poverty of people in Africa, Asia, and Latin America. Like peace, the definition of development was to undergo evolution in the light of experience in implementing a sequence of potential solutions to problems posed by the growing gap between the rich and the poor of the world.

An initial approach was aid in the form of technical assistance, loans, and sometimes grants of capital. It was assumed that this aid would set in motion a process of growth that at some point would enable national economies to "take off" and develop, similar to what had taken place in the industrialized countries in North America and Europe. Growth was measured by gross national product, that is, the national aggregate production of goods and services. Although some countries developed according to this criterion, this strategy failed overall in that at the end of the two development decades the gap between the third world and the industrialized world had increased.

Not only was the gap between rich and poor nations growing, but aid was increasing along with the indebtedness of the third world to industrialized countries. Indeed, increasingly often aid is largely consumed in paying off past loans. In response to the growing gap, criticism has been directed to the character of the international economic system, the ways in which the poor countries are tied to the rich countries. The UN Conference on Trade and Development (UNCTAD) in 1964, transformed into a permanent United Nations body, signified this change of strategy. Increasingly often the cause of the gap was diagnosed as *dependency*; it was argued that the poor stay relatively poor not primarily because of domestic problems but because of the way in which they are tied to rich countries who derive most of the benefits to be gained from their relationship. A New International Economic Order (NIEO) was proposed as a way to eliminate dependency.

International economic equity

While national development remained as a value to be pursued, policy-makers in the third world increasingly often turned to equitable relations with industrialized countries as the means to make this possible and as a value to be pursued for its own sake. The declaration on the establishment of a New International Economic Order at a special session of the UN General Assembly on 1 May 1974 was a culmination of years of third-world frustration at the lack of responsiveness by industrialized countries to their piecemeal demands for change.

Like proponents of functional integration (linking the nations of the world in common pursuits), some advocates of international economic equity view this as a peace strategy. The argument is based on agreement with the functionalists that meaningful peace requires more than simply stopping the shooting. How could third-world shantytowns with unemployment, squalor, disease, malnutrition, and hopelessness be called peaceful? Given the assumption that international economic inequity prevents change in this condition, efforts to create more equitable economic relations between the poor and rich countries of the world then become peace strategies. Ironically this produces contradictions between those who believe functional integration (along with interdependence and free trade) will produce positive peace and those who believe that the free flow of trade (and the accompanying division of labor between rich and poor countries) produces the opposite of positive peace—structural violence.

In a sense, structural violence is the third-world equivalent of incidents in the cold war, except for the fact that the death rate attributable to structural violence is much higher than that incurred in cold war encounters. Structural violence is the deprivation of fulfillment of human potential that takes place as the result of a social structure. For example, those who die on the sidewalks and in the shantytowns of third-world cities each day—before they have reached the average age attained in the industrialized world—have died of structural violence. These deaths could have been prevented had food, medicine, clothing, and shelter available to many people in the world been available to them. These necessities were not available because of the way the world is organized, that is, the social structure. Since their deaths can be attributed to the structure rather than to the direct action of specific individuals, this is called structural violence. On the other hand, war is called direct violence in the sense that the individuals who shoot the guns and drop the bombs, or who order this done, can be more easily identified.

Thus a global dialogue can be said to have produced this formulation for peace thinking:

positive *peace* = no *structural violence*
negative *peace* = no *direct violence*

To many people in industrialized countries this formulation seems strange. To them the words peace and violence are not used in customary ways in the first equation because it is customary to think of peace as absence of direct violence and to think of violence only as direct violence. Why stretch customary and useful concepts to include additional phenomena, thereby making them less precise? Do we not have good words such as social injustice that we already use as labels for structural violence? The answer is yes, but this formulation has value implications in that it appears to make social injustice less repugnant than war. A frequent comment in the industrialized world is: "First you have to stop the shooting. Then we can get on with problems of social injustice." The third-world formulation is an effort to put different kinds of dying on an equal plane, an effort to make the human years lost in the slow death of the shantytown as valuable as the human years lost in death by guns and bombs. In effect, the third world is reacting to the fact that peace is valued in all parts of the world, and violence is generally despised as life-destroying. Noting that far more years of human life are sacrificed through injustice than through war, they find it sensible to apply the terms peace and violence to a mode of dying that is widespread in their part of the world.

The differences between those people who give priority to positive peace and those who give priority to negative peace are instructive. The priorities remind us of how selection of values and the way in which we define them are affected by the life circumstances of those involved. These differences are also instructive with respect to the dialogue on global issues. Problem-solving on these issues requires a global dialogue leading toward common identification and common definition of the values to be addressed. If people from one part of the world insist on imposing their values and concepts on others, then no dialogue can take place. In discussions of structural and direct violence, residents of the industrialized world are forced to ask themselves: "If positive peace is preferred, why do I find fast death (direct violence) so much more abhorrent than slow death (structural violence)?" They will likely conclude that the answer to this question is: "Because the quick death of war is more of a threat to me, my family, and my society than is the slow death of poverty." This admission deepens personal understanding of peace as a value and also provides a better basis for global dialogue and negotiation on issues involving the premature deaths of human beings.

National autonomy and national self-reliance

Historians have sometimes referred to the War of 1812 between Great Britain and the United States as the second war for independence. While the War for Independence did end the rule of the British crown over the United States, it did not prevent Britain from controlling events in the United States in many ways, particularly because of Britain's economic influence and control of the seas surrounding the young republic. Similarly, the demand of the third-world nations for a New International Economic Order marks a continuing struggle for real independence. Increasingly often, they refer to their objective under the labels of national autonomy and national self-reliance. During the First Development Decade (1960s), development for many countries meant doing whatever was necessary to develop in conformity with the economic models of the industrialized countries. Out of their experience in the past two decades, during which most third-world countries believe they have made little progress in gaining on the industrialized world, many of these countries now assert that national autonomy and self-reliance are prerequisites for domestic development. The success of China in providing food, clothing, and health care to its population, while espousing self-reliance (in the context of a centralized, authoritarian political regime), has stimulated a turn toward this approach.

Self-reliance and autonomy are values no more explicit than peace and self-determination. The condition to which these advocates refer is to be found somewhere between dependency and anarchy. Thus they do not mean complete self-sufficiency. But they do mean enough self-sufficiency to make possible autonomous goal-setting and less imitation of the development strategies of the industrialized world. Autonomy and self-reliance could be perceived as antithetical to the priority that many in the industrialized world give to interdependence and free trade. But this is not necessarily the case. Rather, the emphasis is on acquisition of sufficient economic independence to enable external relations to produce a condition of interdependence rather than dependence. Third-world resistance to offers of "interdependence" from industrialized countries is helpful in sharpening definitions of interdependence in the industrialized world where dependency-creating relationships are often called interdependence.

Ecological balance

The First Development Decade began with widespread enthusiasm for spreading the development values and practices of the industrialized world to the third world. By the end of the Second Development Decade the feasibility of extending the practices of the industrialized world to the entire world was questioned increasingly often as was their continued viability in the industrialized world. A new word—over-development—had become commonplace in discussions of global issues, meaning development that destroys air, land, and water resources on which human life depends. The World Conference on the Human Environment in Stockholm in 1972 (discussed in chapter 5) signalled the arrival of (1) the quality of the nonhuman environment as a global issue and (2) balance in relationships between human beings and the nonhuman environment as a global value. This event was soon to be followed by three additional United Nations conferences dealing with environmental problems: the UN Conference on Human Settlements (HABITAT) in 1976, the UN Water Conference in 1977, and the UN Conference on Desertification in 1977.

The impetus for a global approach to ecological issues came from the industrialized world, and much of the preparation for the Stockholm conference was done in industrial countries. These efforts were largely responsive to pollution of the water, air, and land by industries in these countries. Third-world leaders active in efforts to diminish the gap between the rich and the poor countries of the world initially responded with suspicion. Why were leaders from the industrialized world able to move so swiftly toward a global conference on environment when they continued to drag their feet on efforts to mobilize global concern for the growing gap between the rich and the poor of the world? Would concern for environment give the industrialized world another justification for keeping the third world in subservient status based on the conclusion that industrialization there would be harmful to the environment? Some of these suspicions still endure.

Nevertheless, the global attention to environment issues is moving global debate on economic issues to a new plane, making symmetrical debate between the industrialized and third-world countries more possible in several respects: (1) The notion of overdevelopment has undermined the assumption that the industrialized world is a model for the third world. (2) It is no longer assumed that all of the major changes with respect to development issues must be made in the third world. If industrialized countries are overdeveloped, they must change too. (3) The basic philosophy underpinning the industrialized world has been shaken—assumptions about relations between human beings and the nonhuman environment. The view that it is the mission of human beings to dominate and conquer their environment with ever-expanding technological competence has been seriously challenged. Now non-Western values that view human beings as a part of nature and that expect human beings to fit into the whims and cycles of nature have become a respected part of global discussion. These factors are helping to restore symmetry to debate between the third world and the industrialized world, once again demonstrating the benefits to be derived from having participants from a variety of contexts and value systems involved in debate on global issues.

Basic human needs

As a result of the failure of third-world development programs to improve the living conditions of most of the people at whom they were aimed, national development has increasingly often come under challenge as a value to be pursued. Instead, some argue that development programs should serve basic human needs for food, water, clothing, shelter, education, health, and transportation. Increased gross national product, industrialization, foreign aid, increased exports, national autonomy, and national self-reliance might help to satisfy these needs, but they should be treated as means—not as ends in themselves. This emphasis has stimulated yet another reformation of development thinking, reorienting attention from national development statistics to the condition of people in the poorest sectors of society—away from the gross national product piled up in Westernized sections of capital cities and other cities and out to the urban shantytowns and rural villages of Africa, Asia, and Latin America.

It might seem that emphasis on basic human needs is simply a matter of a change in development indicators and in statistical aggregation—that is, a change from indicators measuring production of goods and services. But the implications of the selection of basic human needs as a value to be fulfilled by development policies are much more fundamental. The basic human needs of some have been served rather than those of others because some have access to procedures for defining their needs and implementing them and others do not. Thus emphasis on basic human needs for the world's poor implies participation of the poor in the definition and acquisition of basic needs. This emphasis has implications for which people shall have autonomy and self-reliance. Some third-world development planners are already calling for self-reliance in regions within countries and in local communities. This naturally causes national government leaders considerable concern because it threatens their control over development programs. When basic human-needs terminology is picked up by external authorities such as the World Bank and governments in industrialized countries, third-world government leaders perceive it as a tactic for fragmenting weak nation-states into yet weaker units that will be dominated by outside developers. But some third-world critics of national development strategies are now asking how local regions and communities can define and fulfill their basic human needs in self-reliant ways without domination from any of an array of external bureaucrats—in transnational corporations, international organizations, foreign national governments, or in their own national governments. How can people be enabled to decide for themselves which degree of aggregation of interest really serves their needs—local region, nation, nation-state, international region, or even the globe? Local efforts to define basic human needs will help to answer these questions.

One contribution of the basic human-needs approach to the global dialogue is its applicability to industrialized as well as third-world countries. Despite decades of growing gross national products in the industrialized world, pockets of poverty persist. Meanwhile, much production has not been geared toward satisfying basic human needs but rather toward the production of junk foods, gas-guzzling cars, and seemingly superfluous appliances such as electric can openers. As a result, even the affluent of the world may suffer from malnutrition and a variety of other health hazards brought on by conditions under which needs are generated by producers in the interest of maximizing profits of specific industrial enterprises. Local efforts to define and satisfy needs are as important in industrialized countries as in the third world.

Participation

Emphasis on the possibility and the necessity for the poor of the world to participate in defining their own basic needs reflects a fundamental reorientation of values relevant to global issues. It challenges deep traditions about who is permitted to participate in institutions attempting to solve global problems. For the most part those advocating self-reliance in the satisfaction of basic human needs have not yet understood the full implications of that value. Given the extent of the intrusion of global processes on local communities, self-reliance clearly implies some degree of local control over the individual participation in what have been traditionally labeled as international or foreign policy issues. The development of local control requires a fundamental rethinking of participation in the context of the global succession of demands for participation. These began with the demands by small nation-states (in, for example, the 1899 and 1907 Hague conferences) for participation in international councils, extended to self-determination for dependent nationals in European empires, then to nations in overseas empires. These demands now could be expanded to nations within nation-states and even to regions and smaller communities within nation-states.

New forms of direct participation in global issues are emerging in industrialized countries as well, as exemplified by instances of increased direct involvement of representatives of nongovernmental organizations in international conferences, the refusal of longshoremen to load cargo bound for the Soviet Union, pressures to prevent the marketing of baby food in the third world by multinational corporations, and travel abroad by state and city officials in pursuit of trade and investment. All of these reflect the lessening control of statist ideology over norms for participation in world affairs.

The tendency for wider participation in global issues in all parts of the world is growing, along with an increasing belief in individual participation as the foundation for self-determination in all collectivities. One observer has commented that self-reliance should not end with the word "local": "It should, as is stated in the Arusha Declaration, essentially benefit and be based on the individual, culminating in and deriving from individual self-reliance." Current emphasis on participation recognizes that satisfaction of the needs of individuals by collectivities depends on their ability to define their own needs for collectivities. In the absence of this input, those elites who control institutions with collective labels—whether they are local, regional, national, or global—tend to run them in terms of their interests.

While tendencies do exist to assert the importance of individual participation in global issues in all parts of the world, there are considerable restraints on realizing that priority. These include not only the fact that many peoples live under regimes that limit participation of all kinds, or that powerful corporations control many global processes in decision-making bodies hidden from public view and comprehension. These restraints also include the existence throughout the world of deep-seated traditions against citizen participation in international affairs. Even in democracies, foreign policies have been traditionally handled by a small elite. The public at large has grown accustomed not to participate in foreign policy-making but to accept the policies of that small elite. Change in this state of affairs would require fundamental change in education together with the creation of local organizations through which people could articulate their interests with respect to global issues.

Overview of Value Development

Reflection on this journey through value clarification in the context of global issues could take a diversity of paths, depending on the values and interests of the person making the attempt. Drawing first on the eight values highlighted in the first part of this discussion, we see a struggle for clarification and consensus on six main precepts:

1. The value of *life* in the sense of staying alive.
2. The value of life in the sense of all people acquiring certain *basic human needs*, no matter who they are or where they live.
3. The value of *autonomy* and *self-reliance* for the human collectivities with which people choose to identify themselves.
4. The value of social structures that ensure *equity* in relationships among these collectivities.
5. The value of *participation* by all people in decisions that affect their interests, including global issues and other so-called foreign policy issues.
6. The value of *balance in relationships between the people who inhabit the earth and the nonhuman environment in which they live* in order to conserve this environment.

Underlying these value precepts there seem to be four enduring goals toward which global standards for human life aspire. Two seek to ensure *preservation*:

1. To preserve human life.
2. To preserve the habitat of humankind.

Two seek to ensure *sharing*:

3. To enable all human beings to share the resources of the world.
4. To enable all human beings to develop their individual creative potential.

In a global context, the quests for the first and the third goals are the oldest. The quests for the second and fourth are the newest. Indeed, the fourth is only now being enunciated as a problem in sharing, spurred by growth in the population of the world and in the global reach of human organizations made possible by jet engines and electronic communication. As directors of big, centralized enterprises use these technological inventions to fulfill their personal creative potential, they may deprive people throughout the world of the same opportunity—by destroying their culture and prescribing what they will eat, the kind of housing in which they will live, their working conditions and occupations. Thus the possibilities for human beings to develop their individual creative potential must be shared.

Our effort to portray evolving value themes in this century has dramatized the way in which enunciated means for moving toward a more enduring quest have a tendency to become ends in themselves that may outlive their usefulness and even undermine the original end they were intended to serve. This phenomenon has been particularly well illustrated with respect to the state as a means, as reflected in the eight value themes described earlier in this appendix. Tendencies have emerged more recently to free the pursuit of underlying values from statist ideology. In this way the pursuit of international peace is becoming an assertion of the value of all human life. National self-determination is becoming understood as self-determination, autonomy, and self-reliance for all human collectivities. International economic equity is becoming seen as equity in relations among all human collectivities. Indeed, an emphasis on participation extends concern for self-determination, self-reliance, autonomy, and economic equity to all individuals. This certainly does not mean that territorial units as a prime aspect of human organization will disappear or even that existing nation-states will disappear. But it does mean that there are growing tendencies not to accept specific existing units as ends. It is up to people to decide which collectivities serve their needs.

The value trends that have emerged out of the debate over global issues register the effort toward a better life for most of humanity. They reflect a distillation of the highest impulses in a variety of religious and humanistic traditions. They offer a severe challenge to vested interests in a great diversity of international and national institutions (both governmental and nongovernmental) that exercise power in ways that are creating ever more horrible weapons, rapidly depleting the world's resources, increasing pollution of the environment, increasing the gap between the rich and the poor, and increasing control of global processes by authorities protected against participation or perception by most of the people of the world. These institutions do these things not entirely on purpose, for the powerful too are the victims of inertia. But they are sustaining policies in many places that many feel are pushing the world toward some combination of ecological disaster, nuclear war, endemic poverty for all but a few, and rule of the world by an affluent autocracy.

There is no easy way to avoid these consequences but the values emerging out of global dialogue do reveal that humankind does have strong life-sustaining and life-enriching impulses. The tendency to empower most of the people of the world to participate in governance of the world is critical—reflecting a basic belief in the competence of most people to make life-sustaining and life-enriching choices if they are permitted to participate. Wider participation would require either a new attitude toward the public at large by most people in power or strong demands by the public for wider participation. These changes would require new kinds of participatory education through which most people would no longer defer to elites on issues perceived to be international or global—categories that now of course include almost all issues.

Once the process for widespread participation in global issues is begun, change could come much more rapidly than most cosmopolitan elites expect. They tend to understand that the difference between them and the "country bumpkin" or "redneck" is not a result of intrinsic ability, intelligence, or wisdom, but is the result of power acquired through education and participatory opportunity. Widespread education for global participation would be a revolutionary force in the world. It would mean the fulfilling of participatory value themes emerging out of global dialogue. It would generate new laboratories of activity for defining what a more participatory global system might look like. Only through much wider participation in global issues can we gain insight that will help us to understand how a world of more widespread individual fulfillment might be organized.

C Issues Resolution:
The Policy Context of Global Issues
Richard W. Mansbach

For the better part of five centuries, our understanding of world politics has been conditioned by three simple but critical assumptions:

1. Nation-states constitute the most important set of actors to examine in order to account for political behavior, and the most powerful among them "make policy" for the world as a whole.
2. Political life is divided into "domestic" and "international" realms, each independent of the other.
3. The single issue in world politics is the struggle for power and peace.

It was and remains widely believed that world politics consists of little more than a ceaseless and tireless quest for power, a great game largely played by nation-states that alone are sovereign entities which can marshal the resources to wield power. In contrast, domestic politics was believed to be regulated by a single actor, the government, with sufficient power to order and control other entities within society. In contrast, the international sphere was believed to lack such a center of power and was considered therefore to resemble anarchy, in which each nation-state must strive for power or risk annihilation.

Casting aside the old assumptions makes it clear that global policy-making cannot be dismissed as simply the imposition of power by selected nation-states to assure themselves of security. Once we appreciate that there is a wide galaxy of actors out there (see appendix A), seeking to satisfy a variety of values (see appendix B), it becomes necessary to turn our attention to the manner in which this effort is conducted. In doing so we will find ourselves immersed in the dynamics of politics as central to the "world policy process."

What is policy in global politics? How are issues confronted and dealt with? How is policy made? Who renders key decisions and for whom? How and why are these decisions reached? These are among the knotty questions that must be confronted in analyzing the manner in which global issues evolve. The term *policy* is one that every observer of politics uses with scant regard for its meaning, and as a result the term has come to have many meanings. Sometimes policy is used to refer to action that is being taken in response to the challenges posed by an issue. In other cases, it refers to a set of actions that are promised or intended. At still other times, it is used to prescribe what should be done or what observers hope will be done about an issue, and occasionally it is employed to describe all the actions or proposed actions observers believe to be relevant to an issue, whether or not this is really the case.

Common to all usages, however, is the assumption of intent on the part of actors whether they are aware of such intentions or not.

Still another problem in discussing policy toward global issues is that few observers are certain that it exists at all. We refer to the "foreign policy" of the U.S. government or the "tax policy" of the state of New Jersey, certain that public authorities have an opinion about and perhaps a set of proposals concerning the issue at hand. The notion of "making policy" in such contexts refers to the evolution of opinions and proposals and accompanying efforts to transform the proposals into legislation. The observer may be made aware of the substance of policy through the speeches and testimony of authorities and the actions they take.

The absence of central authority in world politics and the unclear nature of legitimate channels and institutions for articulating grievances and proposals make global policy and policy-making less than self-evident. It is clear that individual actors hold opinions and make proposals about specific issues that define their policies. It is argued here, however, that the consequences of policy-making by individual actors and their subsequent interaction (whether cooperative or not) regarding issues give rise to policy that is global in scope. This does not, of course, imply that such policy is coherent, constructive, or even clear to those who are responsible for it.

Of one thing we can be certain: policy is a process, and studying that process takes us to the heart of politics. It is a process of pulling and hauling, of competition among actors for scarce resources and preferred outcomes. The process determines "who gets what, when, and how," according to one influential definition of politics, and may result in "an authoritative allocation of values" according to another. If policy connotes the articulation of goals and aspirations, it also entails the exercise of influence and the investment of resources by actors in order to persuade or compel one another to accept certain courses of action rather than others. For this reason, policy analysis must examine other areas such as actors, values, and alternative futures.

For several reasons the global policy process bears little resemblance to an idealized procedure in which rational and disinterested persons identify a problem, specify a series of possible options to overcome it, and select the best of these. For one thing the process involves more than a single unitary actor confronting a problem that it wishes to overcome and behaving as a "value-maximizing" individual. Numerous individuals and groups with different resources, information, and value preferences are involved in most significant issues, and the more global the issue the more heterogeneous these are likely to be. These individuals and groups cannot be expected to define and interpret an issue in the same manner because it affects them and their interests in profoundly different ways. This can be illustrated by reference to any issue. In the case of food, for instance, the problem is not simply one of insufficient nutrition for large numbers of people. American farmers and grain dealers see the issue as involving the need for stable overseas markets and high prices for their products. In contrast, the governments of poor countries are preoccupied with increasing their own production of foodstuffs (either for export or to reduce the need for imports) and with obtaining foreign food at the lowest possible price. Starting with such divergent preferences, these actors are unlikely to agree easily on how to define the issue of food or on how to deal with it.

Policy Preferences and Actors

The concerns of human beings naturally change as new issues arise and old issues fade. Earlier it was noted that there has been an increase in "the agenda of issues within societies and between societies,"[1] and this is both a cause and a consequence of the growing participation of people in the policy-making process. But what precisely are "issues," and how are they born in the first place? Politics, as David Easton suggests, entails an effort to allocate "valued things."[2] As intangible constructs, values cannot be sought directly but rather through acquisition of tangible objects that are believed to be relevant to values. Such objects are political *stakes* over which contention occurs. Although all the values mentioned in the previous chapter may be regarded as equally desirable in the abstract, individuals and groups express preferences among them, preferences that change over time as their conditions are altered. At any given moment people are likely to seek intensively to secure those stakes that represent values of which they feel most deprived.

In addition the presence of numerous competing and often autonomous or semiautonomous actors characterizes the policy process even within single societies such as the United States. Roger Cobb and Charles Elder suggest several phases that an issue must pass through on its way to an agenda. These include initiation (articulation of a grievance by a small group), specification (translation of grievances into specific demands), expansion (the attraction of support for demands), and entrance (movement of an issue onto a formal agenda). While the general public may remain uninvolved in an issue, it may attract an "identification group" (those who identify with the deprived), "attention groups" (those who believe they have a direct interest in the outcome), and the "attentive public" (those who are aware of public issues even in the absence of a direct interest).[3]

Global policy-making, like policy-making in a single society, is complicated because any major issue, no matter how it is defined, is linked to other issues in complex ways, and these links are perceived differently by the many participants. The most cursory analysis of an issue such as energy reveals this characteristic. Thus for the third world the sudden rise in oil prices that began in 1973 is seen to be intimately related to the issue of food because petroleum is the basis of much of the artificial fertilizer necessary to grow the "miracle grains" of the Green Revolution. In the industrialized and mobile West, however, the rising price of oil and spot shortages in energy manifested themselves in long lines at gasoline stations and inconveniences in transportation. For all countries the rise in oil prices had a profound impact on their balance of payments and patterns of trade and drove home the centrality of global economic interdependence. Yet for the members of the OPEC cartel this rise in prices meant the accumulation of vast reserves of currency that they find it difficult to spend or invest in a productive fashion. For industrialized consumers it meant chronic balance-of-payments deficits and domestic inflation. And for the poorer countries it has meant such extensive borrowing of hard currency from Western banks and international institutions in order to pay for the oil that many of them are hopelessly in debt.

The actors in global politics also have vastly different priorities among major issues—differences produced by divergent systems of values and real needs. Thus third-world actors have tended to accord a higher priority to issues such as economic development and food than to issues such as the environment, human rights, or military security that are salient to the prosperous West. In the West the concern about human rights is part of a long philosophic tradition that stresses the value and rights of individual citizens as opposed to the government or state. In the Soviet Union, however, Marxism emphasizes the relative unimportance of the individual in relation to society as a whole, and in the third-world individual rights are often sacrificed to produce the political and social mobilization necessary for political stability, national unity, and rapid economic growth.

Environmental degradation, overpopulation, resource depletion, and pollution are viewed as pressing topics in the West. These concerns have encouraged proposals to limit or slow down economic growth and so reduce consumption and regulate the sources of pollution. Such proposals receive little encouragement in the third world. Third-world publics see the West as the consumer of much of the world's raw materials and as the source of most pollution. They interpret pleas for limits to growth as efforts to prevent them from achieving economic development and independence, which are leading priorities for them. Similarly, efforts by the United States and the Soviet Union to prevent nuclear proliferation receive only lukewarm support in the third world. The superpowers view proliferation as a threat to their security and dominance and try to restrict the spread of nuclear power plants and place strict controls on those being constructed in order to prevent their being used for military purposes. These efforts are resisted in much of the third world where such nuclear weapons are considered to be symbols of political independence and where nuclear power plants are seen as critical to overcoming energy shortages and the rising price of fossil fuels that they cannot afford to pay.

The interdependence of actors and issues makes it difficult to isolate single issues for study or to build optimal approaches to them. It is critically important to recognize the relationship among issues and the impact that policy toward any one issue will have on other issues. To study and apprehend fully what lies behind the articulation and elaboration of policy even for a single global issue requires that attention be paid to a vast array of perceptions, definitions, interpretations, interests, and proposals that interact in dynamic fashion. These vary greatly among issues because different sets of actors are involved in each, and each presents a unique set of problems to be overcome. Yet major issues, at least, constitute a global agenda for major actors so that even though priorities among them differ, policy for any one issue will have an impact upon others.

Policy as Process

Policy is really a shorthand way for referring to a whole set of factors that must be understood in order to appreciate the concept. These factors include *goals, proposals, programs, implementation,* and *evaluation.* The first step in analyzing policy for an issue, then, is to summarize and try to understand the sources of the goals of key actors. This entails elaborating the characteristics of those actors that have a stake in the issue and the priorities they have established among the several major issues on the agenda. This summary will assist in distinguishing *possible* policy operations from *probable* ones.

The proposals of actors reflect their goals and give expression to their interests as they see them. Proposals are made by actors to further their goals and maintain or enhance their interests to the fullest extent possible. In the case of arms control the U.S. and Soviet governments have individually and jointly sought for a number of years to win acceptance for proposals to prevent nuclear proliferation and so to perpetuate their near-monopoly of nuclear weapons. They have also sought to assure other governments that they would act responsibly in not using nuclear weapons and would protect third parties if they were threatened. However, some other countries, as has been noted, have been unwilling to accept these proposals or assurances because of their own desires for enhanced security and status in world politics. They have refused to adhere to the 1968 Nuclear Non-Proliferation Treaty and have continued to test and develop their own nuclear weapons.

Every proposal includes a planned course of action and distribution of costs and benefits. Costs and benefits can be distributed in any of four general ways (with numerous specific variations) among actors. Costs and benefits may both be equally divided. Costs may be equally divided and benefits unequally divided, or costs may be unequally divided and benefits distributed equally. Finally, both costs and benefits may be distributed unequally. In the case of nonproliferation, countries without nuclear weapons argue that while the benefits of nonproliferation such as reduced tension may be equal, they have to bear a disproportionate share of the costs by forgoing the opportunity to create their own nuclear weapons. In the case of the proposal to limit growth in order to curb environmental pollution and conserve natural resources, the third world sees itself as having to accept fewer benefits and greater costs than the West. After all, pollution is currently more severe in industrialized than in preindustrialized societies and the former have already achieved a high standard of living. Ultimately, proposals that offer equal costs and benefits cause the least contention, although even their acceptance requires considerable trust and amity among actors. Proposals that promise unequal costs and benefits produce the greatest amount of disagreement.

Actual programs result from actors' decisions regarding the proposals concerning an issue. Such programs may be either collaborative or individual. If agreement among some or all of the interested parties is forthcoming, a single program for action may result. Although this is not uncommon within individual societies, it is unfortunately rare in global politics. Partial agreement sometimes results as in the cases of the Non-Proliferation Treaty and the SALT treaty on the issue of arms control, the GATT (General Agreement on Tariffs and Trade) on the issue of economic interdependence, or OPEC in the area of energy, but the defection or opposition of key actors usually limits the effectiveness of these programs, the rapidity with which they are carried out, and their ability to resolve the problems associated with the issue. Of course, universal programs of action that encourage coordination of effort are preferable, but as these are rare, individual actors often seek to carry out their own programs that may thwart or complement the programs of others.

The implementation of programs depends upon the degree to which cooperation exists among actors and upon the resources and resourcefulness of those who seek to carry them out. In order to appreciate the problems of implementation one should ask a number of questions regarding each policy option and program. These include: (a) What levels of resources are necessary for the program? (b) What types of resources are necessary? (c) What is the source of these resources? (d) What are the scope and domain of the program's objectives? (e) What length of time is necessary to achieve these objectives? (f) Which individuals or groups will carry out the program? (g) What level of national and/or international cooperation is necessary for successful implementation?

In light of the decentralized nature of global politics, the welter of competing proposals, and the existence of many policies and programs for major issues, it may ultimately prove difficult to identify, describe, and evaluate a single coherent policy for many issues. However, individual policies may be sufficiently complementary that we can see, although dimly, a single policy toward an issue emerging within global society—much as the British economist Adam Smith saw an "invisible hand" producing coherent policy in capitalist society under the conditions of the free market. From this perspective, policy is an emergent property that grows out of global interaction, as different actors emulate one another or cooperate quietly and tacitly even in the absence of universally accepted proposals or programs. In time, customs and habits may evolve into something like universal norms.

The Complexity of the Policy Process

The definition of policy as composed of goals, proposals, programs, implementation, and evaluation recognizes that policy is a continuous process with a number of stages or steps. Usually no single point of decision can be identified. Rather, the process features a string of limited decisions, some individual and others collaborative, that collectively create policy in their wake. Any attempt to analyze the process demands answers to questions of *how* things are done. How are issues raised to the agenda? How are goals and proposals formulated? How are programs decided upon and implemented? How may the effects of policy be evaluated?

The sheer complexity of the process and of the issues themselves, and the differences in values, perceptions, definitions, and interests, make the process appear to be slow and uncertain, characterized by what David Braybrooke and Charles Lindblom call "disjointed incrementalism":

> It is decision making through small or incremental moves on particular problems rather than through a comprehensive reform program. It is also endless; it takes the form of an indefinite sequence of policy moves. Moreover, it is exploratory in that the goals of policy making continue to change as new experience with policy throws new light on what is possible and desirable.[4]

What Braybrooke and Lindblom suggest is that the problems that issues pose can only partly be understood and even then in different ways by those viewing them, that proposals to meet them tend to be limited in scope, that consensus on proposals is difficult to achieve within societies and even more so among them, and that the programs that are implemented tend to proceed by "trial and error."

In concluding, a number of observations about actors and issues should be kept in mind that illustrate the degree of complexity confronted. As regards actors:

1. Different actors and individuals are apt to define and interpret the same issue in divergent ways at different times.
2. Actors will assign a different importance and urgency to the various issues on a global agenda depending upon values and perceptions and will rank the significance of issues differently.
3. Actors have different degrees of influence in global politics.
4. Actors include unified national governments, elements in those governments, public and private international organizations, local communities and governments, private groups within single societies, and on occasion even individuals acting on their own behalf.
5. Actors redefine issues and alter proposals *during* the policy process.
6. Most actors have little information about issues and can communicate with one another only intermittently.
7. Actors remain interested in and active toward only a few issues of great importance to them at a given time.

8. Most actors are hesitant to accept rapid change.
9. Actors have different interests that give rise to divergent proposals concerning issues even when they agree about the long-term threats that issues pose for them all.

As regards issues:

1. A single issue may pose numerous problems that affect actors in different ways.
2. The problems posed by issues are rarely "solved" in a permanent fashion.
3. Many important issues exist side by side on the global agenda at any time, and that agenda is in constant flux.
4. Issues tend to have simultaneous domestic and international implications.
5. Many issues are related to one another, and policy toward any one affects others.
6. Issues may remain poorly defined even while programs are fashioned to deal with them.
7. The policy process regarding issues tends to be conflict-ridden.
8. Global issues are usually dealt with in piecemeal fashion, and the process is incremental.

The Issue Cycle

If analysis of the stages of the policy provides insights into the behavior of actors, a focus upon the cycle through which issues pass when they are on the global agenda provides a deeper understanding from a broader perspective. At any given moment active contention occurs over relatively few of the issues that are on the global agenda. Some are forgotten, some are changing in slow and incremental fashion, and a few are the subject of acrimonious debate and even violence.

The complexity of global politics, its decentralized structure, and the consequent difficulty in achieving acceptable resolution mean that important issues remain on the agenda for substantial periods of time. During that time the stakes at issue may change, as may the cast of actors contending over them. During the long period that they remain on the agenda, issues tend to pass through several stages before being resolved. (Not all issues pass through all stages, nor are the stages necessarily in the sequence presented here.) The main stages in the cycle are crisis, ritualization, dormancy, decision-making, and administration.

Important issues tend to reach a *crisis* stage when they first appear on the agenda. A crisis exists in the sense that an atmosphere of urgency is pronounced, existing alignments are breaking down, and new ones must be formed. During this period, misunderstandings may occur with some frequency owing to the lack of established expectations about behavior toward new issues. During periods such as this the probability of violence is greatest.

However, if large-scale violence is avoided, the interaction of actors will in time produce a more stable pattern of expectations. Actors will come to understand and appreciate each other's definition of an issue and perceptions regarding its significance, and will therefore begin to distinguish one another's interests from rhetoric. As this occurs, *ritualization* of behavior may begin. Competition and mutual probing continues, but within understood limits and without the uncertainties that almost assure misperceptions. The evolution of tacit rules of behavior during the cold war reflects the onset of ritualization. The most dangerous crises of that era, at least in Europe, occurred between 1947 and 1949, as West and East began to discover just how many disagreements they had about key stakes such as Germany. By the late 1950s the general sense of crisis had subsided, and the Iron Curtain had emerged as a de facto division of Europe. Rhetoric notwithstanding, it was tacitly understood that neither side would actively interfere in the other's sphere of interest, an understanding reflected by America's refusal to intervene either in 1956 when Hungary revolted or in 1968 when Soviet troops occupied Czechoslovakia.

Dormancy, the third stage, takes place when an issue is relegated to the periphery of the agenda. This may occur owing to a joint realization that continued interaction is likely to cause harm to contenders. In this case not only have efforts to hammer out policy been unsuccessful, but it is not feasible for actors to defeat one another without causing themselves great damage. An issue also may become dormant if it loses its salience, a condition that occurs when other issues arise that are of greater importance or that pose more immediate perils.

The onset of dormancy produces conditions that are suitable for quiet efforts to agree on policy for an issue. Out of the glare of public exposure politicians can negotiate in leisurely fashion without constantly peering over their shoulders at constituents who might object to concessions. *Decision-making* may then occur in an effort to formulate policy, at least about selected and relatively noncontroversial aspects of an issue. Successful decision-making is, of course, the necessary prelude to the final stage, *administration*, during which policy decisions are implemented. In global politics this last stage is perhaps most clearly evident in the quiet, day-to-day activities of the special agencies of the United Nations like the World Health Organization or the Food and Agriculture Organization. For all intents and purposes the issue is not on the global agenda at this time.

This brief description of the issue cycle is intended to illustrate how issues may evolve and how the formulation of effective policy is possible only under certain conditions. Perhaps the greatest virtue a policy-maker can possess is that of patience combined with a sense of timing. Efforts to formulate policy during crises not only will fail but are likely to inflame the passions of other contenders. Efforts to do so during ritualization promise little more, because new proposals are likely to be greeted with suspicions that they represent efforts to defect from the fragile rules of behavior that are developing. Successful proposals are likely to reflect a sensitivity to the needs, interests, and perceptions of adversaries and to be presented when passions have subsided.

The formulation and execution of global policy represent a multifaceted and complex process that defies concise description. In most instances it is neither coherent nor consensual and operates rather differently from the dictates of individual rationality or commonsense. Ultimately, the process is profoundly political and contains all those elements that make politics exciting and difficult to predict.

The process occurs at the intersection of differing perceptions, interests, and needs in a context of decentralized authority. In such a context any significant issue will assume a number of faces and meanings and produce a welter of policy proposals, some complementary and others contradictory. Rational debate and discourse will commonly be replaced by the vigorous efforts of numerous actors to win acceptance of parochial and limited points of view, and such patterns of interaction will be conditioned by a number of characteristics of both the issues and the actors involved.

Coherent policy, particularly in the international realm, is rarely achieved and, when it is, makes its appearance only slowly and painfully. For the most part policy emerges haphazardly as the emergent property of the behavior of a number of actors or groups of actors. And the pulling and hauling of politics continues even while it is administered. Implementation provides new opportunities for altering and adapting

D   The Future of Global Issues
Dennis Pirages

The twentieth century has been a period of large-scale and rapid change in the international system. This century has contained two world wars, the dissolution of a colonial system of political and economic relationships built up over the previous three hundred years, and the emergence of dozens of new nations in the international system. Technology has moved forward relentlessly, remaking the face of the earth. Battles fought with rifles and bayonets have given way to the computerized battlefield, and wars that once were local affairs could now lead to the destruction of four-fifths of the human race in a nuclear conflagration. It is as if the planet is suddenly experiencing an acceleration of history in which the rapidity of changes defies humanity's collective ability to cope.

The last quarter of the century may well herald a period of underlying transformation even greater than that of the previous eighty years. In the early 1970s the OPEC cartel reversed the important historical relationship between consumers and producers of petroleum. Energy-poor industrial countries are now plagued by economic instability as tens of millions of dollars have been routed to Middle Eastern coffers. And demands by less-developed countries for a New International Economic Order threaten to reverse the economic trends that have persisted for the last two centuries. That is, these trends could be reversed if the United States and the Soviet Union can survive the next twenty years without a nuclear exchange.

Given the nature of these tumultuous times, it is logical that scholars and students of international affairs want to learn as much as possible about the future of the planet. A series of global issues must be resolved if a just and lasting peace is to be maintained. Because of the long lead times necessary to begin to solve these problems, it is imperative to use futures methods wherever they can be applied in the analysis of global issues.

The Futures Perspective

The systematic study of the future is a relatively recent undertaking. It is true that decision-makers have always used the past as a guide to future policies, but before the middle of the twentieth century there were few attempts systematically to project futures or to make policy on the basis of these projections. Contemporary futurism had its early roots both in the philosophy of scientific method and in literary science fiction. The former set of roots is related to the Renaissance belief that knowledge can be used to build a better future. This belief was accompanied by the development of the idea of progress, that science would make the future better than the past and that this betterment of the human race was not reversible. The second set of roots is associated with the vision of science fiction writers like H. G. Wells, Jules Verne, or George Orwell, all authors of vivid imagination who graphically called attention to the future as a meaningful topic of discussion.

During the last twenty years interest in and the organized study of the future have flourished. Business leaders, politicians, and individuals want to know something about the future so that present actions will achieve satisfactory long-term outcomes. Since long lead times are required before decisions have impacts in many areas of policy, decision-makers must know something about the future world in which their actions will have an impact.

A futures perspective is essential in studying global issues because of the rapidity with which things change in the international system, the long lead times necessary for decisions to have an impact, and the need to anticipate future events so as to avoid their harsh and perhaps deadly consequences. To illustrate the rapidity of change it is only necessary to reflect on the events of the last four decades. Only forty years ago the United States possessed the world's only nuclear weapons and clearly predominated as the world's most advanced military and economic power. At present there are six members of the nuclear club and the dominant position of the United States in military and economic affairs no longer exists. At the beginning of the 1970s petroleum was considered to be in limitless supply and producer countries were clearly dominated by consumers. Petroleum was selling for less than $3 per barrel. Only ten years later the producers were giving orders to the consumers, and the price of a barrel of petroleum averaged more than $36, only to decline again in the 1980s. In an increasingly interdependent world a futures perspective is essential if military conflict is to be avoided.

A futures perspective is a natural one for social scientists to take. Many scholars in international affairs have begun to think in a futures mode, not living with visions of yesterday but rather thinking of ideas for building a better tomorrow. In international affairs, understanding the factors that are shaping world events and trends that have developed can lead to more accurate predictions of future states of affairs. Once an image of likely futures is obtained, policies leading to more favorable outcomes can be implemented. Preferred futures can be designed and utopias created if the dynamics of change are correctly understood.

A futures perspective offers a useful set of methodological tools for analyzing global issues, but it is essential to recognize initially a major limitation. There does not exist only one certain future that a futurist can "tap into" with the appropriate techniques. Rather, there are many alternative futures dependent upon different chains of events for their realization. Thus the study of the future is the study of possibilities and alternative futures. The intelligent futurist uses sophisticated methodologies to analyze trends that can be expected to create different types of futures. More accurate futurists are better at identifying the more important trends, but every prediction or projection is subject to error caused by the hundreds of unknown events that can change the course of history. For example, world history could be changed in only thirty minutes if key figures in the Kremlin or White House should choose to use the nuclear option. And there is no way of getting inside the minds of the men who will make such key decisions in the 1990s. Thus there is no future world for a time machine to visit since the future does not exist as a reality. Future worlds exist in people's minds as they attempt to shape them to their specifications, an act that makes the future more difficult to predict but more important to know something about.

One observer has compiled a list of six principles that underlie futures research:[1]

1. All social systems exhibit continuity; they do not generally change in discontinuous jumps. The international system can similarly be characterized as exhibiting continuity. If appropriate global trends are identified much can be learned about likely futures.
2. Social systems exhibit cause-and-effect relationships. These relationships permit development of global models with which future possible states of the global system can be probed.
3. Social systems have goals. By understanding the goals (explicit or implicit) of international actors, a series of global futures may be posited.
4. Social systems move forward in a holistic manner. The international system behaves like an integrated organic whole. Human observers can understand these interconnections in projecting futures.
5. Social systems, because of their integration, tend to be self-consistent. Behavior in one sector of the international system will not be contradictory to that in another.
6. Social systems tend to have similarities. In international affairs studying the past behavior of nation-states as well as past systems can be of value in determining what future situations may exist.

Futures methodologies can be divided into two broad categories: explorative and normative. Explorative methodologies represent and attempt to identify existing variables that are causal in shaping likely futures. They make no assumption about what is or is not desirable. Successful use of such methods is denoted by an ability to identify and measure the most relevant trends in shaping futures. All explorative methodologies, ranging from the simple to the complex, are based upon one form or another of trend extrapolation. Some extrapolations are based on historical patterns while others are based on analogy, but they all involve the extension of what exists, or has existed, into the future. Normative methodologies, in contrast, begin with assumptions about desired states of affairs and concentrate on strategies or designs for reaching them.

Simple trend extrapolation is the most basic form of explorative methodology. Relevant variables are chosen and their existing trends will persist and shape the future. Social phenomena exhibit different patterns of change over time. Some increase or decrease in a linear fashion, a constant numerical change per unit of time. Any extrapolation related to population variables, for example, can be expected to change exponentially. Thus world population grows at about 2 percent per year, while global demand for resources, a function of population growth, grows at about 6 percent per year.

Trend extrapolations suffer from some basic deficiencies, the most serious of which is the problem of identifying breakpoints in trends. History is not linear but cyclical. Empires rise and empires fall, economies expand and economies contract. It is difficult for the participant in these cycles not to get caught up in the dynamics of expansion or contraction and to identify correctly the turning points when they occur. For example, in mapping trends in the international system a futurist in the 1950s might have projected increasing American influence over Western Europe and industrial country hegemony over the less-developed economies, entirely missing the great upheavals of the 1960s and 1970s.

Systems dynamics has emerged as a recent, more complex form of trend extrapolation. Heavily dependent upon the simulation capabilities of computers, systems dynamics examines complex nonlinear relationships among systems of variables important in determining future outcomes. Thus the progress of a system can be plotted over time by recourse to mathematical equations derived from past performance. The best-known attempt at using systems dynamics to model global issues is *The Limits to Growth*, a book done at the Massachusetts Institute of Technology in the early 1970s.[2] The study measured changes in world population, agriculture, industrial productivity, natural resources, and population over time in an attempt to peer into the planetary future. The conclusions were not optimistic as the model revealed a variety of negative outcomes given a continuation of current global trends.

Since the study of global problems focuses on goal-seeking people in social settings, normative techniques are also appropriate. This is so because human beings have the capability of understanding their collective future and creating alternatives where necessary. The processes known as *futures design* or *alternative futures* stress an orientation whereby alternatives are created and sequences of steps required to attain them are outlined. Each step of the design process closes up some alternatives while opening up others. Futures design refers to the creative process by which preferred futures are envisioned, collectively debated, and perhaps implemented through a series of steps embodied in a transition strategy.[3] Futures design applied to a global problem would suggest the following types of activities:

1. Analysis of the underlying historical dynamics that create the problem. What are the relevant variables; how have they changed over time?
2. Explicating the linkage between the physical-technological dimensions of the problem and its sociopolitical impacts. For example, what are the human dimensions of "limits" to growth?
3. Outlining the various types of scenarios that have been or could be sketched relevant to the future of the problem. Which are plausible and which are implausible?
4. Creation of a series of futures through a value clarification process. What do people want to optimize? Are these sets of values universally accepted?
5. Development of transition strategies by which these preferred futures could be reached. These strategies must be grounded in a valid analysis of the existing situation as well as relevant social science theory dealing with the dynamics of change.
6. Outlining the social, political, and economic pressure points that exist in the real world and the types of actions that individuals would have to take to implement change. Who are the actors who can do something about a problem? How can they be influenced?

There are many other futures techniques that could be usefully employed in dealing with global issues. No attempt to deal with them can be made appropriately here, and countless books cover this methodological ground in great detail.[4] It should be noted, however, that there have been relatively few applications of futures techniques to the study of international relations. The studies that have been done focus largely on "parameter" problems — climatic change, lack of resources, food production, etc. — and not on global sociopolitical trends. Since designing a viable planetary future is a matter of utmost urgency, more applications of futures techniques can be undertaken fruitfully in the study of global issues.

Origins of Global Politics

A futures inquiry into global issues seeks to isolate the causes of these changes in the structure of international politics in order to understand present problems better as well as to project future developments. There are three factors that go far in explaining the evolution of the present international system: technology, population, and natural resources.

Technology is the most significant of these three factors because it has been responsible for creating a global village. Innovations in transport and communications have shrunk distances among nations. There are no longer any truly isolated areas of the world and what used to be local conflicts often take on global significance. Instantaneous communication among nations is now a reality, and it is possible to travel between almost any two nations in less than a day.

The recent history of the human race has been characterized by technology-related growth; growth in industry, growth in population, growth in resource consumption, and even growth in science and technology. In addition to shrinking the planet into a global village, technology has been responsible in many other ways for reshaping the map of the world. Technology has created demands for resources as well as new synthetic materials. In the former case the global spread of industrialization has created voracious appetites for natural resources such as coal, petroleum, natural gas, iron, copper, etc., that are the building blocks of industrial civilization. In the Western European countries that industrialized early these appetites led to foreign adventures and establishment of a network of colonies that provided them with needed raw materials.[5] In the latter case technology has expanded existing resource bases and created substitute materials through new innovations.

Technology also has had an important impact on population. Human populations living in nation-states are similar to other species in their tendency to multiply until they reach the limits of natural resources at their disposal. Before the Industrial Revolution these tendencies were held in check by natural Malthusian conditions. When individual national populations exceeded the available food supply, populations collapsed and famines frequently occurred. But industrial and medical technologies changed all that, enhancing the carrying capacity of the land and supporting massive increases in population. In 1650, for example, there were only about 500 million people on the face of the earth. By 1850 this figure had doubled to one billion, an increase of 500 million in only two hundred years. The next doubling of world population took only eighty years, and there were two billion people by 1930. Even more astounding has been the most recent doubling of the population to four billion that occurred in only forty years. At present rates of world population growth, another doubling can be expected to take place in only thirty-eight or thirty-nine years, although many factors could intervene to change these estimates. Thus, by the year 2000, barring global disease, famine, or nuclear war, the planetary resource base will most likely be forced to support more than six billion human beings.

Technology assumes additional importance in the analysis of global political issues because of the role it plays in enhancing national capabilities. One study uses the term "lateral pressure" to describe one of the less benevolent aspects of technological development.[6] Technology and related growth create demands for resources as well as the capability to get them, beyond national borders if necessary. Once domestic resources are exhausted, growth gives rise to lateral pressures to obtain them from other sources. Some responses to lateral pressures, such as trade, are quite benevolent. But others, such as war, conquest, or colonialism have been malevolent. Technologically advanced countries historically have met many of their needs for resources or cheap labor through military conquest and various forms of imperialism. The Industrial Revolution thus was a historical period in which the United States and the technologically superior Western European nations were able to use military force or economic domination to spread control and influence throughout the world. In this sense technological developments made global politics a reality. But the growth of interdependence that accompanied the emergence of a global system also gave impetus to the evolution of a series of very complex global issues that threaten the future stability of the international system.

Natural resources are a third factor that help explain the past evolution of global politics and increase understanding of the future of global issues. A resource is anything needed by a nation to increase growth of population and living standards. Fossil fuels, including coal, petroleum and natural gas, currently are the most essential of natural resources because they are the main source of energy used to transform other resources into useful products. When other resources such as water, food, iron, and copper are in short supply, abundant energy can be combined with technology to create new supplies or substitutes. For example, a coastal country without an adequate freshwater supply but possessing abundant energy could use energy to desalinate sea water, thus overcoming natural barriers to population growth.

All nations need an adequate resource base if they are to be significant actors in international politics. Some countries, such as the United States or the Soviet Union, have been generously endowed with natural resources and, at least until now, have not found it necessary to gain access to them through conquest. Others such as Great Britain or France once had adequate natural resources but quickly worked through them and now make up their deficiencies through imports from abroad. Still others, such as Japan, always have been extremely poor in natural resources and must seek the greatest portion they consume from abroad. This, of course, makes these countries vulnerable to their key resource suppliers. Should selected key OPEC countries cut off the flow of petroleum to Japan, for example, the Japanese economy would likely collapse, and there is little that Japan could do to even the score.

In summary, the preindustrial world was composed of hundreds of isolated political units, all of which were reasonably self-sufficient in natural resources. There was very little commerce or communication among these autonomous states. The Industrial Revolution, feeding on technologies developed in Western Europe, remade the political map of the world. As Western European populations and industry grew, these powers moved out to conquer the far regions of the world. By 1939, colonial possessions of the technologically advanced countries occupied nearly one-third of the world's population and land area. Great Britain, France, the Netherlands, Italy, Spain, and Belgium, with a combined population of 200 million, controlled over 700 million people in their colonies. Japan controlled an additional 60 million in its colonies. The Industrial Revolution gave birth to this international politics of expansion and forged a world system of nations characterized by increasing interdependence, and the industrialized countries became increasingly dependent upon the network of colonies for natural resources and cheap labor.

World War II marked the beginning of a change in the expansionist politics of the Industrial Revolution. The historical trend toward greater interdependence has not suddenly been reversed, but the terms or sets of rules under which the technologically sophisticated and less-developed areas of the world interact have changed tremendously. If anything, the events following World War II have increased global interdependence while the colonial empires that were characteristic of the period of the great industrial transformation have been completely dismantled.

Emergence of Global Issues

The study of global issues profits from a futures orientation because there has been very little historical experience with analogous situations. The global viewpoint really did not come into existence until World War II, which was the first explicit recognition that international conflicts could not be isolated in limited geographic areas. But only recently have the growth of communications and transportation given real meaning to the word *global*. Only in the last decade has an image of "spaceship Earth" become accepted as an illustration that the fates of all persons in all nations are now inextricably interconnected. The "issues" dimension is highlighted by recent rapid changes in world population, development of new technologies, and the perception that resources are no longer infinite in the face of human demands. Questions formerly relegated to the economic sphere have suddenly become political issues as well, as proponents of a New International Economic Order have vowed to change the rules that govern international economic affairs.

Global issues are different in several ways from the more pedestrian disputes that have littered the history of relations among nations. Persistence is one big difference; global issues are not likely to be ephemeral. The energy crisis, for example, will be a persisting one that will last well into the twenty-first century. Global issues are also closely linked. For example, solving the world food problem in traditional ways means exacerbating the world energy problem. Global issues are unique in that they have significant impact on large numbers of people. They have an impact on rich countries as well as poor countries. Finally, global issues are distinguished by their importance to the survival of the human race. This is most obvious in the case of arms and security where a single misstep could mean nuclear annihilation. It is less obvious but equally important in energy and environment where lack of attention to basic data and principles can lead to a breakdown of industrial civilization.

To put the emergence of global issues in an appropriate perspective, it could be argued that the face of the world has been shaped by two great revolutions that have had a tremendous impact on the entire human culture. The first, the agricultural revolution, began in the Fertile Crescent about 8000 B.C. and slowly spread out to the rest of the world. At present, almost all of the world's human populations have felt its impact and have moved to or through an agricultural stage of development. The agricultural way of life prevailed over earlier hunting and gathering communities. It was driven by the domestication of plants and animals that in turn provided better diets, dependable crops, and a small surplus of production that could be used to sustain nonagricultural castes—the early beginnings of a division of labor. The agricultural revolution was marked by an increase in the numbers of human beings and the emergence of cultures dramatically different from the hunting and gathering variety.

The second great revolution began to gather momentum in the fifteenth and sixteenth centuries in England and spread over the face of the earth in a relatively short period of time. The Industrial Revolution, the latter stages of which have given rise to global issues, has been heavily dependent upon new technologies that focus on utilization of natural resources, principally the fossil fuels. By harnessing inanimate forms of energy to replace the efforts of human beings and beasts of burden, industrial technology has made each human being much more productive. The result has been a revolution of affluence and rising expectations as each industrial generation has expected and received more than the last. In addition, new technologies and greater affluence have created a global population explosion. A planet that sustained only 500 million people in 1650 may have to support eight billion in the year 2015.

The demands and effects of the Industrial Revolution have created the contemporary context within which global issues are emerging. Many of the trends associated with the Industrial Revolution were quite benign during its early and middle stages, and only during the latter stages have they been perceived to cause problems. For example, population growth was an essential aspect of industrialization. Expanding labor forces were needed to meet manpower needs in new industries. But now in many countries populations have expanded well beyond the capability of the resource base to sustain them. Similarly, technology focusing on the processing of raw materials into finished products led to rapid increases in consumption. But now critical materials, particularly the fossil fuels, are in short supply.

Global issues are emerging in the growing connections between the advanced stages of the Industrial Revolution and the early stages of a postindustrial transformation that promises to be as far-reaching as its two predecessors. The postindustrial revolution is a direct result of the nonsustainable nature of industrial trends. The factors that made the Industrial Revolution work so well are the factors leading to a transition to a postindustrial world. Among the industrial trends that have created the agenda of global issues and that may, in the future, transform the industrial system are the following:

1. Increasing global population density means less "insulating space" among human beings and among nations. The industrial escape to new frontiers is no longer a possibility for most nations.
2. Industrial growth will greatly increase global consumption of natural resources, particularly the fossil fuels upon which industrial activity is based.
3. There is a growing realization that a global ecosystem exists and that it is very fragile.
4. Rapid population growth has accompanied the Industrial Revolution. Populations are growing most rapidly in less-developed areas of the world that can least afford such growth. Coupled with a revolution of rising expectations, this growth can be expected to tax further the world's supply of natural resources.
5. Economies of scale and the related emergence of transnational corporations have created a global marketplace. No parts of the international system can remain economically detached from the others.
6. Growing economic interdependence is linking all countries, rich and poor, into an international economic system in which the fortunes of all participants vary together.
7. Rapid growth in global communications and speed of transportation have combined to create a world best described as a global village. There are no isolated incidents in relations among nations, and conflicts in far corners of the globe have an impact on many other countries.
8. Technological advances have created weaponry with awesome destructive power. The nuclear stalemate among the superpowers has created opportunities for less technologically sophisticated countries to engage in aggression that previously would have been thought to be impossible.

In summary, the Industrial Revolution gave birth to international politics as the term is understood today. During the heyday of industrial growth the politics were those of expansion as population growth and needs for raw materials combined with increasing technological capabilities to permit Western European countries to establish a network of colonies in what is now referred to as the third world. The last two decades, however, have marked a reversal of the politics of expansion as most of the former colonies have now wrested independence from the much weakened colonial powers. A direct result of global conquest and the accompanying growth of population and technology has been increasing interdependence among nations. The world has reached a turning point at which many of the activities responsible for industrial growth are leading to unfortunate outcomes for mankind as a whole. Growth in population and consumption of resources, once considered desirable signs of industrial and economic progress, are now considered to be major global problems in the light of limited resources. In a sense, the emergence of global issues indicates a need to reverse many of the trends of the industrial period before serious damage is done to the planet as a whole.

Analyzing Interrelationships

It has been argued that the planet is now entering a third great revolutionary period that will be just as significant in world history as the agricultural and industrial revolutions.[7] For lack of a better term we have simply called it the postindustrial revolution until its outlines become much clearer. This third great revolution is impending because of problems inherent in the spread of industrialism. For example, the Industrial Revolution focused technological innovations on the use of fossil fuels to run machines replacing human and animal labor. It also created affluent societies in which greater use of natural resources has become necessary to sustain progress. In the 1970s, however, limits to industrial expansion were rediscovered on a global scale.[8] Whether the third great revolution becomes one of despair or of enlightenment feeding on new technologies with benevolent social impacts remains to be seen.

The international system that was a product of the Industrial Revolution has also entered a period of upheaval that marks a transition to a postindustrial system. The first stage of the transition was the complete decay of the Western political empire which came on the heels of World War II. The second stage is now underway and is characterized by attacks on Western economic hegemony left over from the industrial period. This transition has been marked by the formation of OPEC and the emergence of the coalition of third-world nations known as Group of 77 with its demands for a New International Economic Order. The future may well bring demands for a revolt against the social domination of Western culture as a new set of international relationships is formed. Recent events in the Middle East may be an initial step in that direction. The outlines of the new international system are not yet obvious, and it is unclear whether the period of transition will be one of massive destruction given the fact that key actors now have access to nuclear weapons.

The set of global issues explored here is rooted in the transition from an industrial to a postindustrial world system. In most cases they have emerged from the successes of the industrial period. The sources of industrial progress, because of the changing global context, have now become sources of global problems.

The futures dimension, when applied to these global problems, stresses both the obvious discontinuities in the industrial model as well as a comprehensive perspective on them. All of these global issues are linked together. Some issues (energy and food) are obviously more closely tied than others, but none of the problems can be solved by itself. Suggested solutions to individual problems often have unanticipated and sometimes seemingly illogical consequences.

In order to understand each of these problems fully, the relevant *physical science background* must be assessed. In food, for example, this suggests an analysis of the world's arable land and potential crop yield and the problems of bringing more land under cultivation. In energy, attention must be paid to the geological conditions that produce various types of fossil fuels and the resulting global distribution of them. The second major area of investigation is *technological possibilities*. The future of each global issue is partially determined by the implementation of existing technologies and the development of new ones. But a balance must be struck between unwarranted technological optimism on the one hand, and pessimism on the other.[9] Finally, the interaction between technological possibilities and the *sociopolitical environment* must be examined in each area. Broad social and political changes can severely disrupt global food and energy markets. Certain types of technological developments could change the nature of the international system. Thus one must understand a wide range of global sociopolitical futures that could change the rules of the game in each of these three areas.

These perspectives help in identifying the key questions and problems in each of the four issue areas. It is of primary importance to keep the linkages among them as well as the social problems inherent in "unlearning" old patterns of success in mind. To reiterate, it is impossible, in many cases, to solve problems by doing "just one thing." As an example, take the energy-environment-food nexus. Synthetic fuels and coal have been suggested as possible solutions to the energy dilemma in the United States. But to ignore the environmental impact of scenarios relying on these energy alternatives is a big mistake. Similarly, a "gasohol" solution to the energy problem puts fuels in competition with food in the long run. It is not inconceivable that future dilemmas involving a trade-off between feeding people or feeding automobiles could result from that kind of policy.[10] Therefore, a comprehensive "global systems" view of the future is most useful in analyzing each of these global issues.

Energy is the most critical problem in this cluster because cheap and abundant energy would provide resources essential to improvement of world food production and global environmental conditions. Increases in world food supplies are not mainly the result of the injections of more energy into agriculture in the form of fertilizers, pesticides, mechanization, etc.[11] Extrapolation of recent trends indicates that significant additions to world food production could be made based on this formula. But a systems dynamics approach to the future would stress the linkage between energy and food production and raise questions about the ability of the world food market to sustain high levels of consumption while food prices rise because of increased energy costs. Similarly, maintenance of global environmental integrity requires significant energy sacrifices, and environmental standards are now increasingly often under attack as additional energy production becomes a paramount goal.

Assessing the future of the energy issue requires understanding the geological processes by which the fossil fuels have been created and distributed. These processes have been relatively rare, especially those associated with production and tapping of petroleum and natural gas. Most highly industrialized countries (the Soviet Union being an important exception) have already exhausted a major portion of their fossil fuel heritage. Only a few geographical locations now exist in which energy resources are found in large quantities.

Sociopolitical factors are also very important in the energy-environment-food cluster. For example, the 1970s energy crisis was a result of contrived rather than Malthusian scarcity, and, in the short term, energy futures will be determined by political more than economic factors. Assessing energy futures suggests an analysis of OPEC cartel and the political motives of members, the role of transnational oil companies, and the political meaning of significant oil imports. The OPEC cartel is a fragile coalition united mostly by the increased income derived from cooperation. There are significant political, ethnic, and religious disputes among members. The long-term development goals of key actors and attitudes among importing countries differ greatly. The political motives of new key non-OPEC actors in the petroleum market (Mexico and China) should also be assessed. The world energy market can be expected to tighten significantly as world demand approaches production capacity. Given this circumstance, any single significant exporter (such as Iran) will be able unilaterally to throw world energy markets into disarray.

Sociopolitical factors are also important in the environment and food areas. Most significant in the former is the dispute between industrial and less-developed countries over the gravity of and responsibility for global pollution problems. The less-developed countries argue that they are entitled to more pollution, while the industrial countries reply that the global ecosystem cannot tolerate an additional burden. Analysis of world food problems must take account of economic factors such as future global distribution of effective demand (a link to development) as well as sociopolitical changes in key food-deficit countries.

Finally, technological innovations could have a significant impact on all of these problems. Analysis should be made of each of the new technological possibilities as well as the economic, social, environmental, and political costs of implementing them. In the energy area a contrast might be made between the various costs associated with the "hard" paths (nuclear, synfuels, etc.) and the "soft" paths (renewable alternatives). In the food area, reference should be made to the many studies of the Green Revolution and its socioeconomic impacts since some development plans call for the implementation of similar new techniques.

The population area is characterized by an orientation toward the future, and only a few observations are necessary. The starting point in population analysis is the many global and regional projections of future population growth under a number of different assumptions. But reference also must be made to the development linkage and the affluence dimension of population problems. An argument about affluence is becoming more important in negotiations between less-developed and industrial countries. The argument of the less-developed countries is that high rates of population growth are not at the root of population problems, and that the real source is the consumption levels of the highly developed countries. Global limits to population growth then are not a question of numbers but of individual demands. In addition, the less-developed countries claim that population growth rates level off in response to increased affluence. They see little merit in arguments made by developed countries that developing nations must control their populations before industrial growth can take place.

When analyzing the future of global population problems, attention must be focused on the cyclical nature of sociopolitical history. Since population growth rates have been falling in the twentieth century, many observers assume that this is a lasting historical trend. This assumption ignores the possibility of a population resurgence that would upset many of the low-growth scenarios now tacitly accepted. Traditional nationalistic concerns have led a considerable number of leaders in less-developed countries to argue recently for more rapid population growth. The resurgence of traditional religious forces in Iran should be a very sobering fact in this regard. Thus a reversal of trends must certainly be considered a distinct possibility in the analysis of population futures.

Notes

1 The Nature of Global Issues

1 Lee F. Anderson, "Why Should American Education be Globalized? It's a Nonsensical Question," *Theory Into Practice* 21 (Summer 1982): 156.

2 U.S. Arms Control and Disarmament Agency (USACDA), *World Military Expenditures and Arms Transfers 1972–1982* (Washington, D.C.: USACDA, 1984), p. 11.

3 Ruth Lever Sivard, *World Military and Social Expenditures, 1982* (Washington, D.C.: World Priorities, 1982), p. 6.

4 Ibid.

5 Ibid., p. 11.

6 Stockholm International Peace Research Institute, *SIPRI Yearbook 1983* (Stockholm: SIPRI, 1983), p. 161.

7 USACDA, *World Military Expenditures*, p. 11.

8 *SIPRI Yearbook 1983*, p. 237.

9 USACDA, *World Military Expenditures*, p. 53.

10 Sivard, *World Military and Social Expenditures*, p. 21.

11 Michael Ridron and Ronald Segal, *New State of the World Atlas* (New York: Simon and Schuster, 1981).

12 United Nations Department of International Economic and Social Affairs, *Yearbook of International Trade Statistics 1984* (New York: United Nations, 1984), p. 1125.

13 Hanna Umlauf Lane, ed., *World Almanac and Book of Facts 1985* (New York: Newspaper Enterprise Association, 1985), p. 206.

14 John Burton, "International Relations or World Security?" in *The Study of World Society: A London Perspective* (Pittsburgh: International Studies Association, 1974), p. 6.

15 Lynton K. Caldwell, *International Environmental Policy* (Durham, N.C.: Duke University Press, 1984).

16 Ibid.

17 These six strategies are described in detail in Marvin S. Soroos, "The Future of the Environment," in Kenneth A. Dahlberg et al., *Environment and the Global Arena: Actors, Values, Politics, and Futures* (Durham, N.C.: Duke University Press, 1985), pp. 126–38.

18 Council on Environmental Quality and the Department of State, *The Global*

2000 Report to the President (New York: Penguin Books, 1982), vol. 2, pp. 77–78.

2 The Food Issue

1 C. Peter Timmer et al., *Food Policy Analysis* (Baltimore: Johns Hopkins University Press, 1983), p. 3.
2 Lester R. Brown, "Securing Food Supplies," in *State of the World 1984* by Lester R. Brown et al. (New York: W. W. Norton, 1984), p. 187.
3 Timmer et al., *Food Policy Analysis*, p. 6.
4 Council on Environmental Quality and the Department of State, *The Global 2000 Report to the President*, (Washington, D.C.: Government Printing Office, 1980), vol. 2, p. 275.
5 John R. Moore, "World Hunger: Population, Food Supplies and Public Policy." Technology, Resources and Political Economy Program, Occasional Paper no. 3, University of Maryland, 1978, p. 13.
6 International Bank for Reconstruction and Development, *World Development Report 1982* (Washington, D.C.: World Bank, 1982).
7 Robert Paarlberg, "A Food Security Approach for the 1980s: Righting the Balance," *U.S. Foreign Policy and the Third World: Agenda, 1982* (Washington, D.C.: Overseas Development Council, 1982).
8 Paarlberg, "Food Security."
9 Moore, "World Hunger," p. 28.
10 Independent Commission of International Development Issues, *North-South: A Program for Survival* (Cambridge, Mass.: MIT Press, 1980), and *Common Crisis North-South: Cooperation for World Recovery* (Cambridge, Mass.: MIT Press, 1983); U.S. Presidential Commission on World Hunger, *Overcoming World Hunger: The Challenge Ahead* (Washington, D.C.: Government Printing Office, 1980).
11 Carol Goodloe, "Measuring Food Deficits and Undernutrition: An Accuracy Problem" (Staff paper, Economic Research Service, International Economics Division, U.S. Department of Agriculture, Washington, D.C., 1982.)
12 Malcolm Bale and Ronald Duncan, *Prospects for Food Production and Consumption in Developing Countries* (Washington, D.C.: World Bank, 1983).
13 International Bank for Reconstruction and Development, *World Development Report 1982*.
14 Moore, "World Hunger."
15 The Agricultural Development Council, *The Developmental Effectiveness of Food Aid in Africa* (New York: Agricultural Development Council, 1982).
16 International Bank for Reconstruction and Development, *World Development Report 1982*.
17 Ibid.
18 U.S. House of Representatives, *Feeding the World's Population: Developments in the Decade Following the World Food Conference of 1974* (Washington, D.C.: Government Printing Office, 1984).
19 Ibid.

3 The Energy Issue

1 Leon L. Lindberg, *The Energy Syndrome: Comparing National Responses to the Energy Crisis* (Lexington, Mass.: D.C. Heath, 1977).

2   Daniel Yergin, "The Political Geology of the Energy Problem," in *Uncertain Power: The Struggle for a National Energy Policy*, ed. Dorothy S. Zinberg (Elmsford, N.Y.: Pergamon Press, 1983), p. 235.
3   U.S. Central Intelligence Agency, *International Energy Statistical Review* 20 (December 1985): 4.
4   Yergin, "Political Geology." p. 235.
5   *Christian Science Monitor*, 11 March 1983; and *New York Times*, 18 October 1982.
6   CIA, *International Energy*, p. 1.

4   The Population Issue

1   "World Population Growth by the Numbers," *Intercom: The International Population News Magazine* 10 (May–June 1982): 4. The values for each minute and hour have been rounded; thus the latter values are not exact multiples.
2   Barnett F. Baron, "Population, Development, and Multinational Corporations" (speech presented in San Diego, 12 December 1979).
3   Ibid.
4   Population Reference Bureau, *World Population: Fundamentals of Growth*, ed. Patricia H. Cancellier (Washington, D.C.: Population Reference Bureau, 1984).
5   Leon F. Bouvier, with Henry S. Shryock and Harry W. Henderson, "International Migration: Yesterday, Today, and Tomorrow," *Population Bulletin* 32 (August 1979 update): 5.
6   Ibid., p. 8.
7   Ibid., p. 7.
8   Ibid., p. 9.
9   Kathleen Newland, "Refugees: The New International Politics of Displacement," *Worldwatch Paper* (New York: Worldwatch Institute, 1981), vol. 43, p. 5.
10 Rosemary E. Tripp, ed., *World Refugee Survey 1983* (New York: American Council for Nationalities Service, 1983), p. 61.
11 United Nations Department of International Economic and Social Affairs, *International Migration Policies and Programmes: A World Survey*, Population Studies no. 80 (New York: United Nations, 1982).
12 United Nations Department of International Economic and Social Affairs, *World Population Trends and Policies*, vol. 1, Population Studies no. 79 (New York: United Nations, 1982).
13 These examples are taken from Parker G. Marden, Dennis G. Hodgson, and Terry L. McCoy, *Population in the Global Arena* (New York: Holt, Rinehart and Winston, 1982), pp. 88–91.
14 Thomas J. Goliber, "Sub-Saharan Africa: Population Pressures on Development," *Population Bulletin* 40 (February 1985): inside front cover.

5   The Environmental Issue

1   For a comprehensive treatment of the environment issue area, see Kenneth A. Dahlberg et al., *Environment and the Global Arena: Actors, Values, Politics, and Futures* (Durham, N.C.: Duke University Press, 1985).
2   These examples are taken from Michael P. Hoffman, "Prehistoric Ecological Crises," in *Historical Ecology: Essays on Environment and Social Change*, ed. Lester J. Bilsky (Port Washington, N.Y.: Kennikat Press, 1980).

3   The discussion of the five factors is drawn heavily from Robin Attfield, *The Ethics of Environmental Concern* (New York: Columbia University Press, 1983), pp. 9–17.

4   Lester R. Brown et al., *State of the World 1984* (New York: W. W. Norton, 1984), p. 4.

5   Julian L. Simon, *The Ultimate Resource* (Princeton, N.J.: Princeton University Press, 1981), p. 9.

6   Ibid., p. 11.

7   See Parker G. Marden et al., *Population in the Global Arena* (New York: Holt, Rinehart and Winston, 1982), a text that uses the same framework as this volume, for a discussion of the role of population in other issues.

8   Barry Commoner, *The Closing Circle* (London: Jonathan Cape, 1982), p. 139; discussed in Attfield, *Ethics of Environmental Concern*, p. 13.

9   Attfield, *Ethics of Environmental Concern*, p. 13.

10   Dahlberg et al., *Environment and the Global Arena*.

11   Lester R. Brown et al., *State of the World 1985* (New York: W. W. Norton, 1985), p. 99.

12   Robin Clarke and Lloyd Timberlake, *Stockholm Plus Ten: Promises, Promises?* (London: International Institute for Environment and Development, 1982), pp. 31–32.

13   Brown, *State of the World 1985*, p. 104.

14   Robert Allen, *How to Save the World: Strategy for World Conservation* (Totowa, N.J.: Littlefield, Adams, 1980), p. 79.

15   Council on Environmental Quality and the Department of State, *The Global 2000 Report to the President* (New York: Penguin Books, 1982), vol. 2, p. 111.

16   Ibid., p. 341.

17   Ibid., p. 339.

18   Ibid., p. 340.

19   Martin W. Holdgate, Mohammed Kassas, and Gilbert F. White, eds., *The World Environment 1972–1982: A Report by the United Nations Environment Programme* (Dublin: Tycooly International, 1982), p. 21.

20   Clarke and Timberlake, *Stockholm Plus Ten*, p. 25.

21   Erik Eckholm, *Down to Earth: Environment and Human Needs* (New York: W. W. Norton, 1977).

22   Richard P. Rutco et al., "The Climatic Effects of Nuclear War," *Scientific American* 251 (August 1984): 33–43.

23   Holdgate, Kassas, and White, *World Environment*, pp. 194–95.

24   Data on oil spills are taken from Clarke and Timberlake, *Stockholm Plus Ten*, p. 35.

25   *Global 2000 Report*, p. 274.

26   Clarke and Timberlake, *Stockholm Plus Ten*, p. 38.

27   Jonathan Hersch, "Soil, the Crucial Resource," *Christian Science Monitor*, 13 September 1982, p. 12.

28   Holdgate, Kassas, and White, *World Environment*, p. 216.

29   Allen, *How to Save the World*, p. 95.

30   Dahlberg et al., *Environment and the Global Arena*, pp. 31–32.

31   Holdgate, Kassas, and White, *World Environment*.

32   J. P. Robinson, *The Effects of Weapons on Ecosystems*, United Nations Environment Programme Studies, vol. 1 (Elmsford, N.Y.: Pergamon Press, 1979), quoted in Holdgate, Kassas, and White, *World Enviornment*, p. 596.

33 U.S. Arms Control and Disarmament Agency (USACDA), *World Military Expenditures and Arms Transfers, 1972–1982* (Washington, D.C.: USACDA, 1984), p. 11.

34 Carl Sagan, "Nuclear War and Climatic Catastrophe: Some Policy Implications," *Foreign Affairs* 62 (Winter 1983–84): 263–64.

35 Ibid., p. 274.

6 Food: Competition Among Actors

1 Food and Agricultural Organization, *Global Information and Early Warning on Food and Agriculture: Food Supply Situation in 24 African Countries Affected by Food and Agricultural Emergencies in 1984*, 8 February 1984.

2 World Bank, *World Development Report, 1983* (Washington, D.C.: World Bank, 1983), pp. 158–159.

3 Ibid.

4 *Christian Science Monitor*, 27 November 1984.

5 *UNESCO Courier*, April 1984.

6 Carl K. Eicher, "Africa's Food Crisis," *Foreign Affairs* (Fall 1982): 151–74.

7 United Nations Conference on Trade and Development, "Basic Data on the Least Developed Countries," Document #TD/276/Add. 1 (27 April 1983).

8 Lester R. Brown and Edward Wolf, "Food Crisis in Africa," *Natural History* (June 1984): 16.

9 Allan Hoben, "The Origins of Famine," *The New Republic* (21 January 1985), p. 18.

10 Ibid., p. 19.

11 Eicher, "Africa's Food Crisis," p. 161.

12 Ibid., p. 171.

7 Energy: Value Trade-offs for Alternative Sources

1 For a full statement of the role of energy values discussed in this chapter, see James E. Harf, Donald A. Sylvan, and B. Thomas Trout, "Energy Values," in *Energy in the Global Arena: Actors, Values, Policies, and Futures*, by Barry B. Hughes et al. (Durham, N.C.: Duke University Press, 1985), pp. 56–82.

8 Population: Government Policy-making

1 Jyoti Shankan Singh, ed., *World Population Policies* (New York: Praeger, 1979), p. 3.

2 Lester R. Brown et al., *State of the World 1985* (New York: W. W. Norton, 1985).

3 United Nations Department of Technical Cooperation for Development, *Report of the International Conference on Population, 1984* (New York: United Nations, 1984), pp. 2–5.

4 Thomas J. Goliber, "Sub-Saharan Africa: Population Pressures on Development," *Population Bulletin* 40, 1 (Washington, D.C.: Population Reference Bureau, 1985).

5 Robert J. Lapham and W. Parker Mauldin, "The Measurement of Family Planning Effort," unpublished paper, January 1984.

6 Information about Indonesia is taken from Terence H. Hull, Valerie J. Hull, and Masri Singarimban, "Indonesia's Family Planning Story: Success and Challenge," *Population Bulletin* 32, 6 (Washington, D.C.: Population Reference Bureau, 1977).

7   Information about Mexico is taken from John S. Nagel, "Mexico's Population Policy Turnaround," *Population Bulletin* 33, 5 (Washington, D.C.: Population Reference Bureau, 1977).

8   Information about China is taken from H. Yuan Tien, "China: Demographic Billionaire," *Population Bulletin* 38, 2 (Washington, D.C.: Population Reference Bureau, 1983).

9   Information on Bangladesh is taken from Loretta McLaughlin, "In Bangladesh, a Population Treadmill," *Boston Globe*, 22 March 1982.

10 Information on India is taken from Pravin Visaria and Leela Visaria, "India's Population: Second and Growing," *Population Bulletin* 36, 4 (Washington, D.C.: Population Reference Bureau, 1981).

11 David K. Willis, "A Tidal Wave of Humanity," *Christian Science Monitor*, 6 August 1984, pp. 12–13.

12 Information on Eastern Europe is taken from Henry P. David, "Eastern Europe: Pronatalist Policies and Private Behavior," *Population Bulletin* 36, 6 (Washington, D.C.: Population Reference Bureau, 1982).

13 Ibid.

14 Information on the Soviet Union is taken from Murray Feshbach, "The Soviet Union: Population Trends and Dilemmas," *Population Bulletin* 37, 3 (Washington, D.C.: Population Reference Bureau, 1982).

15 Ibid.

16 Cynthia Weber and Ann Goodman, "The Demographic Policy Debate in the USSR," *Population and Development Review* 7 (June 1981): 279–95.

17 Information on migration is taken from United Nations Department of International Economic and Social Affairs, *International Migration Policies and Programmes: A World Survey* (New York: United Nations, 1982).

9   Environment: Strategies for the Future

1   For a brief description of these approaches, see Marvin S. Soroos, "The Future of the Environment," in Kenneth A. Dahlberg et al., *Environment and the Global Arena* (Durham, N.C.: Duke University Press, 1985), pp. 126–38.

2   Kenneth D. Boulding, "The Economy of the Coming Spaceship Earth," in *Toward A Steady-State Economy*, Herman E. Daly, ed. (San Francisco: W. H. Freeman, 1973), p. 127; quoted in Soroos, "The Future of the Environment," p. 128.

3   John S. Mill, *Principles of Political Economy* (London: John W. Parker, 1857), vol. 2, pp. 320–26; quoted in Daly, ed., *Toward a Steady-State Economy*, p. 23, and in Soroos, "The Future of the Environment," p. 129.

4   Robert L. Heilbroner, *Inquiry Into the Human Prospect*, rev. ed. (New York: W. W. Norton, 1980), p. 13; quoted in Soroos, "The Future of the Environment," p. 132.

5   E. F. Schumacher, *Small Is Beautiful: Economics as if People Mattered* (New York: Harper and Row, 1973); quoted in Soroos, "The Future of the Environment," p. 132.

6   Soroos, "The Future of the Environment," p. 137.

7   Anne Thompson Feraru, "Environmental Actors," in Dahlberg et al., *Environment*, p. 58.

8   Ibid., p. 59.

9   Robin Clarke and Lloyd Timberlake, *Stockholm Plus Ten: Promises, Promises?* (London: International Institute for Environment and Development, 1982), p. 32.

10   Ibid.

11   Sandra Postel, "Protecting Forests from Air Pollution and Acid Rain," in *State of the World 1985*, ed. Lester R. Brown et al. (New York: W. W. Norton, 1985), p. 115.

12   Ibid., p. 120.

13   Clarke and Timberlake, *Stockholm Plus Ten*, p. 44.

14   Soroos, "The Future of the Environment," p. 117.

15   Information about DDT is taken from Clarke and Timberlake, *Stockholm Plus Ten*, p. 33.

16   Information is from R. P. Churchill and A. V. Lowe, *The Law of the Sea* (Manchester, Eng.: Manchester University Press, 1983), p. 216.

17   Soroos, "The Future of the Environment," p. 106–7.

18   Churchill and Lowe, *The Law of the Sea*, p. 249.

19   Clarke and Timberlake, *Stockholm Plus Ten*.

20   Information on climate is taken from ibid., p. 25.

21   United Nations Document A/7834 (9 December 1969), pp. 1–17.

22   For a comprehensive discussion of the seabed mining regime, see Werner J. Feld and Robert S. Jordan, *International Organizations: A Comparative Approach* (New York: Praeger, 1983), pp. 264–75.

23   Ibid., p. 273.

24   For an elaboration of these, see William D. Echols and James E. Harf, "Domestic Interest Groups and American Foreign Policy: The Case of the Law of the Sea" (paper presented at the annual meeting of the Western Political Science Association, Las Vegas, March 1985).

25   Clarke and Timberlake, *Stockholm Plus Ten*, p. 40.

26   Norman Myers, *The Sinking Ark: A New Look at the Problems of Disappearing Species* (Elmsford, N.Y.: Pergamon Press, 1979), p. 31, cited in Soroos, "The Future of the Environment," p. 100.

27   Bayard Webster, "Tanzania Asks Rich Countries to Aid Wildlife," *New York Times*, 29 March 1979, p. 16; cited in Soroos, "The Future of the Environment," p. 101.

28   Michael T. Kaufman, "Preserving Rare Species Is an Ironic Success," *New York Times*, 8 March 1981, p. 20; cited in Soroos, "The Future of the Environment," p. 101–2.

29   Anonymous, "Endangered Species Meeting," *IUCN Bulletin* 10 (1979): 17–24; cited in Robert Allen, *How to Save the World: Strategy for World Conservation* (Totowa, N.J.: Littlefield, Adams, 1980), p. 111.

30   This information is extracted from David L. Larson, "Security Issues and the Law of the Sea," *Ocean Development and International Law* 15 (1985): 94–146.

31   For the story of whales, see Clarke and Timberlake, *Stockholm Plus Ten*, p. 40.

32   "An Introduction to National Security" (Washington, D.C.: Arms Control Association, 1983).

10   The Future in an Interdependent World

1   U.S. Congress, Office of Technology Assessment, *Global Models, World Futures, and Public Policy* (Washington, D.C.: Government Printing Office, 1982), p. 44.

2   These five models are (1) World 3, see Dennis L. Meadows et al., *Dynamics of Growth in a Finite World* (Cambridge, Mass.: Wright-Allen, 1974); (2) World Integrated Model, see Mihajlo D. Mesarovic and Eduard Pestel, *Mankind at the*

Turning Point (New York: Dutton, 1974); (3) Latin American World Model, see Amilcar O. Herrera et al., *Catastrophe or New Society? A Latin American World Model* (Ottawa: International Development Research Center, 1976); (4) United Nations Input-Output World Model, see Wassily Leontief, Anne Carter, and Peter Petri, *The Future of the World Economy: A United Nations Study* (New York: Oxford University Press, 1977); (5) Global 2000, see Council on Environmental Quality and the Department of State, *The Global 2000 Report to the President* (Washington, D.C.: Government Printing Office, 1980), vol. 2, p. 275.

3 These conclusions are summarized in Office of Technology Assessment, *Global Models*, p. 304.

4 Herman Kahn, William Brown, and Leon Martel, *The Next 200 Years: A Scenario for America and the World* (New York: William Morrow, 1976), pp. 83, 107; quoted in Population Reference Bureau, *The Environment to Come: A Global Summary* (Washington, D.C.: Population Reference Bureau, 1983), p. 11.

5 Julian L. Simon, *The Ultimate Resource* (Princeton, N.J.: Princeton University Press, 1981), p. 196.

6 Ibid., p. 222.

7 Ibid., p. 348.

8 For a sample of quotations from dissenters Kahn and Simon, see Population Reference Bureau, *The Environment to Come*, pp. 10–11.

9 For a more complete discussion of the Global 2000 model, see Raymond F. Hopkins, Robert L. Paarlberg, and Mitchel B. Wallerstein, *Food in the Global Arena* (New York: Holt, Rinehart and Winston, 1982), pp. 105–13.

10 *The Global 2000 Report*, pp. 77–79; cited in Hopkins et al., *Food in the Global Arena*, pp. 105–6.

11 Hopkins et al., *Food in the Global Arena*, pp. 117–23.

12 *The Global 2000 Report*, pp. 208–98; quoted in ibid.

13 For an analysis of the three future alternatives—solar, coal, and nuclear—see Donald A. Sylvan, "Energy Futures," in Barry B. Hughes et al., *Energy in the Global Arena* (Durham, N.C.: Duke University Press, 1985), pp. 134–55.

14 *The Global 2000 Report*, vol. 1, p. 32.

Appendix A The Role of Actors in Global Issues

1 *New York Times*, 28 September 1980.

Appendix B Values Orientations Toward Global Issues

1 Samuel Shih-Tsai Chen, *The Theory and Practice of International Organization* (Dubuque, Iowa: Kendall/Hunt, 1979), p. 165.

2 The United States has not yet ratified.

3 Material in this paragraph is based on A. Leroy Bennett, *International Organizations* (Englewood Cliffs, N.J.: Prentice-Hall, 1980), p. 11.

4 Cited by Inis Claude, Jr., *Power in International Relations* (New York: Random House, 1962), p. 13.

5 From Nicholas Spykman, *America's Strategy in World Politics* (New York: Harcourt, 1942), pp. 21–22, as cited by Claude, *Power in International Relations*, pp. 14–15.

6   Inis L. Claude, Jr., *Swords Into Plowshares*, 4th ed. (New York: Random House, 1971), p. 287.
7   David Mitrany, *A Working Peace System* (Chicago: Quadrangle Books, 1966).

Appendix C   The Policy Context of Global Issues

1   William D. Coplin, *Introduction to International Politics*, 2nd ed. (Chicago: Rand McNally, 1974), chap. 13.
2   David Easton, *A Systems Analysis of Political Life* (Englewood Cliffs, N.J.: Prentice-Hall, 1965), p. 50.
3   Roger W. Cobb and Charles D. Elder, *Participation in American Politics: The Dynamics of Agenda Building* (Boston: Allyn & Bacon, 1972), pp. 103–9.
4   David Braybrooke and Charles E. Lindblom, *A Strategy of Decision* (New York: Free Press, 1963), p. 71.

Appendix D   The Future of Global Issues

1   Willis Harman, *An Incomplete Guide to the Future* (New York: W. W. Norton, 1979).
2   Donella Meadows et al., *The Limits to Growth* (New York: Universe Books, 1972).
3   See Louis Beres and Harry Targ, eds., *Planning Alternative World Futures* (New York: Praeger, 1975).
4   See William Ascher, *Forecasting: An Appraisal for Policy-Makers and Planners* (Baltimore: Johns Hopkins University Press, 1978); and Joseph Martino, *Technological Forecasting for Decisionmaking* (New York: American Elsevier, 1972).
5   Immanuel Wallerstein, *The Modern World System* (New York: Academic Press, 1974).
6   Nazli Choucri and Robert North, *Nations in Conflict* (San Francisco: W. H. Freeman, 1975).
7   Harman, *An Incomplete Guide to the Future*; L. S. Stavrianos, *The Promise of the Coming Dark Age* (San Francisco: W. H. Freeman, 1976); and Dennis Pirages, *Global Ecopolitics: The New Context for International Relations* (North Scituate, Mass.: Duxbury Press, 1978).
8   Meadows et al., *Limits to Growth*.
9   Herman Kahn, William Brown, and Leon Martel, *The Next 200 Years* (New York: William Morrow, 1976); Orio Giarini and Henri Louberge, *The Diminishing Returns of Technology* (Oxford: Pergamon Press, 1978).
10   Lester Brown, *Food or Fuel: New Competition for the World's Cropland* (Washington, D.C.: Worldwatch Institute, 1980).
11   Maurice Green, *Eating Oil: Energy Use in Food Production* (Boulder, Colo.: Westview Press, 1978).

Bibliography

Agricultural Development Council. *The Developmental Effectiveness of Food Aid in Africa*. New York: Agricultural Development Council, 1982.

Allen, Robert. *How to Save the World: Strategy for World Conservation*. Totowa, N.J.: Littlefield, Adams, 1980.

Anderson, Lee F. "Why Should American Education be Globalized? It's a Nonsensical Question." *Theory Into Practice* 21 (Summer 1982).

Arms Control Association. "An Introduction to National Security." Washington, D.C.: Arms Control Association, 1983.

Ascher, William. *Forecasting: An Appraisal for Policy-Makers and Planners*. Baltimore: Johns Hopkins University Press, 1978.

Attfield, Robin. *The Ethics of Environmental Concern*. New York: Columbia University Press, 1983.

Bale, Malcolm, and Ronald Duncan. *Prospects for Food Production and Consumption in Developing Countries*. Washington, D.C.: World Bank, 1983.

Baron, Barnett F. "Population, Development, and Multinational Corporations." Speech presented in San Diego, 12 December 1979.

Bennett, A. Leroy. *International Organizations*. Englewood Cliffs, N.J.: Prentice-Hall, 1980. 2nd ed.

Beres, Louis, and Harry Targ, eds. *Planning Alternative World Futures*. New York: Praeger, 1975.

Boulding, Kenneth D. "The Economy of the Coming Spaceship Earth." In *Toward a Steady-State Economy*, edited by Herman E. Daly. San Francisco: W. H. Freeman, 1973.

Bouvier, Leon F., with Henry S. Shryock and Harry W. Henderson. "International Migration: Yesterday, Today, and Tomorrow." *Population Bulletin* 32 (August 1979 update).

Braybrooke, David, and Charles E. Lindblom. *A Strategy of Decision*. New York: Free Press, 1963.

Brown, Lester. *Food or Fuel: New Competition for the World's Cropland*. Washington, D.C.: Worldwatch Institute, 1980.

———. "Securing Food Supplies." In Lester R. Brown et al., *State of the World 1984*. New York: W. W. Norton, 1984.

———, et al. *State of the World 1984*. New York: W. W. Norton, 1984.

———, et al. *State of the World 1985*. New York: W. W. Norton, 1985.

———, and Edward Wolf. "Food Crisis in Africa." *Natural History* (June 1984): 16.

Burton, John. "International Relations or World Society?" In *The Study of World Society: A London Perspective*. Occasional Paper no. 1. Pittsburgh: International Studies Association, 1974, pp. 3–29.

Caldwell, Lynton K. *International Environmental Policy*. Durham, N.C.: Duke University Press, 1984.

Cancellier, Patricia H., ed. *World Population: Fundamentals of Growth*. Washington, D.C.: Population Reference Bureau, 1984.

Chen, Samuel Shih-Tsai. *The Theory and Practice of International Organization*. Dubuque, Iowa: Kendall/Hunt, 1979.

Choucri, Nazli, and Robert North. *Nations in Conflict*. San Francisco: W. H. Freeman, 1975.

Christian Science Monitor, 11 March 1983.

Churchill, R. P., and A. V. Lowe. *The Law of the Sea*. Manchester, Eng.: Manchester University Press, 1983.

Clarke, Robin, and Lloyd Timberlake. *Stockholm Plus Ten: Promises, Promises?* London: International Institute for Environment and Development, 1982.

Claude, Inis, Jr. *Power in International Relations*. New York: Random House, 1962.
———. *Swords Into Plowshares*. 4th ed. New York: Random House, 1971.

Cobb, Roger W., and Charles D. Elder. *Participation in American Politics: The Dynamics of Agenda Building*. Boston: Allyn & Bacon, 1972.

Commoner, Barry. *The Closing Circle*. London: Jonathan Cape, 1982.

Coplin, William D. *Introduction to International Politics*. 2nd ed. Chicago: Rand McNally, 1974.

Dahlberg, Kenneth A., et al. *Environment and the Global Arena: Actors, Values, Politics, and Futures*. Durham, N.C.: Duke University Press, 1985.

Daly, Herman A., ed. *Steady-State Economy*. San Francisco: W. H. Freeman, 1973.

David, Henry P. "Eastern Europe: Pronatalist Policies and Private Behavior." *Population Bulletin* 36, 6. Washington, D.C.: Population Reference Bureau, 1982.

Easton, David. *A Systems Analysis of Political Life*. Englewood Cliffs, N.J.: Prentice-Hall, 1965.

Echols, William D., and James E. Harf. "Domestic Interest Groups and American Foreign Policy: The Case of the Law of the Sea." A paper presented at the annual meeting of the Western Political Science Association, Las Vegas, March 1985.

Eckholm, Erick. *Down to Earth: Environment and Human Needs*. New York: W. W. Norton, 1977.

Eicher, Carl K. "Africa's Food Crisis." *Foreign Affairs* (Fall 1982): 151–74.

Feld, Werner J., and Robert S. Jordan. *International Organizations: A Comparative Approach*. New York: Praeger, 1983.

Feshbach, Murray. "The Soviet Union: Population Trends and Dilemmas." *Population Bulletin* 37, 3. Washington, D.C.: Population Reference Bureau, 1982.

Food and Agriculture Organization. *Global Information and Early Warning on Food and Agriculture: Food Supply Situation in 24 African Countries Affected by Food and Agricultural Emergencies in 1984*. 8 February 1984.

Galtung, Johan. "Self-Reliance and Global Interdependence: Some Reflections on the 'New International Economic Order.'" Chair in Conflict and Peace Research, paper no. 55. University of Oslo, 1978.

Giarini, Orio, and Henri Louberge. *The Diminishing Returns of Technology*. Oxford: Pergamon Press, 1978.

Goliber, Thomas J. "Sub-Saharan Africa: Population Pressures on Development." *Population Bulletin* 40, 1. Washington, D.C.: Population Reference Bureau, 1985.

Goodloe, Carol. "Measuring Food Deficits and Undernutrition: An Accuracy Problem." Staff Paper, Economic Research Service, International Economics Division, U.S. Department of Agriculture. Washington, D.C., 1982.

Green, Maurice. *Eating Oil: Energy Use in Food Production.* Boulder, Colo.: Westview Press, 1978.

Harf, James E., Donald A. Sylvan, and B. Thomas Trout. "Energy Values." In Barry B. Hughes et al., *Energy in the Global Arena: Actors, Values, Policies, and Futures.* Durham, N.C.: Duke University Press, 1985.

Harman, Willis. *An Incomplete Guide to the Future.* New York: W. W. Norton, 1979.

Heilbroner, Robert L. *Inquiry Into the Human Prospect.* Rev. ed. New York: W. W. Norton, 1980.

Herrera, Amilcar O., et al. *Catastrophe or New Society? A Latin American World Model.* Ottawa: International Development Research Center, 1976.

Hersch, Jonathan. "Soil, the Crucial Resource." *Christian Science Monitor,* 13 September 1982.

Hoben, Allan. "The Origins of Famine." *The New Republic,* 21 January 1985.

Hoffman, Michael P. "Prehistoric Ecological Crises." In *Historical Ecology: Essays on Environment and Social Change,* edited by Lester J. Bilsky. Port Washington, N.Y.: Kennikat Press, 1980.

Holdgate, Martin W., Mohammed Kassas, and Gilbert F. White, eds. *The World Environment 1972–1982: A Report by the United Nations Environment Programme.* Dublin: Tycooly International, 1982.

Hopkins, Raymond F., Robert L. Paarlberg, and Mitchel B. Wallerstein. *Food in the Global Arena.* New York: Holt, Rinehart and Winston, 1982.

Hull, Terence H., Valerie J. Hull, and Masri Singarimban. "Indonesia's Family Planning Story: Success and Challenge." *Population Bulletin* 32, 6. Washington, D.C.: Population Reference Bureau, 1977.

Independent Commission of International Development Issues. *North-South: A Program for Survival.* Cambridge, Mass.: MIT Press, 1980.

———. *Common Crisis North-South: Cooperation for World Recovery.* Cambridge, Mass.: MIT Press, 1983.

International Bank for Reconstruction and Development. *World Development Report 1982.* Washington, D.C.: World Bank, 1982.

———. *World Development Report 1983.* Washington, D.C.: World Bank, 1983.

Kahn, Herman, William Brown, and Leon Martel. *The Next 200 Years: A Scenario for America and the World.* New York: William Morrow, 1976.

Kaufman, Michael T. "Preserving Rare Species Is an Ironic Success." *New York Times,* 8 March 1981, p. 20.

Lane, Hanna Umlauf, ed. *World Almanac and Book of Facts, 1985.* New York: Newspaper Enterprise Association, 1985.

Lapham, Robert J., and W. Parker Mauldin. "The Measurement of Family Planning Effort." Unpublished paper, January 1984.

Larson, David L. "Security Issues and the Law of the Sea: A General Framework." *Ocean Development and International Law* 15 (1985): 94–146.

Leontief, Wassily, Anne Carter, and Peter Petri. *The Future of the World Economy: A United Nations Study.* New York: Oxford University Press, 1977.

Lindberg, Leon L. *The Energy Syndrome: Comparing National Responses to the Energy Crisis.* Lexington, Mass.: D. C. Heath, 1977.

McLaughlin, Loretta. "Bangladesh, a Population Treadmill." *Boston Globe,* 22 March 1982.

Marden, Parker G., Dennis G. Hodgson, and Terry L. McCoy. *Population in the Global Arena*. New York: Holt, Rinehart and Winston, 1982.

Martino, Joseph. *Technological Forecasting for Decisionmaking*. New York: American Elsevier, 1972.

Meadows, Dennis L., et al. *Dynamics of Growth in a Finite World*. Cambridge, Mass.: Wright-Allen, 1974.

Meadows, Donella, et al. *The Limits to Growth*. New York: Universe Books, 1972.

Mesarovic, Mihajlo D., and Eduard Pestel. *Mankind at the Turning Point*. New York: Dutton, 1974.

Mill, John S. *Principles of Political Economy*. Vol. 2. London: John W. Parker, 1857.

Mitrany, David. *A Working Peace System*. Chicago: Quadrangle Books, 1966.

Moore, John R. "World Hunger: Population, Food Supplies and Public Policy." Occasional Paper no. 3. Technology, Resources and Political Economy Program, University of Maryland, 1978.

Myers, Norman. *The Sinking Ark: A New Look at the Problems of Disappearing Species*. Elmsford, N.Y.: Pergamon Press, 1979.

Nagel, John S. "Mexico's Population Policy Turnaround." *Population Bulletin* 33, 5. Washington, D.C.: Population Reference Bureau, 1977.

Newland, Kathleen. "Refugees: The New International Politics of Displacement." *Worldwatch Paper 43*. Washington, D.C.: Worldwatch Institute, 1981.

New York Times, 28 September 1980; 18 October 1982.

Paarlberg, Robert. "A Food Security Approach for the 1980s: Righting the Balance." *U.S. Foreign Policy and the Third World: Agenda, 1982*. Washington, D.C.: Overseas Development Council, 1982.

Pirages, Dennis. *Global Ecopolitics: The New Context for International Relations*. North Scituate, Mass.: Duxbury Press, 1978.

Population Reference Bureau. *The Environment to Come: A Global Summary*. Washington, D.C.: Population Reference Bureau, 1983.

Postel, Sandra. "Protecting Forests From Air Pollution and Acid Rain." In *State of the World 1985*, edited by Lester R. Brown et al. New York: W. W. Norton, 1985.

Ridron, Michael, and Ronald Segal. *New State of the World Atlas*. New York: Simon and Schuster, 1984.

Robinson, J. P. *The Effects of Weapons on Ecosystems*. United Nations Environment Programme Studies, vol. 1. Elmsford, N.Y.: Pergamon Press, 1979.

Rutco, Richard P., et al. "The Climatic Effects of Nuclear War." *Scientific American* 251 (August 1984): 33–34.

Sagan, Carl. "Nuclear War and Climatic Catastrophe: Some Policy Implications." *Foreign Affairs* 62 (Winter 1983–84): 263–64.

Schumacher, E. F. *Small is Beautiful: Economics as if People Mattered*. New York: Harper and Row, 1973.

Simon, Julian L. *The Ultimate Resource*. Princeton, N.J.: Princeton University Press, 1981.

Singh, Jyoti Shankan. "Introduction." In *World Population Policies*, edited by Jyoti Shankan Singh. New York: Praeger, 1979.

Sivard, Ruth Leger. *World Military and Social Expenditures 1979*. Washington, D.C.: World Priorities, 1979.

———. *World Military and Social Expenditures 1982*. Washington, D.C.: World Priorities, 1982.

———. *World Military and Social Expenditures 1983*. Washington, D.C.: World Priorities, 1983.

Soroos, Marvin S. "The Future of the Environment." In Kenneth A. Dahlberg et al., *Environment and the Global Arena: Actors, Values, Policies, and Futures.* Durham, N.C.: Duke University Press, 1985.

Stavrianos, L. S. *The Promise of the Coming Dark Age.* San Francisco: W. H. Freeman, 1976.

Stockholm International Peace Research Institute. *SIPRI Yearbook, 1983.* Stockholm: SIPRI, 1983.

Sylvan, Donald A. "Energy Futures." In Barry B. Hughes et al. *Energy in the Global Arena.* Durham, N.C.: Duke University Press, 1985.

Tien, H. Yuan. "China: Demographic Billionaire." *Population Bulletin* 38, 2. Washington, D.C.: Population Reference Bureau, 1983.

Timmer, C. Peter, et al. *Food Policy Analysis.* Baltimore: Johns Hopkins University Press, 1983.

Tripp, Rosemary E. *World Refugee Survey 1983.* New York: American Council for Nationalities Service, 1983.

United Nations Conference on Trade and Development. "Basic Data on the Least Developed Countries." Document #TD/276/Add. 1, 27 April 1983.

United Nations Department of International Economic and Social Affairs. *International Migration Policies and Programmes: A World Survey.* Population Studies no. 80. New York: United Nations, 1982.

———. *World Population Trends and Policies.* Vol. 1. Population Studies no. 79. New York: United Nations, 1982.

———. *Yearbook of International Trade Statistics, 1984.* New York: United Nations, 1984.

United Nations Department of Technical Cooperation for Development. *Report of the International Conference on Population, 1984.* New York: United Nations, 1984.

U.S. Arms Control and Disarmament Agency. *World Military Expenditures and Arms Transfers 1972–1982.* Washington, D.C.: USACDA, 1984.

U.S. Central Intelligence Agency. *International Energy Statistical Review.* 20 December 1983.

U.S. Congress, Office of Technology Assessment. *Global Models, World Futures, and Public Policy.* Washington, D.C.: Government Printing Office, 1982.

U.S. Council on Environmental Quality and the Department of State. *The Global 2000 Report to the President.* Washington, D.C.: Government Printing Office, 1980.

U.S. Council on Environmental Quality and the Department of State. *The Global 2000 Report to the President.* New York: Penguin Books, 1982.

U.S. House of Representatives. *Feeding the World's Population: Developments in the Decade Following the World Food Conference in 1974.* Washington, D.C.: Government Printing Office, 1984.

U.S. Presidential Commission on World Hunger. *Overcoming World Hunger: The Challenge Ahead.* Washington, D.C.: Government Printing Office, 1980.

Visaria, Pravin, and Leela Visaria. "India's Population: Second and Growing." *Population Bulletin* 36, 4. Washington, D.C.: Population Reference Bureau, 1981.

Wallerstein, Immanuel. *The Modern World System.* New York: Academic Press, 1974.

Weber, Cynthia, and Ann Goodman. "The Demographic Policy Debate in the USSR." *Population and Development Review* 7 (June 1981): 279–95.

Webster, Bayard. "Tanzania Asks Rich Countries to Aid Wildlife." *New York Times,*

29 March 1979, p. 16.

Willis, David K. "A Tidal Wave of Humanity." *Christian Science Monitor*, 6 August 1984.

"World Population Growth by the Numbers." *Intercom: The International Population News Magazine* 10 (May–June 1982): 4.

Yergin, Daniel. "The Political Geology of the Energy Problem." In *Uncertain Power: The Struggle for National Energy Policy*, edited by Dorothy S. Zinberg. Elmsford, N.Y.: Pergamon Press, 1983.

Index

James E. Harf is Professor of Political Science and
Mershon Senior Faculty, Ohio State University.
B. Thomas Trout is Associate Professor of Political
Science, University of New Hampshire.

Library of Congress Cataloging-in-Publication Data
Harf, James E.
The Politics of global resources.
(Duke global issues series)
Bibliography: p.
Includes index.
1. Natural resources.   2. Population.   I. Trout, B.
Thomas, 1939–   II. Title.   III. Series: Duke
Press global issues series.
HC59.H344 1986   333.7   86-4481
ISBN 0-8223-0583-6
ISBN 0-8223-0623-9 (pbk.)